POVERTY
A HISTORY

MAIN LENDING   **3 WEEK LOAN**   DCU LIBRARY

This edition published 1994
This edition first published in paperback 1997

Blackwell Publishers Ltd
108 Cowley Road
Oxford OX4 1JF, UK

Blackwell Publishers Inc.
238 Main Street
Cambridge, Massachusetts 02142, USA

362·5094 GER

British Library Cataloguing in Publication Data
A CIP catalogue record for this book is available from the British Library

Library of Congress Cataloging in Publication Data
Geremek, Bronislaw
{Litosc I szubienica. English}
Poverty : a history / Bronislaw Geremek; translated by Agnieszka Kolakowska.
p.   cm.   Includes bibliographical references (p.   ) and index.
ISBN 0–631–15425–6 (acid-free paper) — ISBN 0–631– 20529–2 (pbk)
1. Poor—Europe—History. 2. Poverty—Religious aspects—Christianity.
3. Church work with the poor—Europe—History. 4. Poverty—Psychological
aspects—History. 5. Social service—Europe—History.
6. Europe—Social conditions.   I. Title
HC240.9.P6G4713   1994   94–8783
362.5'094—dc20   CIP

Typeset in 11 on 12.5pt Garamond
by Pure Tech India Ltd., Pondicherry, India
Printed and bound in Great Britain by Hartnolls Ltd, Bodmin, Cornwall

This book is printed on acid-free paper

Contents

Foreword

In the Polish political turmoils of the 1980s Professor Bronislaw Geremek was a brave dissident who suffered imprisonment and the loss of his academic post under the regime of General Jaruzelski. Sometime adviser to Lech Walesa and active on the liberal wing of the independent trade union Solidarity, he was one of three candidates proposed by that organization in August 1989 for the office of Prime Minister in the non-communist coalition which came to govern the country – a post which fell, however, to the moderate Catholic Tadeusz Mazowiecki. Geremek's political experience and judgement are highly respected, but he regards himself as a professional historian, and said in a recent interview that 'even as a politician of necessity . . . I maintain an historian's distance'.

Much of his academic life, in which he has formed strong bonds with the École des Hautes Études, has been devoted to the study of people situated on the margins of respectable society, especially in late medieval Paris. Written in Polish in 1978, but not then published, his essay on the history of poverty first appeared in print in 1986, in Italian translation. It has since been translated into other European languages and into Japanese, and is now presented in English, in an elegant rendering by Agnieszka Kolakowska. The Italian version bears the title 'Compassion and the Gallows' [*La pietà e la forca*], which gives a pungent impression of one of the author's major themes, the almost timeless ambivalence in the attitudes of prosperous people, churchmen and magistrates to the poorer members of society. Geremek analyses the conflicting elements of pity and fear which have influenced behaviour towards the poor and which help to explain the harshness of public policy towards those suspected of idle inclinations and rebellious tendencies. With Michel Mollat, for some years director of the Paris seminar on medieval poverty,[1] he argues that even in the Middle Ages there was little sentimentality about involuntary material poverty. A high value might be placed on the spiritual poverty which arose from the deliberate renunciation of worldly goods or from a refusal, even while retaining control of one's fortune, to be ruled by materialistic concerns. But other forms of poverty might well be regarded with contempt and attributed to idle or dissolute behaviour. Not all the ordinary poor were recognized as the poor of Christ, and charity may well have been valued chiefly as a means of legitimating wealth by surrendering a portion of one's riches, without having to forefeit everything essential to one's status. For these reasons, wealth and poverty were believed to be complementary, and the poor had a function in society: on one side stood the alms-giver who needed to earn merit and cancel out his sins, on the other the beggar who contracted to pray for his benefactor's soul.

However, with the great economic crises of the sixteenth century, especially those of the 1520s, mass poverty began to be perceived as a threat to the public good. Hence begging had to be restricted or forbidden altogether, as a danger to good order and public health; the poor had to be provided with enough work to keep them at subsistence level; children had to be educated in industrious habits and schooled in skills which would at least transform the dependent into the labouring poor, beggar boys into cabin boys or apprentices, potential prostitutes into domestic servants or artisans' wives. As Geremek reminds us, many of the principles which govern modern poor relief were formulated at this time through schemes applied first on a municipal or parochial level, then on that of an entire state. Many of these projects foundered in a few years, but with time a much broader community began, at least in principle, to shoulder the burden of disciplining and supporting the poor.

One great strength of Geremek's work lies in its chronological range; few historians have the confidence or the learning to move as he does across the frontier, located somewhere about the year 1500, between the scholarly provinces traditionally called 'medieval' and 'modern'. In the history of poverty and charity, as in other fields, there is a danger of greeting as signs of modernity actions and attitudes which seem to be new, but were actually in being long before 1500. Geremek's long perspective helps everyone to avoid such errors.

Naturally, so concise an essay has had to be highly selective in order to retain its conceptual unity, and some aspects of a vast subject are discussed only briefly in this book. Like Catharina Lis and Hugo Soly, who published some years ago a powerful account of poverty as a consequence of exploitation rather than of underdevelopment or of demographic movements,[2] Geremek concentrates on the links between large-scale economic processes and levels of poverty. These connections are of the highest importance, but other approaches can be adopted, by examining (for example) the family structure and life cycle of working folk, and by looking at the changing balance in families at various times in their collective lives between the number of able-bodied, wage-earning producers and the number of dependent consumers.[3] Informal networks of assistance between patrons and clients can sometimes be traced, and the history of associations for mutual help can sometimes be sketched. It may be, too, that, as Sandra Cavallo has argued in her studies of Turin, much organized relief was not a direct response to dangerous levels of poverty, but rather part of a system of patronage established by well-to-do nobles and citizens in search of prestige and influence. Such people chose to concentrate not on the most abjectly poor, but on certain groups and categories of persons, often drawn from decayed genteel families or from domestic servants, whom they singled out for special favour.[4]

In discussing social action, Professor Geremek understandably gives pride of place to the undertakings of public authorities – to the poor laws, the centralized common chests and general almonries for outdoor relief, the work schemes and workhouses of early modern Europe. Historians have also begun to study private initiatives and voluntary organizations and to examine their interaction with public policy. Lay confraternities were and remained of the greatest importance in Roman Catholic countries. Clerical and lay authorities might struggle to control them, and they were sometimes merged, but they were seldom suppressed and rarely deprived of responsibility for charity.[5] General hospitals were often run by boards of governors nominated by city councillors and prominent churchmen, but they usually retained a certain autonomy. Conservatories designed to preserve the honour of girls and women in sexual danger often originated as private foundations.[6] It may be that, whereas Protestants and Catholics responded to economic crises in broadly similar ways and condemned rogues and vagabonds with equal zest, their institutional structures were in other respects quite different. And the relative

importance of parishes, confraternities and large civic hospitals as agencies
of poor relief varied considerably from one country to another.

Since Geremek wrote this book, some valuable studies have carried
the story further, though they have seldom contradicted his arguments. For an up-to-date account of English policies towards the
poor, readers can now turn to the admirable survey by Paul Slack.[7]
When discussing developments in sixteenth-century Spain, Geremek
was compelled to rely heavily on the famous debate on the ethics of
suppressing begging conducted by the Dominican Soto and the Benedictine Medina in the 1540s, and to describe the projects of reformers
such as Giginta or Pérez de Herrera without exploring their implementation at any length. More can now be known from Linda
Martz's well-grounded study of Toledo and from Maureen Flynn's
lively essay on the confraternities of Spain.[8] Geremek's work sometimes carries the history of poor relief beyond its traditional geographical boundaries and crosses into Eastern Europe, for he discusses
the views of Jan Ludzisko of Cracow and those of Andrzej Frycz
Modrzewski, who conveyed to Poland the opinions of the humanist
Juan Luis Vivés, author of the most widely circulated treatise on social
action in early modern Europe. Light has now fallen on other little-
known regions in the far north, since accounts of poverty and poor
relief in the Scandinavian countries were handily presented in the
latest of several volumes of conference papers on poverty edited by the
Danish historian Thomas Riis.[9]

Most surveys of broad scholarly fields, if they are only summaries of
the latest research, soon become dated and call for new editions. A few
wide-ranging works have the character, lucidity and lightness of
touch to become classics, well worth the reading even as they stand.
Geremek has recorded his long journey through the history of poverty
in one of those rare books, distinguished as it is by qualities seldom
found in the ordinary, sheltered academic world.

Notes

[1]   See M. Mollat, *The Poor in the Middle Ages: An Essay in Social History*, trans. A.
      Goldhammer. New Haven and London, 1986.
[2]   C. Lis and H. Soly, *Poverty and Capitalism in Pre-Industrial Europe*. London, 1979.
[3]   See the useful introduction to the subject in R. Jütte, *Poverty and Deviance in Early
      Modern Europe*. Cambridge, 1994, pp. 36–42.
[4]   See S. Cavallo, 'Charity, power and patronage in eighteenth-century Italian hospi-
      tals: the case of Turin', in *The Hospital in History*, ed. L. Granshaw and R. Porter.

London and New York, 1989, pp. 93–122; 'The motivations of benefactors: an overview of approaches to the study of charity', in *Medicine and Charity before the Welfare State*, ed. J. Barry and C. Jones. London and New York, 1991, pp. 46–62; 'Conceptions of poverty and poor relief in Turin in the second half of the eighteenth century', in *Domestic Strategies: Work and Family in France and Italy 1600–1800*, ed. S. Woolf. Cambridge, 1991, pp. 148–99.

5 Recent works on confraternities include A. N. Galpern, *The Religions of the People in Sixteenth-Century Champagne*. Cambridge, MA, 1976; C. F. Black, *Italian Confraternities in the Sixteenth Century*. Cambridge, 1989; M. Flynn, *Sacred Charity: Confraternities and Social Welfare in Spain, 1400–1700*. London, 1989. On the 'decentralized' character of Roman Catholic charity, stressed by Flynn, *Sacred Charity*, p. 109; see also Jütte, *Poverty and Deviance*, pp. 105, 116, 125.

6 For a broad account of conservatories, see S. Cohen, *The Evolution of Women's Asylums since 1500: From Refuges for Ex-Prostitutes to Shelters for Battered Women*. New York and Oxford, 1992.

7 P. Slack, *Poverty and Policy in Tudor and Stuart England. London, 1988.*

8 L. Martz, *Poverty and Welfare in Habsburg Spain: The Example of Toledo*. Cambridge, 1983; M. Flynn, *Sacred Charity*.

9 *Aspects of Poverty in Early Modern Europe*, III: *La pauvreté dans les pays nordiques 1500–1800*, ed. T. Riis. Odense, 1990. Earlier volumes of *Aspects* were published in Florence in 1981 and Odense in 1986.

BRIAN PULLAN

Introduction

What is Poverty?

Social science has, from its very inception, always recognized the importance of poverty; and the two most vital questions – what causes poverty and how is it to be eradicated – have stimulated a great deal of controversy and an enormous amount of empirical research. At the begining of the modern era the first 'economically unsophisticated' studies of what was the most prominent of contemporary social evils were concerned principally with 'removing the need to beg, directing the idle and finding employment for the poor'. The great increase in the number of poor people that accompanied the rise of capitalism and disrupted society led scholars, ideologues and politicians to see poverty as a social phenomenon. History provided them with examples and arguments. The debates in England surrounding the Old and New Poor Laws were, in the final analysis, historical arguments. Men looked to the past for answers to contemporary social problems as well as for explanations of the causes of poverty. Eighteenth- and nineteenth-century English economists, especially Adam Smith, Malthus and Ricardo, as well as Marx and his disciples, examined the problem of poverty within the context of their studies of political economy, seeing it either as the necessary price of social progress or as evidence of the inefficiency of the system. In each case history appeared as witness for the prosecution. In nineteenth-century thought and criticism, poverty was treated as the 'shameful disease' of modern society for which new remedies were constantly being prescribed, albeit in a volatile atmosphere of differing and evolving opinion. At the end of the century, however, social science, and especially its vocabulary, changed. The uncertain bases of welfare programmes, a greater social and political awareness among ordinary people and changes in the structures of political life combined to remove the words 'poverty' and 'destitution' from traditional economic and social terminology: the idea of poverty had taken on connotations of compassion and condescension, which distorted its meaning, thus limiting its value as a scientific term. Poverty remained, however, an important historical problem: firstly, as a reflection of the changes in psychological and social attitudes that accompanied the transformation of 'traditional' societies into modern ones; secondly, as a framework for research into religious life, doctrine and institutions; and, thirdly, as a subject of debate about the degree to which it is inherent in the development of a capitalist system. In modern social research the study of poverty has focused mainly on the creation of paupers within society and on the transformation of attitudes towards poverty in Europe; examination of the causes of social inequality and of the distribution of national income came to replace traditional questions concerning poverty.

The 1950s and 1960s witnessed a revival of interest in poverty among social scientists. The terms 'poverty' and 'destitution' appeared once more in the vocabulary of economists and sociologists; empirical studies and overviews of the problem were published by the dozen. The optimism of contemporary capitalism is reflected in John K. Galbraith's *The Affluent Society*, published in 1958, in which the problem of poverty in America is presented as eradicable. However, a number of studies and the record of subsequent social policies suggest that Professor Galbraith's optimism may not have been entirely justified. Poverty's reproductive system was, in fact, in very good order, even in highly industrialized countries, and the phenomenon of labour migration, which was creating new islands of poverty in 'affluent' countries, demanded that poverty be considered on a global scale. While the significance of poverty as a serious and widespread problem was unquestionable, the question of where to draw the 'poverty line', and what statistical data to use in establishing it, caused a great deal of controversy. The index of national income adopted by American scholars proved inappropriate as a basis for comparing the widely differing environmental and ethnic circumstances prevailing across the United States. Such an index could not possibly be adapted for the study of other highly developed countries, never mind countries of the Third World, where the situation was completely different. How poverty was to be measured depended on accepted assumptions and aims. The technical limit of poverty was obvious: it was the point at which the survival of the individual and of the family became threatened. Less obvious was the definition of 'relative' poverty, determined by particular social conventions which evolved with time. In a classic study of poverty in York, B. Seebohm Rowntree wrote: 'My primary poverty line represented the minimum sum on which physical efficiency could be maintained. It was a standard of bare subsistence rather than living,'[1] because the line had been drawn at the point at which bare survival could be secured only in the event of all expenditure being directed to that end. This general principle set a precedent for the adoption by scholars of survival 'norms', which, though helpful, could be no more than approximations, subject to regional and cultural variation as well as differences in patterns of consumption. It also became evident that it is not only difficult to choose appropriate indices for measuring material poverty; it is equally difficult to separate material poverty from its extra-material aspects, such as educational opportunities, including professional qualifications, and job prospects.

Disagreement over methods of measuring poverty and some less than satisfactory research, in terms of both empirical results and practical suggestions, obstructed social policy: the authorities needed a reasonably broad base of public consensus as to what it was to be poor in order to develop welfare programmes. Paradoxically, in the social consciousness there was no difficulty in delineating either the social stratification or the topographical limits of poverty. This paradox arises partly from the fact that poverty in contemporary societies is a sign not only of material misfortune, but also of social status. Changes in material well-being and in disposable income, such as occur when children grow up and no longer make demands on the parental budget, are rarely accompanied by parallel changes in social status, position or role. Economic factors do not appear in and of themselves as sufficient criteria for the delineation of poverty. The variety of perspectives from which social scientists may view poverty has tended to obscure the essential unity of the subject. Interdisciplinary studies of poverty have tried to bring together work on economic problems, welfare programmes and the relationship between poverty and deviant behaviour among minority groups, as well as finding room for the social and moral implications of poverty. Viewed in this light, poverty appears as a distinct way of life made up of the interaction of disparate factors – social, cultural, economic, political, psychological, physiological and ecological. Among the features that define poverty as a social phenomenon, commentators found its degrading effect to be the most significant. This did not add anything very new to the understanding of poverty. The nineteenth-century philanthropists, as well as Christian social doctrine, emphasized the moral degradation that poverty brought into people's lives. In the estimation of Alfred Marshall, a distinguished representative of economic thought at the turn of the century who was particularly interested in the ethical aspects of economic development, the connection was quite plain. 'The study of the causes of poverty', he wrote, 'is the study of the causes of the degradation of a large part of mankind.'[2] In modern work on poverty degradation is considered not only in its ethical context, but also – and above all – in relation to society as a whole, including the economic system. For John Galbraith poverty was about 'those who are now excluded from the economic system by accident, inadequacy, or misfortune',[3] but who could be transformed into productive citizens by the right social policy. Considered from the point of view of class structures, associated with the less optimistic 1960s, the degrading aspect of poverty appeared as a part of social inequality, as a result of which the 'dregs of society', comprising between 10 and 20 per cent of the population of industrialized countries, became separated or segregated from the rest of society. In a famous book on poverty in America, Michael Harrington spoke of an 'economic underworld' in American cities, of the 'rejects of an affluent society' who were exploited and unable to participate in that society's life or development.

Behavioural studies of poor neighbourhoods have tended to rely on two theories, known as the 'culture of poverty' and 'ghetto of poverty' theories. The culture of poverty school, associated above all with Oscar Lewis (and of course with Michael Harrington and his work on the United States) emphasizes the specific behaviour of people in deprived urban neighbourhoods. The deviant nature of such behaviour is attributed to an acknowledgement by these people that their values and their cultural traditions, passed on from generation to generation, form the subculture that accompanies low social and economic status. The ghetto theory denies that internal factors contribute to the shaping of behaviour and to the formation of the 'subculture of poverty', and claims that such behaviour is the unavoidable consequence of the social status of the poor, of their place in the social structure. The connection between deviant behaviour and poor neighbourhoods is a result of the sovereignty of social structure, which rejects these neighbourhoods as well as their values and cultural traditions. Although no consensus was reached between the representatives of these two schools, whose ideologies were radically different, their exchanges did show that both internal and external influences are important in the development of deviant collective behaviour. And, most importantly, they revealed that it is not possible to understand poverty outside its social context and without taking account of society's attitudes towards the underprivileged as well as towards material success and failure.

Economic approaches to poverty have emphasized the *exclusion* of the poor from the economic order, from the production process and from the benefits of growth. The sociological, that is the social and cultural, aspects of poverty, its stigma and degradation, should also be emphasized. The American sociologist David Matza divided poverty into three areas, three concentric circles. The largest included all the poor, defined according to income; the second circle included those receiving some philanthropic or state support; and the third those who lived with continuous or recurrent aid and felt the full weight of the stigma of poverty. This last group, including, as a rule, the unemployed and semi-employed, creates its own environment and develops its own brand of deviant behaviour. Among them Matza distinguishes four types: the 'dregs', or rootless individuals and families, especially those from immigrant communities; the newcomers, recently arrived and treated with disdain, even by fellow immigrants of an earlier wave; the skidders, déclassé elements who have, through alcohol, drugs or some such aberration, been reduced from their former social position; and finally the chronically sick, who live on the border between acceptable and disreputable poverty. The 'disreputably poor' are degraded in the opinion of society and are considered to be less than fully human. C. L. Waxman takes up David Matza's notion of the stigma of poverty,[4] and describes the character of that stigma as it appears in various places and under varying circumstances − for example, where immigrants are concerned, poverty is associated with ethnic, racial and religious differences.[5] Both American sociologists attribute the stigma of poverty to the accumulation in history of attitudes that have interpreted poverty as the product of moral weakness and wrong-doing. Matza indicates two paths leading from poverty to disrepute: first of all, widespread poverty, which was handled by charitable, but also repressive, measures, typified in the English Poor Laws; and secondly, 'selective impoverishment', where a proportion of newly arrived immigrants, for example, automatically joins the ranks of the 'disreputable poor'. As regards American society, the English Poor Laws are no longer of any relevance. Prejudice towards immigrants, on the other hand, despite being relatively unimportant in itself, can and does preserve, culturally and ideologically, the stigmatizing effect of poverty.

Work on the disreputable aspect of poverty, which often involves distinguishing between different levels of poverty, has not been helped by the lack of precision shown by scholars in their terminology. Nevertheless, it is worth looking at some of this work, from two points of view especially.

First of all, the type of approach is significant. A portion of a poor neighbourhood is chosen as an example and is examined; it is a portion in which 'poverty and crime are intertwined'.[6] The 'criminal element' is then said to be responsible for the bad reputation, which has often spread, indiscriminately, to all poor people. Attitudes towards poverty and the poor in religious doctrine discriminate in favour of the 'deserving' poor; this point is relevant to and anticipates our discussion of the durability of certain attitudes towards poverty. In the Middle Ages those who were interested in poverty were concerned above all with distinguishing the individuals who received charity from institutions and private benefactors. Modern studies would focus on negative attitudes to poverty and the relationship between poverty and deviant behaviour. However, in both cases, only the attitudes of those who valued the poor are taken into account, and, in the final analysis, it is not the motives of individual medieval or modern writers that concern us (Matza and Waxman explicitly dissociate themselves from adverse moral judgements of the poor), but the social attitudes of their time that they describe or express.

Secondly, the cultural specificity of poor neighbourhoods is seen as a result both of condemnation or fear on the part of society and of the internalization of the stigma within poor communities, who isolate themselves from social change. The tendency of modern man to look at poverty with disdain is unmistakable. Indeed, a peculiar harmony exists between the degrading material and physical effect of poverty, on the one hand, and the negative or pejorative place assigned to poverty in the opinion of society. The romantic interest which mass culture sometimes lends to life in a poor neighbourhood can produce insight into the concerns of poor people and aid research, but is only marginally relevant to the present study.

In a different way and under different circumstances the same economically, socially and culturally degrading nature of poverty is apparent in societies of the pre-industrial age. In the traditions of Judaism, Christianity, Buddhism and Islam poverty was given a saintly face, while wealth occupied a lesser place in the estimation of society and culture. However, in time this scale of values was reversed as ideologies adapted in response to social change. In the fourteenth century European rulers and institutions began to face a need for concrete measures to arrest the spread of poverty and the disintegration of society. The begining of the sixteenth century brought a fundamental revision (*aggiornamento*) of religious teaching, general opinion and social policy relative to poverty. But even in the preceding centuries attitudes towards poverty ranged from glorification to acceptance to censure. Nevertheless, the most important factors in determining ideological attitudes towards poverty, and to a great extent also the social status of the poor, are to be found in the sphere of the sacred, a fundamental source of differences in the medieval and modern approaches to the problems of poverty.

Today scholars consider poverty to be an unambiguously bad thing, irrespective of differences in methodology, assumptions and technique. Even among extremists who cast the poor in a revolutionary role and expect 'desperados' – 'les damnés de la terre' – to bring about a radical transformation of the world, we find the same belief in the degrading effect of poverty. This conviction is more than the product of observation of social reality and the processes that shape it. It is symptomatic of the social attitudes to poverty that characterize contemporary society. And so we come to the subject of this book: changes in the image of poverty and in collective reactions to poverty over the centuries. Above all we are concerned with the changes themselves. Socio-psychological attitudes change slowly and such changes are not easily seen, for they concern what is ingrained in human nature and rooted in the biological foundations of society. It is easier to see changes in methods for producing food, in means of transport, in methods of war or forms of government, than in the sympathies of human beings, their sensibilities, their imaginations. The problem for the historian does not lie only in finding the right tools for research: the very subject, the fabric of history, is elusive. The limits between periods are blurred, differences are obscure, and changes take place in more than one direction. The hanging of beggars did not replace compassion: the gallows and the alms house have stood side by side in good times and bad, in periods of rising and declining fortunes. We find them today, sometimes separated by religious, economic or political barriers, but never far apart. The need to escape, to take refuge from the world's wealth and luxury, has been proclaimed both by members of modern communes and by medieval apologists for voluntary poverty. Just as the son of an eighteenth-century merchant could willingly give up life in a Florentine palazzo and find happiness as a beggar, so in the twentieth century the children of American millionaires may choose to give up the world for a life of poverty in the Himalayas or the Appalachians. Similar analogies can be found in the ways medieval and modern societies have aided and oppressed their poor.

As Europe emerged from the Middle Ages her attitudes and policies towards the poor were undergoing fundamental change. Contemporary accounts have described the shape and dimensions of that change in various ways. According to their various interpretations of the essential forces behind change, scholars associated this 'watershed' with contemporary developments in religion, with the cultural movement, the Renaissance, or with the beginings of capitalism.

In the sixteenth century a new wave of interest in welfare institutions was prompted by interdenominational controversy over urban social reform. This controversy will be discussed in some detail in Part III. It lasted for centuries, to emerge in nineteenth- and twentieth-century historiography as a debate over the role of Protestantism in the reform of charity.

The *terminus a quo* of the reform became the subject of lively debate: Catholic historians attempted to prove that it predated the Reformation and that changes in charitable institutions and their attitudes to the poor were taking place by the begining of the sixteenth century, both on the Catholic and on the Protestant side. It was the German Jesuit Franz Ehrle, subsequently Librarian to the Vatican and a Cardinal, who tried for the first time to write an authoritative and definitive refutation of the thesis that links the transformation of social care and philanthropy with Protestantism. This produced, in German historiography, a heated debate between Catholics and Protestants on the question of the modernization of institutions caring for the poor, a subject which was to dominate the field for the next forty years. Both sides at times displayed a somewhat partisan spirit, but as a result of their polemics the archives were thoroughly investigated and the important documentary evidence isolated, not only in Germany but in neighbouring countries as well.

The arguments of German historians were taken up by Belgian scholars. The case of Catholic Ypres and the reform of philanthropy carried out there in 1525 had already been studied in Germany, where Protestant historians had asserted that the authorities in Ypres had modelled themselves on initiatives undertaken in the towns of southern Germany. In opposition to this view, the Belgian historian Jean Nolf sees the transformation of philanthropy that took place in Ypres in the sixteenth century as completely independent of events in Germany, linking it only with comparable changes that had taken place slightly earlier in Mons-en-Hainaut. A similar position is maintained by Henri Pirenne, who in his monumental *History of Belgium* describes the reform of philanthropy as the work of the Renaissance and emphasizes the social origins – completely independent of the influence of German towns – of the new social policy. Pirenne believed that the reform of 1525 was the product of the intellectual and political influences of three groups – Erasmians, lawyers and capitalists – and that it continued tendencies towards the secularization of charitable institutions and the modernization of social policy which were visible long before 1525. According to this interpretation, then, the sixteenth-century reform of philanthropy was not a child of the Reformation. This position, the view of Pirenne and Nolf, was opposed most vehemently by Paul Bonenfant, an experienced archivist and historian of Belgian hospitals. Bonenfant wrote a lengthy treatise on the origins of the 1531 edict of Charles V on care for the poor, based on an analysis of documentary sources for the reform of philanthropy in towns in the Netherlands and Germany and on the conclusions of O. Winckelmann. Bonenfant insists that similarities in the timing and content of the social reforms that took place at Mons and Ypres on the one hand, and at Nuremberg and Strasbourg on the other, are so striking that the most plausible explanation must be that the towns of the Netherlands followed the general pattern set by German towns. Thus Bonenfant determined that the chain of reform went as follows: Nuremberg – 1522, Strasbourg – 1523, Mons – 1525, Ypres – 1525, Lille – 1527, the imperial edict – 1531. Without denying that certain late medieval developments anticipated reform, he claims that the centralization of care for the poor and the complete prohibition on begging were innovations that sprang directly from the sixteenth-century reform of philanthropy.

Was this reform Lutheran in character? Catholic towns which tried to introduce changes in social policy were certainly so accused. F. Ehrle, on the other hand, says that the Nuremberg ordinance of 1522 was not specifically Protestant, but rather a manifestation of the movement for urban social reform that had grown up in response to social and economic trends of the previous century. One edition of the Nuremberg ordinance actually contains a picture of the Virgin Mary. Bonenfant claims that in the towns of southern Germany the Lutheran inspiration for the reform of social care was for some time concealed or camouflaged, and that Nuremberg had not begun to imitate the model of Saxon towns until 1525. European towns which followed the pattern set in Germany unwittingly adopted a Protestant programme. The sixteenth-century reform of philanthropy was not, in this view, secular in character; the secularization movement had by this time already run its course.

Echoes of this religious and historiographical controversy have emerged in recent historical studies. At the same time a great deal of interest in the Tridentine period, with scholars concentrating as much on the reform of charity in Catholic countries before the Council of Trent as on the results of the Council itself, has had the effect of placing new emphasis on the role of the humanists in the transformation of attitudes towards charity.

This is illustrated in Marcel Bataillon's study of J. L. Vivés as a reformer of philanthropy, published in 1952. Bataillon, a French hispanicist, examines the connection between Vivés' treatise *De subventione pauperum* and sixteenth-century humanist literature, especially the work of Erasmus of Rotterdam. He shows that the political and intellectual urban elites played an important role, independently of the religious question. A similar perspective is shown by Natalie Zemon Davis in her wonderful article on the reform of charitable institutions in Lyons in the 1530s (published in 1968). Even here the reform of charity is treated as an ideological and political urban problem, the subject of much debate and disagreement. What is significant, however, is that those active in the social reform of Lyons in the 1530s were people of different religious persuasions who, in formulating their programme, drew on a vast store of ancient and humanist beliefs. Besides clerics, this humanist 'pressure group' was made up of businessmen, the merchants and entrepreneurs of Lyons. Thus the problem of poverty and beggars can be seen in the context of early capitalism.

The classic studies of Max Weber and Richard Tawney trace a connection between, on the one hand, changes in social attitudes to wealth and poverty and the social ideas of the Reformation, and, on the other, the development of capitalism. Subsequent work on the history of charitable and philanthropic institutions has tended to adopt this framework. The work of S. and B. Webb, and E. M. Leonard, on the English Poor Laws, and of W. K. Jordan on philanthropy in modern England, brought to the surface a great deal of material relating to the modern politics of charity, especially at grass-roots level. Like the French historian Leon Lallemand's monumental compendium of the general history of philanthropy, these works view care for the poor as an autonomous sphere, and the context of social and political administration, legislation and literature as its main reference-points. In the past decade scholars have referred more to the economic and social structures. This type of approach characterizes Michel Mollat's work on the Middle Ages and the research which inspired it. Poverty as a mass phenomenon, however, did not appear until the medieval world was already giving way to a new era; this is why the transition from feudal to capitalist society and from agrarian to industrial structures was such an important period for economic history and the sociology of pauperization.

The classical school of political economy had already considered this issue. Frederick M. Eden's work *The State of the Poor*, published in 1793, makes full use of the sources, the history of English legislation on beggars and tramps and in particular the Poor Laws. This material aimed to define, in the spirit of Smith, the principles of care for the poor. Marx, although sceptical and scornful of Eden's ideas, nevertheless used Eden's work as a major source for his own study of the development of poverty, which he traced to the birth of capitalism. In the chapters of *Capital* dealing with the accumulation of capital, poverty appears in the first instance as one of the factors that contributed to the development of capitalism, and secondly as a tendency encouraged by capitalism. From the middle of the nineteenth century this question inspired much controversy in the social sciences, and, although historians took only a limited part in the debate, the arguments used were for the most part historical ones. Both Bruno Hildebrand, the nineteenth-century historian and economist, in response to Engels, and the contemporary economic historian Wilhelm Abel, in opposition to modern Marxist theories of political economy, have insisted that capitalism actually solves the problem of poverty. Abel, however, does say that this observation applies only to the last hundred years; he acknowledges that from the late Middle Ages to the middle of the nineteenth century poverty was created rather than eliminated. Works of social history have stripped such arguments of their ideological coverings, but differences as to the nature and causes of early modern poverty remain firmly in place. As for the evolution of industrial societies from the middle of the nineteenth century to the present day, there is as much disagreement over methods as interpretations. Scholars have different views on the way in which terms such as 'pauperism' and 'pauperization' ought to be used: whether they should be understood absolutely, as a deterioration of one's material condition, or relatively, as a reduction in one's share of revenue. The dominant view is that the pauperization which accompanied the beginning of the modern era, the first accumulation of capital, commercialism and the first stages of industrialization, was of the absolute kind. The Belgian historians Catherine Lis and Hugo Soly have built a work on 'poverty and capitalism' around this interpretation. From the middle of the nineteenth century, however, the social development of industrialized countries led to the gradual removal of material poverty as a mass phenomenon; the argument of their book is therefore no longer applicable to this period. At the same time, our knowledge of conditions in distant countries and the sense of the unity which modern communication has brought have made us increasingly conscious of what might be described as the 'poverty of under-development'. This concerns above all the countries of the Third World, although labour migration and the exclusion of certain sections of the lower class from the social order are also creating pockets of this 'poverty of under-development' within developed countries.

Thus, although our primary interest is not in the history of poverty as such, in order to interpret changes in social attitudes to poverty we shall constantly have to compare and confront ideas and acts of charity with the social realities of poverty. The first task of this book is to observe the correlation and evolution of these two historical phenomena. It is a task which does not lend itself easily to chronological treatment. We will concentrate, therefore, on the late Middle Ages and the beginning of the modern era, because it is in the development of modern society that the connection between changes in structures and changes in general attitudes and social policies is most clearly perceived. While acknowledging the importance of observing and interpreting these changes as they are taking place in the world today, particularly in under-developed and developing countries, we will focus on Europe, because the unity of European civilization and the traditions of Christianity are central to the problems of this book.

It remains only to acknowledge that the following work is based partly on my own research in libraries and archives, and partly on the work of other historians. Some of the arguments presented here have appeared before in various of my writings and lectures, and I have profited greatly from discussions and critical remarks. I am also grateful to the Woodrow Wilson Centre for Scholars, whose grant made my archival research possible.

1

The Middle Ages: is Poverty Necessary?

In modern European culture the Middle Ages have become synonymous with backwardness; they seem to have existed only in order to provide us with a negative system of reference. Attitudes and opinions deemed inconsistent with modern values tend to be dismissed as relics of the Middle Ages. Our modern values and ideas are rooted in the culture of the Renaissance, and can be traced back to classical antiquity; the Middle Ages, although occupying more than a thousand years of European history, is treated not only as a break in the continuity of this tradition but as a kind of vast and murky mass of obscurantism and opposition to change. This interpretation dominates the history of the ideas of freedom and happiness, the history of attitudes towards work and nature, even the history of political systems and representative institutions. As a result, our image of the Middle Ages is one of uniformity and, when we contrast it with the dynamic changes than can occur within the space of a decade, or within the space of a couple of generations, of a permanent social and cultural inertia.

Needless to say, this picture is distorted, and fails to take account of the dynamics of change proper to medieval society. At the same time, however, it is justified insofar as the various human groups and collectivities which the historian is able to distinguish over this thousand-year period of European history were united by Christian civilization, which was characterized by a high degree of coherence and continuity. The birth of the modern era, the awakening of national consciousness, both cultural and political, and movements of religious reform destroyed the unity and the continuity of the old civilization: it no longer had a place in the new order. Born from a

mixture of 'barbarian' cultures, Christianity and the legacy of antiquity, it died, slowly and painfully, when the collapse of universal-
ism made way for the modern era. It is in these two moments of birth
and death, neither of which can be precisely dated, that the distinctive
features of the Middle Ages are condensed: at its birth the force of a
new religion cut it off from the cultures and societies of antiquity,
while at its death criticism of the existing order brought its essential
characteristics into relief. So vast was the stretch of time that elapsed
between these two moments, and so great the diversity of the ideological needs which shaped the main features of the medieval period,
that there was hardly any resemblance between its initial and its final
stages. The Christian religion provided a measure of continuity: the
scriptural image of man and the universe, of Church and State, of
life on earth and beyond; the promise of salvation, and the doctrinal
precepts which went with it, provided a uniform model of how to
live. What changed, however, was the social context of this teaching.
Christianity, once the religion of a persecuted minority, became the
dominant religion of Europe; once the faith of the poor and oppressed,
it was adopted by the aristocracy. It passed from urban to agrarian
society, and from feudalism to a money-based economy. Each of these
changes posed different moral questions and required a new system of
education for the faithful, a new hierarchy of values, attitudes and
models of behaviour. The metaphorical nature of the Old and the New
Testament made it possible to adapt religious teaching to new requirements, and to absorb new social phenomena into the ideological
framework. Thus within the unity forged by the dominance of the
Christian religion and by the universalist programme of the Church
there was a great diversity of attitudes, scales of values and social
programmes, all nourished, shaped and justified by the same source –
Holy Scripture.

This must be borne in mind when considering social attitudes towards poverty and the poor in the Middle Ages. These attitudes grew
out of early Christianity, which spread because of its teaching among
the poor. Patristic literature, especially Greek, considers poverty not
only from the point of view of voluntary renouncement, but also from
the point of view of the poor themselves. The social circumstances
prevailing in Byzantine towns at the beginning of the Middle Ages
provoked an immediate, complex and compassionate response to the
question of attitudes to the poor; the writings of St John Chrysostom
and the imperial legislation of Justinian scrupulously distinguish

between those among the poor who are capable of work and those who are not. The same distinction is drawn in Western theological, moral and social writings at the beginning of the modern era, when circumstances made it necessary to seek new answers to social problems. In the early Middle Ages, however, people intent on living off charity caused the agrarian civilization of Western Christendom no serious discomfort. It was the Church's mission to help the poor, and a third or a fourth part of Church income was to be allocated to them on a regular basis (one of Charles the Great's capitularies determined that Church tithes were to be divided into three equal parts: for churches and shrines, for the maintenance of priests and for the poor).[1] Poverty itself, however, was not thought to have any intrinsic value or to confer sanctity: wealth and power are bestowed on some by the grace of God, while others are fated to be weak and poor; man must accept his destined condition with humility. Research on the writings of Gregory of Tours has shown that Merovingian society was hostile and contemptuous in its attitude towards the poor. It was not until the eleventh and twelfth centuries, under the influence of the teachings of the Greek Church Fathers and the experiences of Eastern monasticism, that poverty began to be recognized as a spiritual value. At the same time, changes in social structures forced people to confront the problem of increasing poverty and the need to justify moneyed wealth. This situation precipitated the development of charitable institutions and mendicant orders. Charitable work, although motivated by genuine compassion, was at the same time the result of careful calculation: it was an excellent way of 'buying' salvation and an ostentatious way of demonstrating one's wealth and Christian principles.

In the critical view of those engaged in the Catholic and Protestant movements for the reform of charity, these changes represented a serious threat to society by making a life of begging attractive. The Reformists presented medieval charity as an intrinsically defective system which failed, not only because of embezzlement and misappropriation of funds on the part of individuals and institutions, but also because it was fundamentally flawed: the sums disbursed in charity were quite enormous; alms were given indiscriminately, not according to need; and the administration of charitable institutions was entirely in the hands of the clergy — the secular authorities and indeed all laymen being excluded from the organization of charity. The exaltation of poverty and alms-giving that lay at the foundation of this system undermined or even denied the work ethic, which ought to be the fundamental principle guiding the lives of the masses.

Medieval literature and Church policy provide plenty of evidence to refute this thesis. It was a constantly recurring theme in the teachings of the medieval Church that work is a duty which must be assumed with humility. The Church Fathers, as well as many medieval theologists and canon lawyers, emphasized the need to distinguish between different kinds of poor and to deny alms to those capable of work. Vagrancy is constantly condemned and attacked by ecclesiastical authorities and in social and legal writing. The Church also approved measures taken by the municipal authorities to deal with the problem of beggars and root out vagrants, and in 1311 the Council of Vienne ordered, in its constitution 'Quia contingit', the reform of refuges, hospitals and other charitable institutions, forbade their use as a source of prebends for the clergy, and recommended that their administration be entrusted to competent authorities.

If, however, we turn from the teaching and policies of the Church, from doctrine and legal principles, to social attitudes as they are presented in literary sources, chronicles and town records, we can see quite clearly that the exaltation of poverty as a spiritual value went hand in hand with an increase in the practice of charity. The poor knew their place and their role in the social order: they were there to enable others to buy salvation through alms-giving. The question we must now consider is how this attitude fared when confronted with the realities of the lives of the poor.

1.1 The Medieval Idea of Poverty and the Social Reality

The history of cultures, attitudes and social structures does not easily admit of clear divisions into well-defined periods or eras; any such division must be arbitrary. In the history of ideas, doctrines and ideologies, on the other hand, such divisions are easier to define: historical analysis allows us to trace the evolution of concepts and ideas, to discern semantic changes as well as continuities of meaning and connotation. But changes in collective attitudes and value systems are hidden and elusive, and they occur slowly, over a vast time-scale. Our points of reference when attempting to trace and define changes of this kind are the great structures of civilization; but when such structures disintegrate, at times of profound crisis, changes in attitudes and behaviour are not always clear and immediate. Nor can civilizations easily be distinguished by clearly defined hierarchies of values, for in each civilization many different value systems coexist, along with vestiges of earlier stages in the development of its culture. But if, in spite of this, historians persist in studying changes in collective attitudes, it is not because their diachronic view of human events leads them to slice up history into periods and eras where no natural periods and eras exist, but because of the internal dynamics of cultures. In every civilization praise of wealth may be found alongside its condemnation, pacifism alongside the glorification of war, the exaltation of physical work alongside the praise of reflection. But the hierarchy of values changed at different periods, constantly reshuffled by ideological programmes intended to justify or to condemn the existing social order and to promote or repudiate a particular set of values.

In medieval Christian civilization all such programmes and ideologies were rooted in Holy Scripture. A variety of doctrines developed concerning the idea of poverty, but all were built on the social teaching of the gospels, and their divergences were the result of varying interpretations of that teaching. Differences in interpretation were, indeed, hard to avoid, given the fact that the same conceptual framework was used to describe both social and spiritual events. Both in the gospels and in patristic literature poverty is exalted as a spiritual value, accessible to rich and poor alike. The fundamental values of the 'economics of salvation' are humility and renunciation. In biblical terminology and in early Christian literature *pauperitas* is clearly assimilated to *humilitas*; humility and weakness are defining characteristics in the early Christian exaltation of poverty. Crucial to this doctrine was the belief that poverty, in order to be a virtue, must be voluntary; this belief was to play an important role in the practice and interpretation of the ideals of the gospels throughout the Middle Ages. The poverty of Christ was voluntary: it was a renunciation of his power as King and Son of God. Those who follow his example by renouncing power and wealth are therefore praiseworthy. The literature of the early Christian period also exalts the external signs of humility and renunciation which characterize true poverty, such as poor clothing, a life of austerity without possessions, an income or a home, a low social status (sometimes assimilated, significantly, to that of a foreigner) and the daily hardship and suffering of a life of want.

Complementing the doctrine of poverty was the exaltation of charity, which was considered to be a universal duty. In Christianity the notion of a gift, the universal means of creating bonds between individuals and groups, acquires a new dimension, both spiritual and institutional. Alms-giving comes to be seen as a way of redeeming one's sins, and the existence of the poor in Christian society is consequently a natural part of God's plan of salvation. The classic formulation of this doctrine may be found in the *Life of St Eligius*: 'God could have made all men rich, but He wanted there to be poor people in this world, that the rich might be able to redeem their sins.'[2] The doctrine of Christian charity soon gave rise to charitable institutions; some of these continued the traditions inherited from antiquity, while others were founded on new principles as Church structures evolved. Thus the duty of charity, in addition to affecting the daily lives of the faithful, also made Church institutions collectively responsible for social compassion and generosity and for safeguarding the interests of the poor.

Thus the ethos of poverty, both in its early Christian and in its medieval form, entails a conflict between two incompatible ideals: the heroic life of renunciation on the one hand, and the duty to help the poor on the other. Renunciation, held up as the Christian model of the ideal life, was the path to perfection, but it was a path reserved for the elite few; the duty of charity assumed that differences of fortune were inevitable, and that wealth and poverty must necessarily continue to exist side by side. Indeed, the words from the *Life of St Eligius* quoted above might equally well have been reversed: God wanted there to be rich people in this world in order that they might help the poor. The exaltation of charity not only offered the rich the opportunity of buying their salvation; it effectively sanctioned wealth and justified it on ideological grounds. The exaltation of poverty therefore concerned only a select group of those who aspired, by adopting a life of renunciation and refusing to fulfil their social role, to an ideal of Christian perfection. But for the majority of the rich the normal model of Christian life consisted rather in seeking salvation through good works, such as aiding the Church, funding new shrines and donating money to charitable Church institutions. There is a distribution function in the economics of salvation – a sort of division of labour within the framework of the *societas christiana*. The Church, as well as all those who strive to realize the Christian ideal of renunciation within its religious communities, is concerned with the salvation of souls. The tripartite division of Christian society into those who pray, those who wage war and those who work – a division reflecting the accepted medieval view of the world during the agrarian era – sanctioned, among the other functions of the Church such as the care of the poor, its role as manager of salvation. For the masses, the principal duty of life was work, valued more or less highly in Christian doctrine over the centuries but always treated as a divine duty, to be fulfilled within this tripartite distribution of functions. The Christian social ethic which exalted poverty as a search for perfection through humility varied in its translation into practice according to the social setting. For the working masses it meant accepting one's lot with humility; for them, abandoning their social role by renouncing work would be an act not of humility but of pride.

The Christian doctrine of poverty had little to do with social reality; poverty was treated as a purely spiritual value. Thus the medieval exaltation of poverty did not alter the fact that the pauper was treated not as a subject but as an object of the Christian community. The models of ascetic life presented in hagiographic literature concerned only the aristocracy, of whose lifestyles they were negative mirror-images; for them, the path to salvation lay in rejecting the social reality. It is in this context that the semantic value of the concept of poverty in the early Middle Ages becomes apparent, for it was determined by the relation between the opposing concepts of *potens* and *pauper*; thus the criterion of poverty was not material wealth or its lack, but rather power, privilege and social position. Karl Bosl has shown that the *potens/pauper* opposition has its linguistic and conceptual roots in the Psalms, and later occupied a crucial place in the collective consciousness of feudal society. In the course of the first millennium Christianity radically overhauled its social ideology, adapting it to a new situation in which structures of domination had to be sanctioned, and in which relations of dependence based on land ownership played a primary role.

The models of the ascetic life found in early medieval patristic and hagiographical literature were drawn from the gospels. Poverty as a spiritual value was glorified by invoking the external signs of poverty in the lives of Christ and the Apostles, and the metaphors employed in the argumentation referred to the concrete realities of a life of poverty and want. Holy Scripture (Matthew XIX.24) presented poverty as a condition in which salvation was more easily obtained than in a life of opulence. Tertullian was equally succinct in expressing this idea:

'*Deus semper pauperes justicavit, divites praedamnat*'[3] ('God has always looked with favour upon the poor and condemned the rich'). The first Christian communities, and above all that of Jerusalem, were also presented as models of the ideal life. These two ideals – the ideal of poverty in the gospels and the way of life of the first Christian community of Jerusalem – both served, sometimes together and sometimes separately, as models for the eremitic and monastic life, initially in the East, and later in the West, where they defined the rules and basic principles of life in monastic communities. But the image of life in the Jerusalem community was also a prefiguration of the future 'heavenly Jerusalem', and as such it played a much more important role; for it was not merely a model of the ascetic life, but a representation of Christian utopia. In the Acts of the Apostles, in which its principal features are outlined, what is exalted above all is the community of spiritual and material life ('*sed erant illis omnia communia*') and the poverty of its members, who sold their houses and possessions to lay the fruits of the sale at the feet of the Apostles.

Both the ideal of the gospels and this 'form of the first Church' played an enormous role in the spiritual life of Christian Europe from the beginning of the second century, in unorthodox reform movements no less than in the new forms of religious life, particularly monastic life, introduced by the Church. The development of trade in the eleventh and twelfth centuries created a new situation which, as Lester K. Little has shown, transformed the ethos of poverty. In this new situation wealth loses its former 'social' quality: it is no longer the result of privileges conferred by power, land ownership and military conquests. It is now based on money, and expressed solely in money. The birth of urban civilization created new moral problems, and new rules were needed for the plan of salvation. *Fuga mundi*, escape from the world, was a rejection of the new social structures, a spontaneous expression of individual discontent. As long as voluntary poverty remained an expression of individual aspirations it was tolerated by the Church; but when it began to assume the form of a collective movement and spread to entire communities it became a threat. The creation of mendicant orders was a way of 'taming' and controlling such movements, and at the same time of sanctioning, ethically and religiously, the urban world of money.

The new ethos of poverty was based on the same principle: like the old, it sanctioned both wealth and its renunciation and derived its meaning from their opposition. In the new stereotype of symbolic virtue and vice, avarice (*avaritia*) supplants pride (*superbia*) as one of the antitheses of poverty; this change reflects the changes in the social situation. In the constant process of adapting models of Christian life to reality, the ethos of poverty and its translation into practice by the spiritual elite conferred legitimacy upon wealth and sanctioned its place in the social structure.

Charity, in the form of alms-giving and donations to the Church, was presented as a way of redeeming one's sins in this world, and was to be practised constantly. It was the solemn duty of those who exercised power – at the courts of kings and great feudal lords it became customary to feed a certain number of poor on a regular basis, and to distribute alms on journeys – and of those involved in lucrative activities, especially activities of a morally dubious nature, such as money-lending. It became highly ritualized and institutionalized, and the Church was its main beneficiary. Entries in Italian trade and banking registers headed '*per Messer Domeneddio*' in practice represented donations to the Church, used, in the thirteenth and fourteenth centuries, mainly for the upkeep of monasteries, hospitals and religious orders. The poor themselves, to whom alms were distributed both by individual benefactors and by monasteries and religious brotherhoods, came last on the list.

The age of great expansion and blossoming for charitable institutions in Western countries of the Christian world came in the twelfth and thirteenth centuries; most of the hospitals in the Paris region, for instance, were founded between 1175 and 1300. It was now principally by and through charitable institutions that the duty of charity was performed. Their blossoming was connected with a renewal of religious feeling – an 'evangelical awakening', in the words of M. D. Chenu – and the forms of charity in which this new religious fervour was expressed were intended primarily to benefit religious life. Thus the network of hospices endowed by private benefactors and administered largely by the Church was strung out along the great medieval pilgrimage routes, in order to provide temporary shelter to the pious on their pilgrimages. Charity was at that time a way of strengthening the social bonds between religious institutions and the faithful. Private citizens began to get involved in charitable work: there is an excellent study of this type of initiative in twelfth-century Anjou. Religious institutions extended their activities into the towns, where they funded the building of hospitals and hospices which they also ran themselves. One of their functions was to provide a framework for the charitable and social work of the faithful. There was also another: in Venice, for example, the brotherhood complemented the secular elite structures, providing dignity and position to those for whom there was no place in the hierarchy of local government. The social scope of charitable activity, as well as the selection of those for whom it was intended, left no doubt as to the marked class character of the theory and practice of charity in the late Middle Ages. Italian charity of the fourteenth and fifteenth centuries openly privileged the 'shame-faced poor' ('pauperes verecundosi' or 'verecundi' in Latin, 'poveri vergognosi' in Italian): the noble origins which naturally made them 'ashamed' of their poverty and prevented them from stooping to begging also seemed to endow them with exceptional moral qualities. Indeed the Florentine brotherhood Buonomini di San Martino, as well as the foundations of the Monti di Pietà, selected recipients for aid primarily from among the middle and upper strata of society; as Richard Trexler has observed, the ideal of Christian 'fraternity' was in practice marked by the spirit of class solidarity and singled out for special privileges the impoverished members of the social elite. Hagiography was also influenced by this sort of poverty. Hagiographical models, from the oldest – St Alexis – to the most recent – St Francis – promoted voluntary poverty, the renunciation of power or wealth by those who possessed them. In the same way the model of the deserving poor was taken from the impoverished social elite: St Nicholas offers aid to a noble whose indigence is such that his daughters are in danger of resorting to prostitution; St Dominic helps a ruined noble, constrained by poverty to turn his daughters over to heretics.

From the twelfth century onwards the theological doctrine of charity begins to distinguish between two categories of poverty. According to Gerhoch von Reichersberg, a twelfth-century theologian and social theorist and one of the most remarkable thinkers of the period, we must distinguish between the 'poor with Peter' (*pauperes cum Petro*) and the 'poor with Lazarus' (*pauperes cum Lazaro*). Among the former we find, first and foremost, the clergy, whose poverty ought to be their distinctive feature, inherent in their condition; voluntary poverty, which according to Reichersberg should be an integral part of Church discipline and convent life, is a spiritual value conferring legality on 'power within the Church' and on the mediating role between man and God which those who have attained 'perfection' may assume. St Lazarus, on the other hand, represents the other category of poverty. The *pauper Lazarus* of the gospels is a model of secular and material poverty (*paupertas quae est in penuria*);[4] the poor in this category are treated not as active subjects but rather as objects of help provided by the Church and its faithful. The model of the pauper Lazarus which reappears in theological thought in this context attests to a certain openness, on the part of the Church, to the reality of material need. It would be natural to suppose that the recognition of poverty as a spiritual value entailed a similar recognition of the dignity of the pauper as such; I have already remarked on the significance of the external signs of poverty in this context. Clearly, there was a link between these signs and the moral valuation of poverty as a condition. However, in placing too much emphasis on this valuation we are liable to overlook the realities of a world in which the pauper is no more than an object of charity and the bearer of a humiliating condition. Christian doctrine is concerned, from the moral point of view, mainly with the giver of charity, not with its object. Medieval charitable practice is full of examples of acts of genuine compassion. But there is an ostentatious side both to the distribution of alms at convent gates and to individual acts of charity, which appear as mere trappings of piety, flaunted by the benefactors for the better external expression of their own social prestige.

Theological controversy and debate surrounding the doctrine of poverty presents the poor as no more than objects of charity; and although canonical thought has certainly contributed to a better understanding of the realities of material poverty, it has done nothing to propagate the moral or ideological value of that condition. The view that the egalitarian model of charity must be rejected in favour of one which introduces distinctions between different kinds of poor is not an invention of modern welfare: as Brian Tierney has shown, it first found expression in Gratian's *Decree* and in the writings of decretists in the twelfth century. Their interpretation of the teachings of the Church Fathers, especially of St Ambrose and St John Chrysostom, tried to show that beggars fell into two categories, the 'honest' and the 'dishonest', as Ruffin of Bologna put it. The dishonest beggars are those who, although able to work, prefer to beg and steal. Physiological poverty, understood as a state in which an individual has no means of supporting himself and his family, is treated as a priority where immediate aid must be given. Theological debates of the time also reveal the view that theft, when committed in a situation of 'extreme necessity', is not a crime but the exercise of a right. As a result, the starving (and the social history of the first centuries of our millennium shows that this was no mere rhetorical turn of phrase, but had a firm basis in reality) were able to enjoy the same status as widows, orphans, prisoners and madmen, all of whom could claim support in any situation. The strength of the entitlement of these groups to receive support was directly proportional to the poverty of their condition and legal status.

In the eyes of those living at the time, the social structures of that period were becoming increasingly fragmented. The traditional tri-partite division of estates into clergy, nobles and peasants was giving way to a more complex and developed picture of the professional roles and functions to be found within particular groups. The Church gradually began to lose its monopoly as mediator between man and God, and a clearer division of roles emerged within the Church itself: between lay and monastic clergy, for example, and between different orders. The structural changes within secular society brought into relief, independently of the professional diversity, the basic structure of power, the rift between the dominating and the dominated classes. If these latter, whose everyday lot was poverty, put into practice the model of Christian life, it was because they accepted their fate and displayed humility in the face of the duties imposed on them by their legal and social status and by their material condition.

In this context, and in light of the teachings of Christian charity put into practice through the policies of Church institutions and the dominating classes in the period between the twelfth and fourteenth centuries, material poverty becomes associated with social inferiority. Gratian evokes the distinction between *hospitalitas* and *liberalitas*, which we may interpret, in modern terms, as the distinction between alms-giving and welfare. According to Stephen of Tournai, one of the twelfth-century decretists, *hospitalitas* is unconditional: its principle is that 'we provide for all those for whom it is in our power to provide'.[5] *Liberalitas*, on the other hand, must distinguish between the 'honest' and the 'dishonest', 'kin' and 'strangers', old and young, humble and arrogant, and provide aid to the first in each of these categories. Whatever the subtleties of interpretation of these two terms (*liberalitas* may be understood both as hospitality and as aid within hospital institutions), this kind of thinking sanctioned the practice of charity of the late Middle Ages. Hospital institutions functioned as places of refuge for the sick, the handicapped and the poor; they also took in pilgrims. These institutions of social aid were for the most part concerned with people suffering from social and material degradation; when pilgrims from higher classes appeared among them, they voluntarily renounced their status, in the full knowledge that here, among the genuinely impoverished, they would find suitable conditions for their act of humility. In theory, the practice of charity extended to all beggars, whether on the streets or wandering from door to door, but uncertainty as to their 'honesty' and moral qualities cast doubt both on the validity of compassionate behaviour towards them and on the effectiveness of their prayers on behalf of their benefactors. The medieval canonists elaborated subtle distinctions between the usefulness of alms-giving to the beggar and its advantages to the benefactor, and this confirmed, in the mentality of the time, the need to distinguish between different kinds of poor. Guido de Baysia, who approved of this type of analysis, wrote that an act of charity is truly an act of virtue when it is performed rationally, in other words when its consequences both for the benefactor and for the recipient of alms are taken into account. It was therefore rational to support people one knew – impoverished members of one's own *milieu*. This is the type of reasoning that sanctioned the class orientation of charity. The fundamental distinction between 'social aid' and charity was already present in the Middle Ages; modern debates about welfare reform have simply resurrected it.

In considering the significance of the ethos of poverty in medieval consciousness and behaviour, we should bear in mind not only its practical limitations but also the fact that, even in theory, the exaltation of poverty as a spiritual value conflicted with the low social status of the truly poor.

Ecclesiastical writing alone contains many examples of this conflict. Already in the tenth century, the Benedictine Ratherius of Verona, a theologist well schooled in patristic writings, dedicated a whole chapter of his *Preloquia* to the problem of beggars. The main conclusion of his arguments is that poverty is not a value in and of itself and does not by any means guarantee salvation. On the contrary, a pauper who sins will be damned, as many examples in Scripture testify. Moreover, the duty of charity extends also to beggars, even to the handicapped or the infirm, insofar as their condition allows. They should 'offer up to God' what they can; in their search for salvation, they, too, must look to the expiation of their own sins. Indeed Ratherius seems, in the severity of his judgements, to harbour a clear dislike for beggars. The beggar should, he says, be content with the basic necessities for survival and avoid *superaffluentia*. If he is healthy and able to work, he may not beg. Even if he is unable to work and has no means of support, he should make himself useful through charitable works, such as tending the sick or burying the dead. Ratherius' severity can best be seen in his rejection of large families as the cause of poverty; the poor man should be able to feed his family through work and 'abstinence'.

This degree of severity towards the poor is clearly exceptional in the social attitudes and theological thought of the early Middle Ages. Nevertheless a change in the tone of Christian writing on the subject did not become visible until the twelfth century, as a result of profound transformations in Christian attitudes towards poverty; Rotherius' mode of discourse would sit badly with the growing sensitivity to social problems and the 'new perspective on the poor' that emerged in Western Christianity in the twelfth and thirteenth centuries. But polemical writings, aimed primarily at heretical sects which advocated poverty as a Christian value, contain analogous arguments seeking to present it as a degrading condition.

The degrading aspects of poverty were frequently stressed in ideological attacks on movements of voluntary poverty and mendicant orders. Innocent III made explicit his opposition to mendicancy as a shameful and undignified condition which ill befits the clergy and degrades all who practise it. When deliberating the case against Bernard, Dean of the chapter of Nevers, who was accused of heresy, he decided to restore the latter's *beneficium* in order that he should not be forced to beg, thus 'bringing shame upon the clergy'. The same argument was invoked in the decision to accord a pension to the Bishop of Toulouse, removed from his post for simony, that he should not 'bring shame upon his status as a man of the cloth'. Begging was seen to be humiliating not only for the beggar but also for the social group to which he belonged, to everyone linked to him by 'solidarity of status'. The polemics against mendicancy of the thirteenth and fourteenth century, and especially the violent attack on it by William of Saint-Amour, invoke scholastic reasoning and interpretations of Scripture in their attempts to emphasize the degrading nature of poverty and mendicancy; they also invoke the realities of poverty, arguing that, while it should be borne with dignity, it does not confer dignity on one's life.

For poverty, on the moral plane, gives rise to specific sins. Humbert of Romans, emphasizing, in the thirteenth century, the social aspects of pastoral work by weaving into his sermons elements of the everyday life – and everyday sins – of the lower classes, remarks that poverty 'born of necessity' does not confer a state of grace because 'it is not poverty itself that is a virtue but the taste for poverty'. The people, however, have no taste for poverty, and for this reason it is 'the rich of this world that they deem happy (*beatos*)'.[6] The remark is significant not only because it is a succint summing-up, by a great French Dominican, of the essence of the ethos of poverty, distinguishing between physical poverty and the 'taste for poverty', but also because it clearly states the attitudes of the masses towards indigence and wealth. People like wealth; they do not like poverty. Poverty gives rise to the mortal sin of jealousy; covetousness, envy and the refusal to accept one's condition lie at its root, and are widespread among the poor. By this refusal they oppose the divine will and defy God, a defiance they also express by stealing, in an attempt to escape their condition. The acts of rebellion invoked by Humbert are low in the hierarchy of crimes; but he also criticizes the habits of the poor: idleness, debauchery, drunkenness and dishonest dealings are an integral part of their lives.

Needless to say, the views of a thirteenth-century moralist and preacher concerning the poor – from peasants through town labourers to beggars and lepers in hospital refuges – are one-sided and limited by the aims of religious teaching. But the issue is not the extent to which this description corresponds to reality. What is important is the negative attitude towards poverty which it reveals in the ecclesiastical literature of the period, and hence in the social consciousness. The brunt of the preacher's sarcastic criticism is directed against the secular world in general (although it does not spare the clergy, the monks or the converts), but it is based on the conviction that the sins of secular life are born of poverty and wealth alike. The origins and the nature of the sins in each case, however, are not the same. The sins of the rich lie in the abuse of power and wealth, privilege and dignity of position. The sins of the poor, on the other hand, arise from the poor man's rejection of the humiliations and privations imposed by the social and material condition which is his lot.

Criticism of the poor was a frequent theme in medieval literature. Particularly widespread was the satirical portrayal of peasants, where the main element of ridicule was the social and cultural inferiority of the peasant masses. Twelfth- and thirteenth-century literature on vagrants abounds in this type of writing. But poverty is only a secondary element here. The main object of criticism is secular society as a whole, seen from the point of view of this self-styled 'proletariat' (or perhaps 'plebs' would be a better word, in order to avoid etymological confusion); all social groups were criticized from the point of view of the elite from which the readers and listeners of this literature were drawn. However, it is in moralistic literature and in writings on moral theology, two closely linked genres, that the significance of poverty as a model in medieval society can best be evaluated.

Moralistic literature from the early Middle Ages to the twelfth century contains much criticism of the *pauper superbus*, the pauper who refuses to accept his condition with humility. In later periods, as the professional divisions of society became more widely accepted in the medieval consciousness, moral criticism of the poor became part of the 'review' of the socio-economic conditions of various groups. Much of the criticism was admittedly directed more often at the rich than at the poor, who tend to appear either in the guise of victims, abused by the rich of this world, or as the recipients of charity, which the rich have a duty to provide. But by the thirteenth century the poor, too, had become the object of attack. The French satirical poet Guillaume de Clerc argues in his *Besant de Dieu* that the poor are no better than the rich because they are 'treacherous, envious blasphemers, proud and full of jealousy and lust';[7] they cheat at work, work as little as possible, and drink away their earnings as soon as they are paid. A century later, Jean Le Fèvre's outburst is typical of the tone of moralistic literature:

> Au voir dire,
> nulz home ne doit le pauvre faire
> s'il a ce qui est necessaire.[8]

In other words, one should be content with the bare necessities of life; no one in this condition can be said to be poor. Contempt for poverty is clearly at the root of this claim. Elsewhere, a French rhyme-maker sneers at the cupidity and greed of beggars when they crowd and jostle for places at alms distributions.

'Fa spessamente povertà fallire' – 'poverty often leads to ruin' – declares Francesco da Barberino, a fourteenth-century Italian poet. Poverty goes hand in hand with greed: if one is content with what one has, one is not poor. In this context the only connotations of poverty are pejorative ones. Francesco da Barberino seems to assume that it is everyone's desire to become rich, and claims that this end can be reached by the spiritual path of renouncing greed. The negative attitude to poverty is also expressed in the theme, frequent in Italian literature of the fourteenth century, of the moral vices which it engenders. An anonymous work from the period portrays poverty as a cloak which conceals anger, envy and other sins, and contains the cry: 'O povertà – cosi sis despersa!' ('Poverty, be thou accursed!'). It goes on to describe the humiliations and indignities which make poverty a fate worse than death:[9]

> La morte può ben l'uomo privar di vita,
> ma non di fame e di virtude altera;
> anco felice e vera
> riman perpetual nel mondo e viva.
> Ma chi a tua foce sconsolata arriva
> sia quanto vuol magnanimo e gentile,
> e pur tenuto è vile
> e perciò chi nel tuo abisso cala
> non speri in alcun pregio spander l'ala.[10]

Death does not rob man of his dignity or his virtues, but poverty does; such is the Italian poet's conclusion. The poem was clearly written in the context of anti-mendicant polemics, and its style can be placed within the trend to reject poverty as a moral value; its validity as a piece of testimony is therefore doubtful. But it is important as one among the great variety of attitudes and doctrines concerning poverty which existed and developed side by side in medieval society. The programmes of the Church and the demands of waging an effective struggle against heterodoxy within Christianity brought out different elements of these doctrines at different times. But regardless of these ideological fluctuations, the rule was that poverty could reach its apotheosis only as a spiritual value, while real, physical poverty, with its visible degrading effects, was perceived, both doctrinally and by society, as a humiliating state, depriving its victims of dignity and respect, relegating them to the margins of society and to a life devoid of virtue. The medieval ethos of poverty did not exalt the state of material need, nor did it oppose the view that the poor were superfluous in society. St Bonaventure, in his response to critics of the mendicant orders, of which he was an advocate, invoked arguments characteristic of the medieval doctrine of poverty: after all, he said, praise of chastity does not entail hostility to marital life, just as praise of the solitary life of hermits does not entail a condemnation of the communal life. This argument reveals something of the relationship between the ethos of poverty and the social reality.

The pauper evoked fear and suspicion because he rebelled against his condition, but also because he posed a threat to property. The Czech chronicler Cosma took it for granted that the 'golden age' of the past which he described in his utopian vision contained no beggars. But the context of his assumption was significant: 'There were no bolts on the stables and doors were not closed to the poor, for there were no thieves or brigands or beggars.'[11]

Finally, we should consider the social consequences of the ethos of poverty when it was put into practice by an elite seeking salvation through a Christian life of ascetic perfection. Setting aside theological controversies about the poverty of Christ and the apostles, or poverty as it was practised by the mendicant orders, it is clear that, in medieval Christianity, voluntary poverty commanded respect, and was even enveloped in an aura of sanctity. The very real expulsion from society which it involved was nevertheless accompanied by a high degree of prestige. In cases of genuine poverty there was a direct relation between the pauper's way of life, which infringed generally accepted norms, and the disgust, hostility and rejection of which the poor were objects. In cases of asceticism and voluntary renunciation, on the other hand, the attitudes were reversed: the deliberately 'asocial' condition of ascetic groups evoked the admiration, an admiration sometimes amounting almost to idolatry, of society. Can it really be said, then, that the ascetic life was an 'asocial' one?

I have already remarked on the ambivalence inherent in a life lived according to Christian models: such a life, if strictly observed, would be detached from, indeed opposed to, socio-cultural realities. We must now consider the effects of putting into practice the ascetic ideal of Christianity on the way of life of its followers. One of the ways of accomplishing this ideal involved mortification and breaking with the habits of one's past life. This was sometimes done covertly: Robert d'Arbrissel, when he was studying at Angers, wore a hairshirt underneath his 'fine' outer clothing before opting for the openly ascetic life as a hermit in the forest. The life of the hermit, the recluse, the wandering preacher (who preached among people as well as in the desert) were all, in the first centuries of our millennium, forms of a movement to revive the ideal of Christian life; the external signs of poverty were adopted in order to imitate the 'nakedness of Christ', and to express the break with a previous way of life, whether secular or clerical.

This break consisted primarily in abandoning settled areas and farmland and moving away from 'civilization'. The flight towards forests and deserts was the expression of a choice to live on the margins of Christian society. Medieval literature contains some terrifying images of this kind of existence 'at the ends of the earth', which were nevertheless within sight of villages and towns. In the medieval imagination forests and deserts were realms of perpetual darkness where evil forces reigned and brigands and ferocious beasts stalked by night. Into the midst of this evil the hermit entered, a hero come to wrest the desert from the clutch of dark powers, to Christianize the forest, conquer fear and break the sway of wild beasts, men as well as animals – brigands, fugitives and exiles living 'in the wild' after breaking the rules of Christian life within society. Such is the hermit encountered by Tristan and Isolde in the forest of Norrois: he preaches to them from the gospels and gives them absolution. Jacques of Vitry, in one of his *exempla*, describes the missionary activity of hermits among brigands: a brigand, having confessed, undertakes, in penance for his sins, to recite the Pater Noster at every cross he comes to on the road. At the first cross he is killed by a relative of one of his victims, but the hermit sees his soul being carried up to heaven by the angels. In Wolfram von Eschenbach's *Parzival* the hermit similarly acts as teacher and adviser; he is described as a 'good man', and his sanctity is due to a life of renunciation: he eats neither meat nor fish and is dressed in rags.

The harsh diet, impoverished appearance – the body almost naked, barely covered with rags – and neglect of hygiene figured prominently in descriptions of the lives of medieval hermits. They were not only the signs of perfect poverty, as seen in the context of the ideology of renunciation; they also assimilated the hermit, externally, to the common vagabond. (Critics of eremitism use this resemblance as an argument against the ideology as a whole.) The hermit's way of life places him in the category of those who exist on the margins of the organized life of society.

Finally, hermits are cut off from society by their solitude, for their way of life, especially when accompanied by a vow of silence, involves the rejection of all social contact. The only remaining link between the hermit and society is the functional relation involved in the cult of his sanctity. But even this must be weighed against the fear or revulsion evoked by his appearance, his isolation and his way of life. St Haimrad of Swabia, for instance, was constantly rejected and chased away because people were frightened and angered by his appearance and manner of address; it was only when he found refuge in a hermitage that he won the trust and sympathy of the local population.

This break with ordinary life was characteristic not only of individual hermits but also of ascetic groups and various forms of convent life. The eremitic rule laid down by Étienne Muret and applied in Grandmont was inspired by the words of St Paul enjoining the chosen to 'die for the world'. Practical rules were laid down to ensure strict adherence to the evangelical model of non-participation, or highly restricted participation, in social and family life, and in the life of secular institutions: in Grandmont, for instance, begging at mills and private houses was allowed; and as for family life, it was preferable, if a choice had to be made, to come to the aid of a dying stranger abandoned by his own kin than to attend the funeral of a relative. Communities of hermits and ascetics represented a wide variety of social classes: members of the elite who had renounced their former privileges joined genuine paupers and social outcasts to form groups around the advocates of the new religiosity (the entourage of Robert d'Arbrissel, for example, is known to have included vagabonds, thieves and prostitutes). As the Church gradually came to accept these forms of piety, until at length, through the 'taming' of their proponents, they became institutionalized, a phenomenon described by Max Weber as the 'routinization of charisma' could be observed: the refusal to live one's life according to the recognized social norms was sanctioned by the Church, the leading institution of the prevailing social system, which had the power to dictate rules of coexistence and to control their application.

Externally, then, the way of life chosen by aspirants to Christian perfection was similar, in its essential features, to the life of the genuinely poor. But poverty is instrumental here: what is important is the spiritual life. The voluntary act of renouncing society, whether spontaneous and individual or ritualized and collective, played a functional role: it was a path of merit, a means towards an end, and as such it involved a symbolic rise in status. Similarly, *fuga mundi*, the flight from the world, was not a simple and unambiguous escape from society; it was an escape from social structures that were in conflict with the Christian ideal, from a way of life which prevented the propagation and fulfilment of that ideal. Hermitages were established in spots where they could be seen and easily visited, at roadsides and crossroads; and hermits, and even recluses, often wandered from place to place, preaching the gospel wherever they could, even in towns.

Indeed, urban development was an important factor in the social genesis of voluntary poverty. There is no doubt that the choice of such a life was primarily a protest against the wealth accumulated by the Church and the clergy, against the social position of ecclesiastical institutions and of the people connected to them within the structure of wealth, domination and power. But a new kind of wealth was beginning to make itself felt, concentrated in the towns. Both the urban way of life and the economic activities associated with it evoked anxiety on the moral plane. The medieval anti-urban doctrine treated the city as the work of Cain, the biblical patron of individuals and groups tainted by sin, outcasts condemned to a life of exclusion until they atoned for the sins they had committed in opposing the will of God and the principles of human coexistence. It is significant that monasticism and eremitism had their beginnings in Eastern Christianity, where the old city structures, places of wealth and luxury, still survived. Thus voluntary poverty, in its quest for Christian perfection, was above all an escape from urban civilization.

The exaltation of poverty was a permanent element of religious teaching. Its function varied with the audience: for the poor, the stress was on the merits – with the prospect of salvation – of accepting their lot with humility; for the rich, it was a reminder of the need to atone for their sins by deeds of charity. Preachers drew liberally on the hagiography of poverty in presenting this double message. A typical parable, often used by preachers, was that of the hermit St Macarius: travelling through Mayence, he saw a poor man (*hominem pauperrimum*) lying on the ground in a city square; he was dying alone, and 'no one cared about him because he was poor'.[12] It was then that the hermit had a vision: he saw a host of angels gather around the dying man, while around the nearby house of a rich man, a house resounding with joy, he saw a crowd of demons. The point of this *exemplum* was not to condemn wealth; it was a reminder of the many dangers of sin to which the rich man is exposed, dangers symbolized by the demons crowding around his house, and of the constant vigilance which a life of riches requires: the rich man must look to his salvation by observing the ideal of the Christian life. There is another message in this *exemplum*, still addressed to the rich man, in the spirit of the gospels: it is a reminder of God's benediction of the poor. Finally, the moral tale sheds some light on the social reality of the day in presenting the pauper, abandoned by all, dying alone in a public square.

The medieval ethos of poverty did not promote material poverty either as a social reality or as a transcendental perspective. There was no attempt to diminish the degrading aspects of poverty. The most famous ascetics and their followers did indeed practise the ethos of poverty through voluntary degradation and rejection of society, but they were seen as being doubly privileged, both by the prospect of future salvation and by the aura of sanctity which gave them the respect and dignity of high social status. There is no link, on the moral plane, between the practitioners of voluntary poverty and the genuinely poor. But sometimes, by virtue of the external similarities of dress, appearance and way of life, the aura of sanctity was extended to the latter group. Finally, the heroism of renunciation, doctrinally presented both as an end in itself (although such a perfect model was almost impossible to put into practice) and as a means to salvation, played another role: it stimulated compassion. Thus it was beneficial both to professional beggars and to the poor in general.

1.2 Alms and Beggars

Recent research has brough forth a large number of studies, both general works and monographs, of charity and charitable institutions in medieval and modern times. The picture they paint varies from country to country, but in general the evolution of charitable institutions and hospitals, closely linked to the activities and politics of the Church, follows the same course everywhere in the Christian world. I shall consider here only the social consequences of this activity and the sociological profile of the recipients of alms and beneficiaries of charitable institutions.

The collective distribution of alms remained a widespread custom throughout the Middle Ages. For a long time it took place mainly in monasteries, but it was also a part of secular life: it was the rule, for example, at the funerals of sovereigns and men of great wealth, and in time also became common practice at the funerals of rich members of the bourgeoisie. Sovereigns maintained a custom of liberal alms distribution on tours of the country and certain holidays. The chronicles which describe the life of Robert II, King of France until his death in

1031, mention the fact that it was his custom to distribute, in each of his residences, wine and bread to a number of poor which varied from three hundred to one thousand; and that in the last year of his life, during Lent, he gave alms to between a hundred and two hundred poor every day. The monasteries, in accordance with the rule of their order, regularly distributed alms, especially on holy days. Services in memory of the dead were also generally accompanied by a distribution of alms, and sometimes wills made in favour of churches contained a clause stipulating that part of the legacy be distributed as alms. One of the monks from the monastery of Reichenau specified that after his death ceremonies in his honour should continue for thirty days, and should be accompanied not only by prayer but by four distributions of alms, to benefit, on successive days, one hundred, two hundred, three hundred and four hundred poor. The periodic alms distributions at the gates of the monastery of Cluny took place on an enormous scale: at the beginning of the fast meat was distributed to hundreds of poor, while the number of poor people who sat down to eat at table during celebrations in honour of dead monks was at least ten thousand per year; and on certain holy days, between fifteen hundred and two thousand poor gathered at the monastery gates to receive alms. The statistics given in later documents concerning alms distribution in towns, in the form of money or food, are no less impressive, and sometimes astonishing. In 1355 the will of a well-to-do townsman of Lübeck contained instructions for the distribution of alms to nineteen thousand poor, the entire population of the town being at that time between twenty-two and twenty-four thousand. The distribution of bread at Rodez, organized by the local brotherhood, was intended for six thousand people; the population of that town was around five thousand. The most common type of will contained provisions for aiding between several hundred and several thousand people.

Some of these statistics, especially those taken from narrative or hagiographical literature, should obviously be taken with a grain of salt. But more reliable documentation concerning alms distribution by monasteries, sovereigns and men of great wealth is to be had from account books. Although it is not always clear from these documents whether the numbers given refer to recipients of alms or to the amount of alms distributed, in general it can be said that, in the case of regular alms distributions taking place during one day, the amount of alms does correspond roughly to the number of recipients. In the fifteenth century a Parisian townsman left instructions in his will for alms to be given to nearly four thousand poor, spread out over different areas of the city, and provided a list of these. In the fourteenth century the brotherhood of Or San Michele in Florence, according to its account books, provided partial support (three or four times a week) for five to seven thousand paupers, and watched permanently over their welfare; in addition it saw regularly to the needs of about a thousand poor. Where a large concentration of people was involved, this required a uniform and well thought-out system of control, a system which, from its origins in the thirteenth century, was to spread beyond the towns to become an integral part of medieval charity. It was in the thirteenth century that the first attempts were made to work out a method of identifying and keeping track of those who were entitled to aid by the distribution of special tokens; this had the added advantage of preventing the beneficiaries from collecting alms twice, or several times, in the course of a single distribution. The use of tokens is first mentioned in around 1240 by Richard Fishacre, a Dominican from Oxford, who, in his commentary on Pierre Lombard's *Sentences*, makes use of the following example: a king ordered one of his courtiers to distribute tin 'numbers' among a group of poor, entitling them to a meal at the king's table on a particular day. On the appointed day, another courtier distributed identical 'numbers' to a different group, thus ensuring that both groups received royal alms even though they had been given their 'numbers' at different times. This example served to illustrate a theological argument about the nature of the sacraments, but its significance lies in the fact that the distribution of tokens to the poor is treated as normal practice. The token system signals a trend towards stricter control, both of the poor themselves and of the distribution of alms; it is thus in conflict with the traditional conception of the good deed, where the most important element was the psychological intention of the alms-giver. Giovanni Villani, a Florentine chronicler, notes that in 1330 a citizen of Florence left his entire fortune to the poor, specifying that each poor man was to receive six deniers; but, in order to prevent false claims, all the poor of the city were made to gather in the churches at a given hour, and received their share as they filed out of church one by one. In this way seventeen thousand poor were benefited.

In order to estimate the number of poor in the city one would have to take into account, in addition to this seventeen thousand, residents of hospices, prisoners, and monks who lived by begging for alms:

about four thousand in all. But even these figures are not sufficient to establish the total number. Beggars were constantly on the move, their movements guided by a particular sort of calendar composed of days on which alms were distributed. These distributions took place mostly in monasteries; the dates were often fixed and known in advance, and beggars often travelled long distances to be at the right monastery on the appointed day. This wandering from monastery to monastery made up the substance of their lives; in addition to the great alms distributions on holy days, which the beggars particularly appreciated, they could always expect some modest daily support at the gates of a convent. Distributions which took place as a result of testamentary bequests also had great drawing power, attracting the poor from the whole region through which the news had spread. It can be seen from wills in Forez at the beginning of the fourteenth century that alms were generally distributed after the harvest, a practice convenient for the heirs, and word of the occasion spread within a radius of ten to fifteen kilometres from the place where the deceased had lived. Urban charitable institutions also organized alms distributions on a huge scale, particularly at the time of the annual banquet of the local brotherhood, which sought in this way to reaffirm its prestige and provide a spectacular display of its piety. In the case of the brotherhood of Or San Michele of Florence, however, it is clear that the main object of the exercise was to impose more rigorous controls on the poor population: all the poor who were given tokens, and entitled to claim their share of assistance, were listed in a register in which, alongside their names, various details concerning them were inscribed. It appears from these registers that this assistance was not limited to citizens of the town but extended to include peasants, and that it increased when the harvest had been poor: in the latter half of March 1347 the names of peasants from two hundred and twenty-three villages in the *contado* of Florence were listed in the registers.

But who were these people? What were the origins and status of those who received charity in the Middle Ages? We might suppose that, given the humiliation and loss of dignity which begging involves, only those who lived in extreme poverty would have recourse to it. But this was not always the case. The medieval distinction between the 'shamefaced poor' and other types of paupers is significant precisely because the former term denotes members of the middle or even upper classes who have lost their social status and been reduced to poverty; it is never applied to the mass of working poor for whom indigence was a normal condition. For them, the acceptance of charity involved no loss of dignity. The crowds which gathered on the great distribution days did so not only in order to claim their small – often negligible – share of the money, but to participate in what was also a social occasion, and to meet others like themselves. Thus the mere fact of accepting charity is not sufficient to define beggars as a sociological category.

The distribution of alms, however, has great significance in its own right, not only as a means of estimating the number of beggars or paupers. The forms it assumed could change, just as changes took place in the relations between secular and ecclesiastical charitable activity; but the essential fact about it remains the enormous quantity of alms which continued to be distributed and the ease with which the poor could obtain aid. It was, of course, insufficient in times of natural disasters and famine; but at normal times the generosity of the benefactors made begging an attractive way of life. It will be useful briefly to sketch the main features of the medieval system of alms-giving and its relation to the psychology of charity.

To give alms is to display compassion; but the institutional role of the Church in this regard was such that it acted as a kind of screen, which frequently shielded such displays from the public eye. The mediation of the Church between rich and poor was the basis of medieval Christianity. It was, in fact, the Church which provided direct aid to the poor: in the first place by allotting a third or a quarter of ecclesiastical revenues to the support of the poor, and secondly by undertaking the management of charitable donations and legacies to monasteries. The monasteries would then distribute these funds in the form of alms. The first form of mediation involved donations made to the Church by society as a whole; the individual act of charity was lost to view in what had become a general duty. And yet these individual contributions formed the basis of the support which parishes were able to offer their poor; as the expenses of the parish increased, this support diminished, and parish priests gradually shifted the burden, in addition to the usual donations for the Church and the parish, to their parishioners. The second way in which the Church mediated in matters of charity, in managing donations and legacies to monasteries from well-to-do citizens, involved something more: such gifts, while they remained the means whereby the benefactor could demonstrate his piety, as well as his riches and power, were clearly a way of satisfying the aspirations of great lords and sovereigns to attain a dominant position with regard to the Church. Compassion for the poor and the desire to better their lot play a very minor role among the psychological motivations for charitable gifts. For the monasteries, providing assistance to the poor was a duty, one of the functions imposed upon them by liturgical practice and by the statutes of their order. But the funds for this, too, became more and more restricted as the internal expenses of the monasteries continued to grow and to take over an increasing proportion of their budget. If the budget was a large one, a proportionately small part of it, set aside for the poor, would suffice to organize alms distribution on a large scale; but when this was not the case, the monastery's charitable activity became no more than a marginal part of its work. At the end of the thirteenth and the beginning of the fourteenth century, the revenues of the abbey of Saint-Denis, near Paris, amounted to thirty-three thousand Parisian pounds, of which a little under one thousand was spent on assistance to the poor; this modest 3 per cent of the budget hardly reinforces the image of the monastery as a mediator between generous benefactors and the poor, although it did enable some alms distributions on a grand scale to take place on holy days and during Lent.

The expansion of individual charity in the twelfth and thirteenth centuries had the result of expanding the class of benefactors to include the elite of the towns. At the same time the model of charity described above suffered some changes: the mediating role of the Church was somewhat restricted, individual charity could flourish more freely and benefactors were often able to provide assistance directly. Donations were made to hospitals, lepers' colonies and refuges, and it seems that in many cases these direct acts of charity were the expression of a genuine desire to help the poor. The broader social framework within which acts of charity took place was also reflected in the increasingly significant role of religious brotherhoods. The appearance of mendicant orders changed the nature of donations to monasteries; the custom of giving alms directly and in response to specific requests became a general one. As a result of these changes the act of charity became almost a mass phenomenon. It is difficult to say, on the basis of our present knowledge, to what extent the poor were able to benefit from this expansion of individual generosity; it seems probable that a very limited proportion of the funds donated to monasteries was actually distributed to the poor. In this way the ethos of poverty and the 'evangelical awakening' were to a great extent subject to abuse and institutional exploitation.

The system of medieval charity was such that a certain number of the poor were assured of permanent assistance; these were groups attached either to the court or to the house of their benefactor. The liturgy of alms-giving, which defined the place, the nature and the value of the assistance given, also gave rise to the principle of continuous assistance, a sort of 'poor man's prebend'. The monastic *consuetudines*, which set down in detail how and in what circumstances the poor were to be given aid, distinguished, among the categories of the poor, a group which was to be under the permanent and total care of the monasteries; it is to members of this group that the liturgy refers when it commands that their feet be washed, that they be given shelter for the night and that they be invited to share the meal of the monks. The liturgical nature of this kind of aid is further accentuated by the fact that the number of poor participating in this rite was strictly defined. It was a symbolic number, and as such one of the ways in which the ritualization of ecclesiastical charity was given expression. The charitable activity of sovereigns was also distinguished by this ritual character. The biographer of St Louis notes that the king was in the habit of distributing alms with great generosity: '. . . wherever he went in his kingdom, he would give money to churches, hospices, hospitals for lepers and refuges for monks, and to impoverished gentlemen and gentlewomen.'[13] In addition to this – a form of alms-giving of limited advantage to beggars, for only those residing in hospital institutions could benefit from it – it was also the king's daily custom to distribute food among the poor; not to mention '. . . those who ate in his room; and often . . . he himself would cut their bread and pour their drink.' The custom of offering the poor the shelter of one's house and the food from one's table was not limited to palaces and monasteries; it was also practised by great lords, both secular and clerical, and in time, as the contents of wills confirm, was even taken up by the bourgeoisie. This ritualized and institutionalized form of charity was useful in expiating the sins of wealth and power; at the same time it assured a stable existence, in the form of a prebend, to a number of people, for whom poverty was in a sense the professional justification of that stability.

In the same way the permanent assistance provided by hospitals and religious institutions created a group of 'pensioned poor'; medieval hospitals and hospices, besides offering shelter to wandering paupers, primarily pilgrims, also served as permanent residences for some of the poor of the region. Setting aside the question of the extent and density of these hospitals (where the functions of a hospital in the modern sense, understood as the providing of medical care, played a very minor role), it should be noted that various types of such hospitals existed, described in the fifteenth century by Antonin of Florence. He lists them as follows: the *syndochium*, which gave shelter to pilgrims and to the poor; the *procotrophium*, where the poor were fed; the *gerontocomium*, which sheltered the old; the *orphanotrophium*, or orphanage; the *brephotrophium*, which provided food for children; and a number of others. Historical research has shown that this list is more than a theoretical canon: these specializations were reflected in the practice of charity in the late Middle Ages. These specialized hospices also provided permanent support to a number of paupers – further instances of 'pensioned poverty'. The criteria of selection for this kind of permanent support are fundamental to the definition of poverty in the Middle Ages: its recipients were above all the infirm and disabled, orphans and the elderly, in other words those whom material poverty had placed in a particularly wretched social condition.

If, on the other hand, we now turn to those who relied on charitable institutions, such as religious brotherhoods, for their subsistence, or who received permanent support from the municipality or from professional bodies, and whose names therefore appeared regularly in the registers of alms distributed, we find that, although the elderly and the infirm did of course appear, most prominent were those who had sunk into poverty as a result of unfortunate circumstances: children from large families, people whose support had been cut off by the death or illness of the family breadwinner, victims of natural disasters such as fires, and so on. The majority of those who relied on professional bodies for support belonged to the category of the 'shamefaced poor': impoverished members of the social classes represented by these bodies. There were a number of such people among the 'pensioners' of the Florentine brotherhood of Or San Michele: their poverty was justified in the eyes of the brotherhood by their illness or by the difficulties of their family situation – reasons considered honourable enough to account for the state of poverty to which they had been reduced. The system of tokens distributed to the poor, a confirmed practice in many late medieval cities, may be considered as an attempt to extend the 'poor man's prebend' to a broader class of people; it served to put into practice an important principle of the doctrine of alms-giving in the late Middle Ages, that of distinguishing between different categories of poor people and supporting only those no longer able to live in a way befitting their social rank. In the Netherlands, in the fifteenth century, it was even possible to buy such tokens, and thus to guarantee oneself a sort of old-age pension for the rest of one's days.

The holders of these prebends, poor people receiving permanent — although not always total — aid from secular or religious institutions, made up a category of people whose regular lifestyle and stable position in the social hierarchy were assured. Incapable of subsisting unaided, they owed their support and stability of existence to the medieval doctrine of charity.

Hospitals, as we have seen, were among the places offering this kind of stability. Before they became places of compulsory detention for beggars, hospitals had provided temporary shelter and organized the distribution of alms. In 1403 the hospital of the Holy Spirit in Cologne supported about fourteen hundred beggars each week; this figure did not of course correspond to the number of permanent residents of the hospital, but to the number of alms distributed. In 1475 the same hospital appears to have supported seven hundred beggars daily, and this figure, too, refers to the distribution of alms. Medieval hospitals fulfilled their function as places of refuge for the poor in two ways: by providing shelter for the night and by distributing food, daily or at regular intervals. It was often stipulated in the founding acts of a hospital that its function was to relieve the growing overcrowding of the city by beggars, or by certain categories of poor. Such was the motivation, for instance, behind the many privileges and subventions accorded to the Lucerne hospital in 1419 by Count Wilhelm von Arnberg, who, in setting down the arguments on which he based his aid, at the same time manages to shed some light on the lives of the poor: '. . . since I have seen with my own eyes', he says, 'how many poor, crippled, infirm and needy people live in the hospital in Lucerne, and how each day new ones are brought in from the street.'[14] The striking fact which emerges from eyewitness accounts such as this is that the lives of the poor oscillate between the hospital or refuge and the street. The fourteenth century saw the idea of centralized aid for the poor, based in hospital institutions and run by the municipality, beginning to take hold; by the fifteenth century it had been put into practice in many European cities. But throughout this period hospitals and refuges nonetheless remained places where aid was regularly distributed, fixed stations in a beggar's life. Indeed, in the late Middle Ages hospitals tended to close their doors to beggars when their number was too great, pleading insufficient resources to deal with such quantities of people, and arguing that the presence of wandering beggars would disrupt hospital life and lead to drunkenness and debauchery among the residents. But even as the hospitals continued to distribute alms, the city's streets and churches remained the main places of begging. The first steps to centralize the administration of aid to the poor and place it in the hands of the municipality often consisted in a hospital's assumption of responsibility for the city's poor. In 1458 the city of Antwerp set up a Chamber of the Poor, a secular charitable institution which was nevertheless based on the parochial system of charity and maintained some of the forms of that system, such as, for example, the so-called Tables of the Holy Spirit. In the distribution of alms the Antwerp Chamber adopted the use of the metal tokens mentioned above.

While it is doubtful whether the 'begging aristocracy' – those who received prebends or some other form of permanent aid – can really be described, judging by the life they led, as beggars, a large proportion of those who received alms from hospitals and monasteries were professional beggars. Most of them were vagabonds, guided by the calender of Church alms-giving, by distributions on holy days and by legacies to the poor; those who lived in the country went begging from one village to another, since the countryside could provide no stability for them. In cities, on the other hand – both modern and medieval – they were rapidly integrated into a stable structure.

This is borne out above all by iconography. In representations of urban life, beggars seem to be a permanent element of the social landscape, as much an integral part of what characterizes a city as architecture and the activities of tradesmen and craftsmen. Similarly, in iconographic representations of church scenes, beggars are always among the crowd of people gathered outside, as well as inside, the church. They are present in literary descriptions of cities, if only to emphasize the miserliness or generosity of the citizens. As to their number, the figures cited are often unreliable: the author of a fifteenth-century description of Paris claims, for instance, that the city contained eighty thousand beggars. They are obviously absent from tax lists, which is why they do not appear as a separate category in financial statistics. Exceptional in this regard is the tax list of Augsburg for 1475, where beggars are singled out as a professional group; of the four thousand, four hundred and eighty-five tax-payers, one hundred and seven were listed as beggars. They paid the same taxes as day-workers. The tax records of Basle in the mid-fifteenth century include, in the lowest revenue section, three beggars and three blind men; but on the whole beggars do not appear on tax lists, as the estimation of revenues and capital on the basis of which tax was calculated was hardly possible in their case. Nor is it clear whether the Augsburg list took account of all the city's beggars. What is certain, however, is that this group of a hundred-odd beggars led a relatively stable life – although, like day-workers, they probably moved around more than other categories of the urban population – and that this life was seen by their contemporaries as a sort of profession, since they were singled out as a tax group. The fact that they were subject to taxes implies, in addition, that they were permanent residents of the city, ordinary people with neighbours and acquaintances, and that their places of 'work' and residence were sufficiently stable and defined to enable the taxman to control their income and to collect his due.

By the fourteenth and fifteenth centuries municipal authorities had begun attempts to establish a legal framework to regulate aid to the poor. The first to do so were cities in South Germany, which served as the first models for the reforms of charity which the sixteenth century went on to implement. Already in the fourteenth century, a municipal ordinance at Nuremberg restricted begging to those in possession of a metal token. A special functionary (*Bettelherr*) was appointed by the municipal authorities to control beggars, distribute tokens to those genuinely in need, keep a register of beggars and, twice a year, look into their situation. Non-local beggars who came to Nuremberg might stop there for no longer than three days. No doubt the effect of such measures was not very great, but they do establish that by the late Middle Ages municipal authorities were already attempting to control beggars and define a centralized social policy concerning them. Still, the legislation often failed to keep pace with reality, as most municipal authorities were occupied largely with the running of charitable institutions, both hospitals and centres of alms distribution, and preventing large numbers of beggars from entering the city. Analogous measures were taken during epidemics, when legislation forbidding beggars to move from place to place was a basic hygiene precaution. Similar efforts were made on a national and regional level to deal with the problem of vagrants. Measures against vagrants were also aimed at beggars, firstly because the distinction between beggar and vagrant was a fluid one, and secondly because the effectiveness of these measures depended on restricting alms distribution, limiting access to support and subjecting it to some kind of control. But such legislation could not touch those beggars who had lived in a town long enough to be treated as local residents; they could not be assimilated to vagrants. Its real function was to prevent the influx of impoverished peasants into the towns; as a measure aimed at the 'professional' beggars who crowded the streets and the churches it was mostly ineffective.

Paupers of every category, recipients of 'prebends' and street beggars alike, stood in a very particular relation to their benefactors: in exchange for material gifts, the poor man promised spiritual support – alms for prayer. The huge sphere of doctrinal controversy concerning the essence and definition of alms and of the good deed, although it loomed large both in medieval theology and, later, in polemics at the time of the Reformation, is best avoided here. One aspect of these debates which it would nonetheless be well to bear in mind is the injunction to distinguish between worthy and unworthy poor – a distinction which naturally reinforced the idea of a contract, with alms representing its material, prayer its spiritual, side. If only the fact of giving alms counts, charity is a one-sided affair, concerning no one but the giver; it is an entirely disinterested act of generosity, motivated by the sole desire to help one's fellow man. If, on the other hand, it is seen as a way of expiating one's sins, with the additional hope that the recipient of charity will intercede with God on behalf of his benefactor and pray for him, the disinterested purity of the act of alms-giving is severely weakened. The doctrine of the 'deserving' poor suggests another solution, in which both parties involved in the act of alms-giving – the recipient as well as the benefactor – receive due attention. St Thomas Aquinas condemns all those who solicit alms without being forced to do so by dire necessity; and Geiler von Kayserberg, a fifteenth-century preacher and moralist from Strasbourg, develops this argument further, claiming that giving alms to the 'wrong' sort of pauper – in other words to one who is not deserving – is harmful to the giver as well as to the recipient of charity. This view of alms as a contract finds expression in some remarks by the thirteenth-century Italian chronicler Fra Salimbene, who strongly criticizes the crowds of beggars who gather mutely in front of churches, palms outstretched: they should be chased off, for they are useless. Coming from the pen of an Italian Franciscan, these words have a particular significance: they suggest that giving alms to mendicant orders would be preferable as a form of charity, since the benefactor could then be sure of a return on his 'investment' in the form of prayer on his behalf.

In the sermons of Giordano di Rivalto (1260–1311), a Dominican from Pisa, alms-giving is explicitly presented both as a contract and as an exchange: the beggar who receives material aid is bound, in exchange, to pray for his benefactor. This view of alms-giving as a contract was not fully formulated until the twelfth century, but it lies at the roots of the psychological motivation of charity. It also had a significant influence on the behaviour of beggars, who became conscious of their usefulness. These two aspect of alms-giving, the material and the spiritual, determined the place of beggars in the social 'division of labour', and defined the external forms of their existence. Begging, viewed as a profession, created its own methods, techniques and customs, with an organizational structure similar to that of craftsmen's guilds.

A beggar's external appearance was not only a reflection of his genuine need but a part of his professional technique. Clothes were the main thing. Medieval iconography portrays beggars barefoot and in rags; often, in the many images of St Martin offering his own clothes to a beggar, they are also naked – as, for instance, on the eleventh-century capital in the abbey of Saint-Benoît-sur-Loire. In iconography the evangelical commandment to clothe the naked is variously interpreted: beggars are offered outer clothing, such as coats, or their rags are exchanged for something more solid. In the satirical literature of the time one frequently comes across the motif of the beggar who sells off the clothes which he has received, prefer-ring to keep his rags in order that he might the more effectively attract the attention and pity of passers-by and possible benefactors. It seems, indeed, that beggars' clothes were subject to certain regional variations: Boccaccio, for instance, speaks of some beggars' clothing as typically French – although this might indicate no more than a particularly ingenious fashion of disposing their rags about their bodies. The common accessories of the wandering beggar, such as the staff and the sack, were both functional and symbolic.

Equally important in the beggar's appearance is his body: it, too, crippled and racked with illness, old age or poverty, is part of his professional technique, and must be exposed to public view in the right way. Both the literature and the legal statutes of the time provide many satirical examples of the ingenious tricks and artifice resorted to by beggars in this regard. In the circumstances, however, it was quite natural for a beggar to flaunt his physical degradation: the right to solicit alms was granted primarily to the sick, and beggars resorted to ostentatious displays of their infirmity in order to confer legitimacy on their begging as well as to inspire pity. The works of Hieronymus Bosch contain numerous cruel and horrific examples of human infirmity which arouse both revulsion and compassion. The insistence with which beggars demand alms seems to go hand in hand with their insistence on providing a spectacle for the public.

The theme of infirmity as a professional strategy appears frequently in medieval literature in the form of parables about cripples miraculously healed. Variations on this theme are a peculiar synthesis of folklore and hagiographical tradition. It may be found in different versions of the life of St Martin of Tours (beginning with the so-called pseudo-Odon version, which dates from the end of the eleventh or the beginning of the twelfth century). The description of the miracles which took place during the transfer of the saint's relics from Auxerre to Tours is accompanied by the story of two paralytics (*paralitici* in the Latin version, *contrets* in a twelfth-century biography in verse, finally *contrefaictz* in a fifteenth-century version) who learn of the miracles. They are frightened, and one of them says, 'Brother, we live lives of comfortable idleness. No one bothers us, everyone pities us, and we are free to do what we will – in short, our days are spent in well-being.' But if a miraculous cure were to take place, 'we would be forced to do physical work, which we are not used to, and as for begging, that would be out of the question.'[15] In two other versions – the verse biography by Péan Gatineau and a prose version from the end of the fifteenth century – the theme of the happiness of the beggar's life is further developed: he can sleep when he likes, he always has enough to eat and drink, etc.: a miraculous cure would only make his life difficult. The two paralytics therefore decide to flee and, in their haste, throw the crutches on which they leaned while begging over their shoulders: thus the miracle was accomplished nonetheless. Other versions of this story, found in collections of *exempla*, contain a paralytic and a blind man, but the essentials – infirmity as a justification for begging, and a fear of having to work – remain the same. In these versions, too, the beggars attempt to flee, but cannot get through the crowd, and are cured against their will.

The beggar's profession requires that he publicly expose the reasons for which he is seeking assistance; this is what distinguishes professional beggars as a social category among other types of poor. The 'deserving' poor find help among personal acquaintances, but beggars, while the causes of their downfall are often the same – the break-up of a family, or just a stroke of bad luck – must rely on strangers for aid, and expose to them all their miseries. And while the need to support a large family was a frequent reason, among both professional beggars and the 'deserving' poor, for soliciting aid, the professional beggar was forced to exhibit his numerous and miserable family members in the street. Small children were a particularly useful professional tool, for they inspired the most pity and compassion; for this reason they were often used for begging, especially by women, who then had no more need to provide further justification, such as sickness or infirmity, for asking for alms.

Professional begging often imitated the various organizational structures of urban professional guilds. A significant example of this is the contract entered into between two beggars in Brittany at the end of the fifteenth century. One of them, acting the role of employer, agreed to pay the other a regular salary for a year in exchange for whatever the latter could earn from begging. Another form of contract is described by Sacchetti in one of his novellas: three blind men from Florence decide to form a 'company', a sort of beggars' collective in which all the profits from alms would be pooled and shared out equally between all the members once a week. They beg with the aid of guide dogs and sing religious songs as they wander from village to town.

Singing belongs to what one might call the 'artistic production' side of the beggar's craft. Indeed, there are many similarities between beggars and wandering artists in their way of life and their methods of earning a living. Beggars played a variety of instruments (some of them were even called 'beggars' instruments'), sang and told stories. They also had an idiom of their own which included a wide range of cries and appeals used to attract the attention and pity of passers-by. It is significant that in 1317 the bishop of Strasbourg issued an edict forbidding Beguines from crying 'Bread, in God's name!' to passers-by, and ordering them to use the forms of address in common use among other beggars.

Beggars were integrated into urban life to such an extent that they founded their own corporate organizations, which gave them a legitimate place in society. The most frequent among these seem to have been brotherhoods of the blind. The statutes of brotherhoods of the blind in Barcelona and Valencia in the fourteenth century specify the forms which solidarity and mutual aid within the community could take: thus they might share the services of a guide (*lazarillo*), visit each other at times of sickness and share out the alms collected among their members. This last clause is reminiscent of the Sacchetti novella mentioned above, which also sheds some interesting light on the customs prevalent among the blind of Florence: it seems that they used to congregate each day at noon at a tavern near the San Lorenzo bell-tower, and appear for the most part to have lived in that area. In Strasbourg a 'brotherhood of poor blind men' was formed in 1411, to become, twenty years later, the 'brotherhood of Strasbourg beggars'. There was another beggars' brotherhood in Lvov, presided over by one of the 'elders' of the trade and functioning as a professional organization for members of the 'rag-picking' class. The professional organization founded by beggars in the parish church of Kutna Hora in 1443 was probably also some sort of brotherhood. An organization of their own, run along the lines of a religious brotherhood, allowed beggars to establish a network of contacts, participate in a more active 'social life' and benefit from various forms of collective action and mutual aid. It also allowed them to exercise a corporate monopoly and an anti-competitive policy, principles characteristic of medieval craftsmen's guilds as a whole. The social consequences of such organizations were of course considerable: they legitimized the role of beggars in urban life and in its professional structures.

Several conclusions may be drawn from all this. Above all it is clear that the role of beggars in medieval society was well defined: they were an integral part of the social 'division of labour' and participated in organized forms of corporate professional life. At the same time the peculiar nature of their 'professional' activity led to a certain amount of ambivalence concerning their social status.

As we have seen, the beggar's professional technique essentially involved a public display of his external 'weaknesses'; his misery or infirmity justified his appeal for aid. In the general spectacle of ostentatious misery it was often difficult to distinguish the genuine cripple from the impostor: deceit or its suspicion, then as now, invariably accompanies the beggar's profession.

The oldest sources describing fraud and fraudulent techniques used by beggars are literary. The fact that they were composed principally

in order to amuse an audience does not detract from their value: they
are important testimony, confirmed by legal documents as well as by
court and police archives of the time. What they reveal is primarily
the many areas of professional specialization. This aspect of beggars'
lives was first described in medieval Arabic literature; later, in the
fourteenth and fifteenth centuries, it was developed in Europe. The
spread of information about the fraudulent practices of beggars
diluted the zealous compassion with which the poor were regarded
and reversed the trend of exalting the life of misery. At the same time,
however, it does testify to the professional stability of beggars.

The formalization of alms-giving on the one hand and the pro-
fessionalization of begging on the other created the equilibrium in
which 'functional' poverty existed in the Middle Ages. This equilibrium was disturbed by poverty as a mass phenomenon, by the crowds
of paupers who gathered from time to time at large-scale distributions
of alms, their lives a precarious and impermanent balance between
poverty and work.

1.3   The Rural Poor and the Urban Poor

Poverty in the Middle Ages had various sociological connotations. Its
vast terminology lends an air of unreality to questions about genuine
poverty or about the categories of people for whom material need is a
part of daily life: such questions seem to have no basis and no possible
response. The terminology of a given period is of enormous importance in shedding light on social awareness and mentality, but less
useful in reflecting reality. In the medieval consciousness the idea of a
pauper had various associations, although its range of meaning nar-
rowed with time: initially denoting all those who did not belong to
the privileged elite of a feudal society, it gradually came to refer only
to those who lived from alms or from some kind of welfare. During
the period of its widest range of reference it was an element of the
potens/pauper dichotomy, but during the Carolingian period it was also
used to distinguish between various categories within the lowest
reaches of the population: the term *pauperes* referred to free men as
opposed to serfs. Thus it was not used exclusively to designate the
lowest elements of the social hierarchy. As the terminology of poverty
evolved, its shifts of meaning reflected the increasing significance of

social *déclassement*: the meaning of *pauper* came to encompass someone no longer able to support himself or his family in the style to which they had been accustomed or in a way befitting their social position. As material poverty – the need to subsist on alms and social aid – and *déclassement* gained in prominence in the late medieval terminology of poverty, and finally came to dominate the range of meaning encompassed by the term, so the uses of the word began to reflect the social process of pauperization.

The scale of this process was the result of social and economic conditions. In demographic terms pauperization may be seen as the symptom or the result of relative over-population, in economic terms as the result of short- or long-term crises and periods of depression. The difficulties of historical research in this field lie not in the nature of the sources but rather in the relative nature of the phenomenon itself, for it has meaning only in particular situations well defined in time and space. On the one hand, we have a process of social and material degradation in which groups and individuals are faced with the prospect of no longer being able to live in accordance with their social status; on the other, we have groups and individuals whose very survival is threatened and whose need is extreme. According to Eric Hobsbawm, the term 'pauperization' applies to a category of people who are incapable of procuring for themselves even the minimum necessary means of subsistence without external aid. It is this aspect of poverty which is of interest here. It might take place on a mass scale without lasting sociological effects, in other words without involving the impoverishment of particular groups; or it might determine, in a continuous way, the standard and way of life of a specific category of people. Both these model situations are reflected, in different ways, in the rural and urban life of societies of the agrarian era.

Because of the very limited yields from medieval agriculture, the peasant masses lived in permanent fear of hunger. Attempts to revise this gloomy picture have succeeded in refuting the 'black legend' of peasant life in the early Middle Ages, but without taking into account periods of crisis: a small farm with few reserves could not survive a bad harvest, especially if this was repeated year after year. And in spite of the gradual development of medieval agriculture (confirmed, for example, by comparing the Carolingian with the Merovingian period), the problem of famine and physical survival continued to be a serious one for the peasant masses. The demographic expansion which took place during the first centuries of our millennium was far more rapid than the evolution of agricultural techniques. The low productivity of agriculture, combined with the system of feudal exploitation, made poverty endemic in rural life.

At the same time, however, no category of people who might be described as being 'proletarianized' appeared in Western rural society, at least until the latter half of the twelfth century. According to Georges Duby, sources for the period 'describe a rural society which is certainly hierarchical to a great degree, both by law and by wealth, but it is a society in which life was stable and affluent.'[16] This feeling of security seems to concern mainly the various categories of servants in great houses, where large stocks of provisions were protection against bad harvests; peasants were more vulnerable. But peasant solidarity in 'normal' times seems to have been sufficiently strong to prevent the extreme impoverishment which certain families would otherwise have suffered. The peasant masses, although differentiated by legal status and wealth (land as well as human and animal labour), were less differentiated socially. When famine came it was local; however dreadful its consequences (and the horrific accounts of cannibalism, of human flesh laid out for sale in meat markets and of death from starvation given by medieval chroniclers do reflect, albeit with some exaggeration, the scale of disaster), when it was over life returned to normal.

The lives of peasants were sometimes so precarious economically that they voluntarily subjected themselves to serfdom; in the official forms which they filled out in order to do this they gave their extreme poverty as a reason. This voluntary serfdom took various forms of dependence. At the beginning of the eighth century it meant the protection of a feudal lord. The appeals for protection were as follows: 'Since it is common knowledge that I have nothing to eat and nothing to wear, I have asked for your pity so that I might clothe myself and entrust myself to your protection, which you have granted.'[17] By the terms of such a contract the person asking for protection is promised food and clothing, and promises in his turn to work for the noble's *familia*, to serve and to obey. These are obviously conventional formulas; the social reality behind them did not always conform to the principles of such contracts, nor was the decision always as voluntary and spontaneous as one might think. (Significantly, one of the clauses of the contract stipulates that the service and obedience into which the petitioner enters should in no way infringe his *libertas*.) In the eleventh century, the case of a peasant family from Anjou who ap-

pealed to the Saint-Florent convent in Saumur to take two of their
children as serfs, for they could no longer feed them, was still characteristic. But it is clear that the transition from freedom to serfdom did
nothing to better the peasants' material lot, and the process was soon
reversed: one sees, especially in the twelfth and thirteenth centuries,
a large number of families, and even whole villages, trying to buy back
their liberty. But the fact that voluntary serfdom did persist, as the
last and only possible resort in situations of economic necessity,
testifies to the constant precariousness of the peasant's existence. At
times neither rural solidarity within communities nor the various
forms of assistance available from the parish were sufficient to maintain the survival of the poorest. But throughout the Middle Ages and
until as late as the twelfth century such cases were rare; it was
extremely unusual for a family to become so impoverished that it was
forced to leave the village to seek other means of subsistence.

From the middle of the twelfth century the structure of peasant life
was considerably changed by the penetration into the countryside of
a money-based economy. The extent of its influence in Western
Europe varied from country to country. In France, the fact that
peasants were buying back their liberty was a good illustration of the
extent to which money-based commercial transactions were gaining
in importance; feudal lords were becoming more interested in the
money which came in from the letters of franchise they had granted
than in the feudal services they had traditionally obtained from
peasants. The price of freedom was sometimes exorbitant, but the
relative ease with which peasants managed to obtain the credit to
finance their release shows the faith of creditors in the stability of
their monetary income. The social consequence of these changes,
however, was that financial disparities within peasant society became
increasingly pronounced; and as this stratification proceeded, the
poorest categories of the peasant population were impoverished to
such a degree that they were reduced to the level of a rural proletariat.

In the course of the fourteenth and fifteenth centuries these groups
became more numerous. Their existence was a struggle for survival.
For the peasant masses, helpless in the face of changing fortune, life
was a farm with three or four hectares, few draught and farmyard
animals and very meagre reserves, barely enough to last until the
next harvest. Their economic insecurity is reflected in the fact that
they took short-term loans based on future harvests. The existence of
casanae, small lending establishments set up in the countryside of

eastern France by creditors from the north of Italy, and of Jewish money-lenders in the south of France, shows the extent to which the system of credit penetrated the most economically vulnerable peasant groups. This middle stratum of peasantry was regularly depleted as whole families dropped away to join the category of village indigents, who could no longer survive from farming their own land. In such situations it was the village craftsmen who came to their aid, by offering additional sources of income for the men and the possibility of work for the women and children. Thirteenth-century documents contain increasing amounts of information about 'landless' peasantry who manage to eke out a living on the margins of village life by tending to flocks, and about 'children', younger sons whom the family farm, having been parcelled out in small lots among various members of the family, no longer had the resources to feed. One finds increasing numbers of 'gardeners', landless or almost landless peasants who earned their living by hiring out their services; the majority of them had only enough land for a 'garden', a small plot insufficient to provide more than minor additions to their basic needs. In southern France the 'brassiers' lived entirely by 'selling' the strength of their arms ('bras') and hiring themselves out as day-labourers to richer peasants or landed gentry. From the beginning of the fourteenth century the tax registers show a marked increase in the number of impoverished peasants, who appear in these documents as 'indigents', 'poor men' or even 'beggars'; these technical terms, used by the tax authorities to refer to those who were unable to pay their taxes, covered mainly the rural proletariat and certain groups belonging to the traditional category of rural 'poor', such as widows and orphans. As a result of these changes the countryside became a place of permanent 'relative over-population', with serious social consequences: for the over-population was not hidden, as might typically be the case in an economy where a surplus workforce is used for extensive production, but, on the contrary, blatant, with immediate and shocking effects for the mass of people desperately looking for work in their own village and not finding it. Accordingly, as a large part of the rural population was forced to buy food with the money they earned as hired labourers, the wages of day-workers in the countryside fell sharply, while grain prices rose. Migration brought only partial relief. Part of the surplus population was absorbed by undercultivated countries or regions, but this was only the part with enough money to finance such a move, and the possibilities of colonization were in any case limited. Short-term migration, on the other hand, became a characteristic feature in the life of the rural proletariat, although its rhythm was determined not so much by seasonal work opportunities as by periodic crises: in Provençal villages at the beginning of the fourteenth century, one in three families went away for the winter to seek work elsewhere. The rural proletariat in the late Middle Ages struggled for survival in dire poverty.

Studies in medieval agrarian history reveal the vast scale of the process which reduced a proportion of the peasantry to a proletariat; equally large was the intermediate group, the mass of peasants living under the constant threat of joining them. Robert Fossier, in his study of rural Picardy, reconstructs the social make-up of the countryside at the end of the thirteenth century:

Indigents and beggars	13%
Owners of small parcels of land, so unstable economically that a bad harvest is a threat to their survival	33%
Peasants with more land but without draught animals	36%
Wealthy farmers	19%

This study also shows that the significance of the amount of land owned by a peasant is relative: in Picardy the high quality of the soil allowed a whole family to lead an independent existence with only two or three hectares. Of the 'wealthy' peasants, only 3 per cent owned more than three hectares of land. The Picardy countryside provides a telling picture of social stratification among the peasantry: between the two extremes, the rural proletariat and the wealthy farmers, lies the overwhelming majority (more than two-thirds). Their lives are precarious, unstable and vulnerable to changes of fortune; and they are the group most cruelly hit by the process of pauperization in the Middle Ages. Other parts of Europe present an analogous picture of the structure of peasant society. The figures concerning English peasantry show that, in 1280, peasants with less than three hectares of land – not enough, in other words, to feed a family – represented 46 per cent of the population. In Cambresis, at the beginning of the fourteenth century, 13 per cent of the peasantry lived in poverty and 33 per cent owned only small plots of land. In maritime Flanders, of the one thousand and seventy-two peasant landowners who took part in the 1328 revolt and died in the battle of Cassel, a little over 1 per cent were wealthy farmers, 23 per cent had between 2.2 and 4.4 hectares, and 59 per cent farmed parcels of land smaller than 2.2 hectares.

The size of a farm is not in itself a sufficient criterion for evaluating a family's economic status. Equally, the tax registers which designate certain families as 'beggars', on the basis of their estimated income from land, should be treated with a certain amount of caution. In both cases the information is insufficient, and one can only speculate about the role of other sources of income, such as day work in town or a craft practised at home, in their total revenues. Nonetheless such documents do give us some indication of the extent of 'landlessness' in the countryside, and reveal the existence of a sizeable group of peasants no longer able to earn their living from agriculture. They provide a glimpse into the process of pauperization which had begun to affect the countryside.

The idea which statistics give us of the dimensions of rural poverty is not entirely accurate. This is mainly because the documentation on which they are based is not always reliable and does not respond well to quantitative methods of historical research. On the other hand it is pushing scepticism too far to deny any possibility of estimating the extent of poverty in the Middle Ages: statistics do reliably establish an order of magnitude which serves as a framework for the data. However, broad generalizations often fail to take account of regional differences. Economic life in the Middle Ages was extremely local in character: long-distance trade was hindered by lack of transport, and economic conditions consequently varied even within a specific region. A more general pace of development was imposed by climatic conditions, although it took long evolutionary cycles for their effects to make themselves felt. The different local economic and social structures also created an international division of labour: thus circumstances unfavourable for one region might represent an opportunity of economic development for another. This was apparent during the great crisis of the fourteenth century, which affected most of Western Europe but spared the Eastern and Central regions, enabling them to profit from the new economic situation. Economic stratification among the peasantry was also determined by local conditions: natural disasters, while not necessarily entailing general poverty among the peasant masses, often widened economic differences between them. L. Génicot has made a statistical study of the economic situation of peasants in three villages in the duchy of Namur in 1289, according to the size of their farms; the poorest peasants, whose plots of land were insufficient to provide for their needs, represented 38 per cent of the population in the first village, 54 per cent in the second and 73 per cent in the third. The discrepancies are huge, and they appear within a single region. Barely a quarter of the inhabitants of the third village are able to subsist on the profits from their land; the rest must look elsewhere for additional sources of income. In this same village, moreover, there are no landed gentry, and the number of wealthy farmers is extremely small (barely 6.5 per cent, compared with 20 per cent and 26 per cent respectively in the two other villages – which shows that the extent of pauperization in the countryside is not always the result of a process of polarization); work opportunities are accordingly very limited.

These examples are not meant to suggest any general tendencies in the social evolution of the countryside. They serve only as models of specific situations in which more and more farmers, unable to make a living by cultivating their own land, either join the ranks of the proletariat or continue to farm their land under the constant threat of having to do so. This type of situation may be observed at various times throughout medieval Europe.

As rural poverty progressed in the Middle Ages it took one of two distinct forms. In the first, despite fluctuating social circumstances, natural disasters, feudal land rents and variable relations between feudal masters and peasant farmers, there is no real pauperization. Impoverishment, temporary or long-lasting, is local, and affects the entire village population. Cases of profound impoverishment, so extreme that the family cannot continue living as it has done and is forced to look for other resources, are isolated, and even then the aid and solidarity of the community softens the blow: various forms of social assistance enabled the aged, the infirm and families without support to remain within the community and protected them from becoming wandering beggars.

In the second model, poverty is the result of the expansion of money and the market economy, which created huge discrepancies in financial status among the rural population. The peasants who could no longer survive by cultivating their own land became a huge category of people. In the agrarian structure of the countryside the middle-ranking farmers were still the most numerous, but they were also the most vulnerable to changing conditions, and their numbers were continually being depleted as one by one they joined the ranks of the rural proletariat. From the thirteenth century onwards the various forms of rural solidarity were dominated by the richest groups, and thus did nothing to weaken the process of social polarization. Poverty came to mean the reduction of a large group of peasants to a proletariat, characterized by permanent insecurity and a hand-to-mouth existence, a constant search for work to maintain survival.

These latter, while certainly victims of the process of impoverishment, in that they were unable to continue living the normal life of the peasant classes, are nevertheless not to be confused with the beneficiaries of medieval institutions of charity. Most likely they attended the great alms distributions. Some of them became beggars or tramps, but for the most part they remained in their village and worked for a living. They were not the main object of medieval charity, in particular of its evangelical awakening in the twelfth century; they were not 'shamefaced poor', for their poverty did not contradict their social status; they were not poor from choice; nor, finally, could they 'rightfully claim' alms because of sickness or infirmity. They were working poor. Nor were their lives entirely bleak: they were sometimes able to earn enough from temporary work to rise above a life of basic survival. Granted, wages were low in the country, in the villages as well as on the estates, but the cost of living, too, was proportionately low. And there were among them those who managed to live slightly above the general level of utter poverty. But since the opportunities for hired work were limited, and jobs as well as wages seasonal and temporary, life was for most of them precarious and full of uncertainty.

This second model of rural poverty reflects the gradual disintegration of the social system while remaining within the structures of agrarian society. As long as the rural proletariat remained an integral part of village life – the life of the family, the neighbourhood, the community and the parish – it continued to exist within the organized framework of life in the countryside.

The process of pauperization in rural society is closely linked to the expansion of the market economy and the use of money. These factors also play a role in another aspect of medieval poverty: urban poverty.

It should be stressed at the outset that this was not merely the same phenomenon reproduced in a different social and topographical context: it was not a case of the rural poor migrating to the cities. As long as the traditional agrarian structures held, the rural poor stayed where they were. Indeed, impoverished rural families were often so deeply attached to their villages that they preferred, despite their poverty, to stay put; a sense of security was more important than the possibility of finding a better life in a new and unknown place. In addition, migration requires money, and those who tried to move without sufficient means soon found themselves reduced to a life on the margins of society. Certain periods of increased migration, such as those noted, for example, in the Florentine *contado* in the fourteenth and fifteenth centuries, were signs that the traditional social structures of the countryside were already disintegrating; the Florentine migrations show, moreover, that only the wealthiest migrated to the cities, while the poorer peasants simply moved to other villages in the area. The 'proletariat', the impoverished and the marginalized, played a very small role in the development of medieval cities; detailed research on the subject has not confirmed Henri Pirenne's claim that European cities owed their expansion to the masses of 'desperados', tramps and vagabonds (as in the famous example of the Milanese *pannosus*, typical of this new class of 'vagabond-turned-bourgeois') which they absorbed. The city was not seen as a haven, a means of escape from rural poverty. It held out, to those with a certain amount of money and social prestige, the promise of a better life, perhaps even wealth and a higher social status. Research on the social origins of the rural population flooding the cities of northern and central Italy clearly shows wealthy peasants to have been the dominant group; the rural poor were less easily accepted. The influx of people uprooted from their old surroundings was greatest when urban centres were just beginning to form, and probably included both fugitive serfs and impoverished nobles. The medieval city in the first stages of growth naturally offered great hopes of success and social stability to those who had lived on the margins of society; but above all it attracted those who were most active and felt restricted by the immobility of agrarian society. Carlo Cipolla has compared medieval urbanization to the European emigration to America in the nineteenth century, pointing out the similarity of the migrants' collective hopes. The comparison can be taken further: in both cases it was the wealthiest and the most active who emigrated, not those who were poorest and without resources. In later stages of urban development this process continued, so that the influx of peasants into the cities entailed a corresponding flow of wealth from the country into the city. The German saying *Stadtluft macht frei* ('the air of the city makes you free') reflects one of the main attractions of the medieval city: here was a chance to free oneself from personal dependence and servitude – although personal dependence was quickly replaced by a whole network of economic and corporate constraints.

The city creates a new type of poverty which is different from the rural kind. Its nature is determined by the city's socio-economic structure and by its particular environment. This is not the place to go into the topology of the medieval European city; but even a brief glance at its main features cannot fail to reveal the huge variety of relations which exist in urban centres between wealth and poverty, and which are determined both by the size of the city's population and by the role of the production sector in its professional structure. Small urban centres tend for the most part to retain the social structures of the countryside: agriculture maintains its leading role, and within the city walls as well as in its immediate environs residents continue to breed livestock and cultivate the land, thus ensuring a certain amount of self-sufficiency. In social life, too, the old customs are retained, and with them the traditions of rural family life and village solidarity. Agriculture and the country way of life maintain their presence in cities, whatever their size, throughout the Middle Ages, although their extent and influence naturally change with time and vary from place to place. Great cities, with populations of over fifty thousand, were few in medieval Europe: in Italy, a highly urbanized country, they were Florence, Venice, Genoa and Milan; north of the Alps there was Paris, the largest city of medieval Europe, and in Flanders Gent and Bruges. In the Arab world there was Constantinople and certain cities of the Iberian Peninsula. Great cities such as these naturally fostered the growth of specifically urban ways of life, which continued to evolve into the modern era. They were distinguished, in their social structures, by the anonymity which comes from size, by their emphasis on what American sociologists call 'secondary group relations' and by a considerable degree of social disorganization; in economics, by a system of interdependence based on a highly developed division of labour. This handful of large cities obviously forms an inadequate basis for the drawing of general conclusions. Nevertheless it seems that all the cities of medieval Europe which reached a certain stage of development reproduce the patterns one observes in the great urban centres. If we adopt the historian's statistical scale, which (although in this case the statistics are arbitrary) sets a lower limit of two thousand inhabitants for a 'medium-sized' town, we can say that, with a population of this size, and *a fortiori* with one of five or six thousand, the traditional mechanisms of social life break down. Personal contact disappears as a basis for life in a community, and in professional life corporate solidarity is weakened as hierarchical and class differences are emphasized. On the scale of the community, the feeling of solidarity and shared responsibility is very much weakened, and makes itself apparent only when some external danger threatens the city. The new forms of solidarity which gradually take over the social life of the city, such as religious brotherhoods and professional organizations, are based on groups, and therefore divide as well as unite. Their politics are defensive, and in order to protect their own interests they will create legal or material obstacles, or sometimes both, to deter new members. Craftsmen's and merchants' guilds try to restrain economic competition among their members, but city life, despite its group structures, is guided by a spirit of constant competitiveness. The development of money and market mechanisms which left their mark on the countryside make their consequences felt much more intensely and dramatically in the city.

A city's economic and professional structure does not always correlate with its size or population. In small towns, whose merchants and craftsmen provide for the needs of the local market, social and material contrasts are not very marked. Their social structure is defined largely by the principles of small-scale production, where the craftsman is helped in his work by his own family, and the occasional apprentice or helper becomes a member of an enlarged household. Studies of the social structure of pre-industrial society reveal a particularly large number of household servants – over 13 per cent in England between the sixteenth and the eighteenth century, and over 20 per cent in London by the end of the seventeenth century. Various functions are covered by this category, depending on the production structure of urban crafts: where only the local market is involved, the relation of personal dependence within the craftsman's *familia* is maintained; but in cases where the production is intended for more distant markets, and quantity as well as greater skill and specialized technology are required, the craftsman begins more and more to employ wage-earners. This latter group was composed of craftsmen's helpers, apprentices and pupils, but also, and increasingly, of craftsmen themselves, who thus renounced their economic independence. The cost of raw materials and the instability of the market, coupled with increasingly complicated technology demanding specialized skills and an extensive division of labour, often forced the craftsman to submit and work for the merchants and entrepreneurs who organized production. In certain branches, the policy of hiring wage-earners was dictated by the technological nature of the work; this was the case, for example, in mining and construction. In others, it was the consequence of economic and social changes. The role of the wage-earner in the structure of production continued to increase as the late medieval city evolved, gradually eroding the foundations of its social equilibrium.

In addition to the social elements which played a role in the evolution of the early medieval city, a number of institutional mechanisms gradually took shape; their function was to soften and restrain the emerging social contrasts and to protect the small producer. Studies of the structure of medieval cities have revealed specific characteristics of two very different urban centres, both typical of their age – Frankfurt am Main and Ypres. Frankfurt was one of the largest German cities of the time and played a significant role in international trade, although it was not a centre of any specialized industry: the list of its crafsmen, who supplied principally the local market, encompasses all the branches of industry. Ypres, on the other hand, with a much smaller number of inhabitants and without Frankfurt's reputation as a centre of trade, was nevertheless a highly specialized centre of the textile industry, the leading industry of Flanders. Its socio-economic structure in the fifteenth century was already typical of an industrial city: the number of its wage-earners was far greater than Frankfurt's, while the percentage of independent craftsmen and small producers was considerably lower. Ypres was not exceptional in this regard: in the regions of medieval Europe where the pace of industrial evolution was most rapid, such as northern Italy or Flanders, similar structures were frequently to be found even in quite small cities. Dinant, for instance, despite a population of barely six thousand, was famous as a specialized industrial centre producing metal tools and household implements (the latter known as *dinanderie*). Most European cities of the time, however, adopted the Frankfurt structure, with relatively few wage-earners and a social structure that guaranteed the independence of the direct producer.

Municipal institutions and craftsmen's guilds tried to develop a policy of regulating professional relations and limiting, by non-economic measures, the action of market mechanisms governing the workforce. Throughout the late Middle Ages, however, two processes conspired to weaken and obstruct the successful implementation of this policy. The first was the evolution of specialized industry and the division of labour which it entailed, the growing role of trading capital and the increasing independence of direct producers. The second was the ever-growing role of unskilled hired labourers. Both these processes gradually opened the way to the formation of a proletariat. At many points they converged: in a system of organized production, the small producer lost his independence and became reduced to carrying out a very small and restricted stage of the production process; as a result his professional qualifications were no longer needed, and the fact that he had his own tools of the trade or a well-equipped workshop ceased to have much importance. In this way he was gradually absorbed into the proletariat: all he had to offer was his physical ability to work.

Unskilled labourers, however, were under a particular disadvantage in medieval urban society. There was no professional institution to which they could belong to protect their interests; unable to defend themselves against society's scorn for manual labour, they were relegated to the margins of society. They were a group which comprised many categories of people and a variety of trades. Those who felt their lack of status most keenly were the women workers. The medieval city had very few corporations for typically female professions; a woman could become a member of a 'male' institution only after the death of her husband, as the widow of a master craftsman. For the most part women were employed in auxiliary or household tasks. Historical documents describe the situation of those who did have a profession – as spinners, for example – as typically proletarian. The song of the silk spinners in *Yvain ou le Chevalier au Lion* is strikingly perceptive of their lot:

> Toujours tisserons draps de soie
> Jamais n'en serons mieux vêtues
> Toujours serons pauvres et nues
> Et toujours aurons faim et soif.[18]

> (Always spinning sheets of silk
> We shall never be better dressed
> But always naked and poor,
> And always suffering hunger and thirst.)

In the rest of the poem the spinners continue to complain of hunger; they can barely earn their bread, and even of that they have very little in the morning and less still in the evening. In the detailed description of the abuses perpetrated on his workers by Jehan Boine-broke, a Flemish entrepreneur at the end of the thirteenth century, the complaints of women predominate: he was brutal, he frequently cheated them and refused to pay them. Both in France and in Italy there were frequent cases of women spinners being drawn into economic dependence by loans, early payments and salary advances. Women's wages were notoriously low: they were paid the same as children.

Unskilled male labourers did occasional work, and sometimes also found employment with craftsmen, or in some branches of trade. And although the porters' guild was jealously protective of its monopoly, and the work demanded no particular skills, there was no lack of occasional jobs, such as loading shipments and transporting merchandise. There was also some agricultural work to be had in the city, especially at tilling and harvesting time, and city maintenance and cleaning also created some demand for workers. Construction, and some crafts requiring simple manual labour, offered perhaps the widest field for the unskilled labourer. All these jobs were temporary, and the fact that there was no official organization to define and protect the workers' interests always maintained their wages at a minimum.

Thus their social position was marginal. For women, in addition, the very fact of being reduced to earning a living was a social degradation, even when they only did a little extra work to swell the family purse. Both municipal legal archives and literary descriptions assimilate women workers to prostitutes – a stereotype which had its practical consequences. The fact that unskilled labourers had no professional organization of their own not only excluded them from the life of the city, which in medieval times was organized and defined by brotherhoods and guilds; it also made them objects of scorn or outright hostility on the part of craftsmen, for whom they were potential competition. It was this exclusion, more than their lack of professional qualifications, which prevented their integration into urban society. Domestic service, after all (also a solution for this category of people without a profession), did not demand any special skills or professional training; but as servants they became dependent, and their social position was both stable and socially recognized.

The situation of wage-earning craftsmen was quite different. Their numbers grew rapidly, particularly in centres of developing and increasingly specialized industry; and apprentices, unable to surmount the increasing difficulties of becoming master craftsmen, found themselves condemned to remain in a fixed role of auxiliary worker, while craftsmen gradually lost their autonomy to entrepreneurs. Unlike manual labourers, however, wage-earning craftsmen were well integrated into the organized structures of urban life: as members of professional guilds, they benefited from a well-defined legal status and could protect their interests as a group. However, their possibilities in this regard were sometimes restricted: some guilds were composed of associated entrepreneurs together with the craftsmen who worked for them, others still of craftsmen who, already as a group, had found themselves relegated to the status of wage-earners, dependent on entrepreneurs. More homogeneous among professional organizations were journeymen's brotherhoods. In all these cases there is no doubt, however, that wage-earning craftsmen were well integrated into the social structure and organized life of the city. *Déclassement* and dire poverty were the only two causes of pauperization among them.

Despite the existence, in cities, of certain forms of agriculture, pursued in order to bring in a little additional income, most wage-earning craftsmen had to buy their food; only the town's elite could afford their own garden, let alone a plot of land outside the city walls. Economic fluctuations, bad harvests and rising prices had immediate repercussions on the city's poor. In 1475, when peasants from the *contado* of Verona complained of heavy taxes, they were told that even the poorest of country folk did not need to buy food, whereas if the city's poor, who had to buy their food, were obliged to pay taxes, the cities would soon become depopulated. The wages of most city labourers were very low and were spent mostly on food; they were also quite firmly fixed, so that they failed to keep pace with the rising cost of food. Economically, the life of a city craftsman was as unstable and precarious as that of a small farmer or landless peasant.

Studies of family budgets among the wage-earners of Flanders and Tuscany, which will be discussed further in the following chapter, confirm that material instability was a permanent and inevitable feature of the lives of a substantial part of the population of the medieval city in the early stages of capitalism. The policies of the traditional medieval institutions, corporative and municipal, succeeded to a great extent in keeping economic disaster at bay, primarily by controlling the labour market and the influx of new inhabitants to the city. The effects of such policies, however, were very much diluted by the contending forces of demographic pressure, the spread of suburbs housing new inhabitants and the number of craftsmen who worked at home or were not members of any corporation.

To the impoverished masses, both in the city and in the countryside, the social and cultural elite were profoundly indifferent. Poverty was treated as a normal part of their lives. There were charitable institutions to help poor families. In Florence, for example, this was done by distributing alms to women, even if their husbands worked. The Dominicans, too, would from time to time appeal to the faithful to show compassion towards the working poor. But on the whole the poor received no help unless and until they were reduced to a state of impoverishment so great that they were prevented from doing the duty imposed on them by their social status – working. Poverty in itself certainly elicited no pity, either in the city or in the country. The question is whether it was seen purely as a stigma, and whether it provoked contempt.

The answer to this question is more usefully sought in literary images and in the writings of the Church than in the realities of the relations between different social groups. But neither literature nor reality can provide the sole and definitive response. The stigma of poverty in the city can nevertheless be seen to give rise to two distinct tendencies: first, the refusal to accord to the poor their full rights as citizens and their exclusion from membership in professional brotherhoods and guilds; and second, the topographical delineation of poor areas within the city.

Impoverished craftsmen were not excluded in this way. Even those who could no longer work remained members of their guild, thereby retaining their legal status, even if they could no longer take advantage of its privileges. Those who had never been accepted as members of a professional guild, on the other hand, fared rather worse. The tax registers of Basle for 1429 list a large number of craftsmen who were guild members but who had sunk very low on the financial ladder or, in some cases, become totally impoverished. At the same time, however, the Basle registers distinguish a group of four hundred and eighty-four tax-payers classed as 'non-incorporated' (*nicht zünftig*), most of them women. The lowest category of tax-payers (from zero to ten guilders) generally accounted for no more than 20 per cent of the membership of particular guilds (there was one exception, a guild with 36 per cent), but made up 60 per cent of the 'non-incorporated' group. The 'non-incorporated' were not only poor in the financial sense; their social and legal status was also much weaker, and prevented them from participating fully in the life of the urban community. Unskilled day- and manual labourers, who drifted from one job to another, were in a similar position. They, too, lived outside the organized structures, with unstable jobs and irregular earnings, frequently on the move. None of the people in this 'non-incorporated' category enjoyed full rights as citizens. The medieval city exploited them and treated them with contempt and hostility, for their very existence was a threat to the organized professional structures which governed and formed the basis of life in the urban community. The newcomers among them, migrants from the countryside unused to city ways, were additional cause for hostility, awakening the city's stereotyped attitudes of contempt and distrust towards the 'yokel'.

The topography of the city also reflected the degradations of poverty. Where a family lived was determined primarily by profession or membership in a guild, and there was always a tendency for members of the same profession to live in the same area. Sometimes this was dictated by the nature of the work; for instance, if the work was 'dirty' or water was needed for production, the municipal authorities would set aside an appropriate area for members of that particular trade. Most striking, however, was the social division of the city's topography into rich and poor. It was concentric: the closer a family lived to the religious and economic centre of the city, the higher its position. The price of land was dictated by this arrangement, by which means, of course, the system was protected and maintained. The social topography of Toulouse and Paris in the late Middle Ages testified to its permanence: the poor quarters remained in the same place for a long time, even though, as the cities expanded, the poor were gradually pushed out into the suburbs, and the concentric layout itself was also somewhat disturbed. Some of the city's poor zones began to be interwoven with the 'basest' elements of society, criminals and prostitutes.

The city walls were also an element in defining zones of poverty. In the late Middle Ages, cities expanded by building outside the walls, creating suburbs. Most striking in the social structure of the 'suburbanites' was the complete absence of an upper class. In general, residents of the suburbs were poorer, their rights more limited and their zones of poverty large, encompassing tramps and vagabonds as well as the lowest categories of workers. During a conflict between 'burghers' and 'suburbanites' in Iéna in 1404, the city council denied the 'suburbanites' the right to brew beer on the grounds that they were too poor to fulfil the necessary conditions, these being the payment of a tax (*Schoss*) and the possession of arms and a cuirass. But the suburbs evolving on the outskirts of towns should not be regarded as being composed only of social outcasts. They gradually created an organizational structure of their own to rival that of the city, although they continued to be weighed down, in the eyes of city dwellers, by the social stigma attached to living on the periphery.

The way in which one lived was also a factor in determining one's place in the hierarchy of wealth and prestige. Owning a house was of course symbolic of stability and a certain social status, but failure in this regard did not automatically make one a social outcast. In the late Middle Ages the practice of renting lodgings became widespread among both the poor and the middle classes, and a new dimension was added to the topography of poverty: for the poor were now distributed not only horizontally, among the various quarters of the city, but also vertically, in attics and cellars. In densely populated cities, the appearance of many-storeyed houses was soon followed by the building of lodgings adapted to the social position of their future inhabitants. Workers' lodgings, cramped and meanly equipped, began to appear as early as the fifteenth century. In the suburbs, on the other hand, houses with rented flats were rarer; more frequent were poorly built, sometimes even temporary, shoddy structures, some of which, in the fourteenth and fifteenth centuries, were also to be found in the Temple district of Paris. The number of people living in cellars was large; sometimes, to judge by research into the structure of certain northern German towns in the fifteenth and sixteenth centuries, it comprised as much as 10 per cent of the population. In some medieval cities the living conditions were almost a prefigurement of the nineteenth-century Manchester described by Engels. It was in the Middle Ages that slums first made their appearance, and continued, throughout the various stages of urban development, to characterize the living conditions of the poor. The lines of demarcation which governed social topography, and therefore also social relations, were drawn in such a way as to separate the poorest from the rest of the urban community.

From this general picture one may conclude that poverty, both rural and urban, and even in the proportions it had assumed by the late Middle Ages, remained bound by the existing social structures. It continued as the normal condition of the working classes. Its permanent presence, however, brought them no stability, and they lived, as before, with the constant threat of being reduced at any moment to utter penury. With the fluctuations of the economy, more and more people found themselves out of work and in danger of starvation; wages, which did not keep pace with inflation, proved inadequate to feed a family. Urban life was particularly difficult; in order to survive, one needed money to buy food. Poverty was also more striking in the city, where luxury and famine lived side by side, and where crowded streets and public meeting-places – the church, the marketplace, the tavern – made it stand out. Finally, urban poverty was accentuated by low social and legal status, exclusion from organized community life, topographical restrictions and the general contempt which it inspired.

Faced with this very real need, the need of the worker, both the medieval ethos of poverty and the system of alms distribution and hospital aid proved indifferent or, at best, inefficient. The poor relied primarily on spontaneous acts of solidarity on the part of neighbours and family members, but such efforts were effective only when numbers were limited; they could do nothing to alleviate poverty on a large scale. Some forms of social aid became common-law traditions: in England, for example, 'manorial' custom had it that farmers who were childless and too old to work the land were entitled to keep the profits from a small plot, while the land was cultivated by the new leaseholder. Widows, until they remarried, had the right to inherit land without paying for the usufruct. Professional guilds also provided occasional help to members who had become impoverished as a result of accidents or other blows of fate, and among urban brotherhoods the provision of such aid was a statutory rule. The amounts, however, were meagre, barely enough to cover a tiny fraction of basic needs: in Gent, for example, in 1330, the poor received from the Table of the Holy Spirit, a parish charitable institution, just over two and a half kilos of bread per year. The municipal authorities, charitable foundations and private individuals made some effort to help. It was surely no coincidence that donations to the hospital in Ypres in the thirteenth century were greatest at times of economic depression. In 1423 the municipal authorities of Brussels decreed that everyone between the ages of ten and sixty must work, and even offered to lend working tools to those who did not have their own, but threatened to banish from the city anyone who 'stubbornly' chose to remain unemployed. Ten years later they ordered the arrest and imprisonment of 'healthy beggars' (*mendiants valides*) on charges of arson, inciting riots and disturbing the peace. This attitude to 'healthy beggars', a tradition going back to ancient and early medieval times, aimed to keep the 'working poor' outside the range of the ethos of poverty and made them objects of scorn, distrust and hostility.

2

The Disintegration of Medieval Society

The French historian Henri Hauser once remarked on the peculiar 'modernity' of the sixteenth century. He was speaking not so much of the culture of that age as of its socio-economic mechanisms.[1] Most of the problems which were to characterize the life of modern societies were already there, *in statu nascendi*: the birth of the working class, conflicts between workers and employers, strikes, economic crises, inflation and poverty. The sixteenth century also witnessed the great religious controversies which were to divide the Church for the rest of the millennium, and the ideologies which were to mark the whole of modern social thought.

Because macrohistorical studies present a continuous picture of the past, historiographers and philosophers of history must slice up the past into a succession of periods, and the divisions they make are always to a great extent arbitrary. From a microhistorical perspective, however, the past arranges itself much more readily into 'natural' chronological chunks: the dates of birth and death of individuals, for instance, or of the founding or dissolution of an institution. But even here an element of randomness creeps in, when, for example, we speak of a person's 'youth' or 'maturity', as if these were not relative terms which vary with the era or the social context; or, again, when we refer to the 'flourishing' or 'decline' of an institution, as if we were not thereby imposing our own value-judgements on a historical narrative in order to slice it up in a certain way. And once we come to the study of large groups – social classes, nations or societies – it becomes quite impossible to find divisions which could in any way be considered 'natural'. When we try to slice up history chronologically, it is as if we were sectioning live tissue. The fabric of mass phenomena is continuous; dramatic events remain the epiphenomena of history, and cannot by themselves be taken as indicators or expressions of collective change. It is only when we have situated the origins and consequences of an event within their context that we can begin to assess the extent of that event's significance.

The continuity which we observe in collective processes does not mean that change does not take place. On the contrary, it is here that the most clear and striking changes occur. The lives of individuals follow different and changing paths, shaped by historical possibilities but at the same time woven into the fabric of the 'natural history' of humanity, a level on which change takes place so slowly that the historian's tools and methods cannot discern it. Changes in collective sensibilities, ways of communicating and forms of expression are more perceptible. But such changes cannot be precisely fixed in time; the temporal scale within which they take place is vast, its approximate limits discernible only as probabilities, by calculating the quantitative preponderance of certain characteristics at different points on a continuum of evolution.

The twentieth century abounds in dramatic breaks in continuity, but ordinary observation has shown them to have had little effect on social attitudes or ways of life. At the same time, a violent 'acceleration of time' in certain historical conditions, the particularly swift development of a country or a region, has accentuated differences between societies, not only in their material conditions, technological development or global production, but also in their internal social structure. The twentieth century has allowed us to establish two things. First of all, a system is determined by the elements which predominate within it; they define its distinctness as a 'model'. A 'model' is not merely an intellectual construct which we impose on the complexities of reality in order to arrange them more simply; it is also a genuine reflection of that reality. For not only does it bring out the distinctive features of a society (such as, for example, its preference for a free labour market rather than non-economic coercive measures), it also allows us to view that society as a structure which constantly affirms, strengthens and regenerates those features. Secondly, systems which differ fundamentally in their social structure may coexist in one epoch. As a result, any division into periods on a typological level must be based on 'historical time', in other words on a chronology which is not absolute but relative. Nomadic societies or feudal military structures are separated from modern economic systems not by the years of the calendar but by evolutionary stages.

These two observations are of fundamental importance in social history, for they define its basic principles of research. When we look at the way in which past societies have evolved, we must also look closely at those historical processes which involve a transition from one mode of social coexistence to another, a sort of mutation of the dominant structure. The pace of these processes, however, is not everywhere the same, although in earlier epochs the evolutionary differences between particular areas were not so great as they are now. The Swiss economic historian Paul Bairoch has examined the disproportions in the evolution of particular countries in the industrial and pre-industrial eras, and has shown that, in the latter, evolutionary disparities did not exceed a relation of one to three, while in the former they attained proportions of one to twenty-five. What is important, however, is not so much the scale of these disparities (which shows that areas of under-development in large parts of the world are a largely modern phenomenon) as the fact that they appear or become sharper precisely at moments of transition and radical change in the socio-economic structure. Thus differences in social organization exist not only in a temporal but also in a spatial, geographic, dimension.

It is for this reason that the view of the sixteenth century as a peculiarly 'modern' era in the social history of Europe cannot be fully embraced. It would be more acceptable if the field of observation were limited to the domain of social consciousness, and in particular to its expression in economic doctrines and social thought. For it was in the sixteenth century that people became aware of a new dimension to social problems. In theological controversy, in the Catholic and Protestant reform movements, in humanist thought, the problem of attitudes towards beggars and widespread poverty reflected a collective anxiety about the direction in which society was evolving. But the changes at the root of this intellectual movement, and its acompanying reforms of charitable institutions, began much earlier than the sixteenth century. The process which was to give birth to modern society, or rather to the 'first modern age', began to emerge during the hundred years between 1320 and 1420, the age of the first 'great crisis' of feudal society; while the second such crisis, in the seventeenth century, laid bare both the inadequacies of the old social system and the social problems inherent in capitalism.

This examination of the place of poverty and the poor in medieval society has taken little note of the way in which attitudes changed from year to year and decade to decade. This does not mean that short-term changes in attitudes towards collective and individual wealth did not take place in the Middle Ages. The annals of bad harvests and famines provide an outline of a very particular set of social circumstances, for they trace the extent of dire poverty. But blights of this kind were temporary and did not influence social status; they did not lead to a permanent segregation of the impoverished as a group. More significant in its effects was the expansion of the money-based economy and urban growth. These were factors which sped up the creation of extremes of wealth and poverty and accentuated divisions between social groups; they were responsible for the growth of poverty on a mass scale. The social circumstances provide a framework for situating these factors in space and time.

2.1   The Social Circumstances

The period spanning the late Middle Ages and the beginning of the modern era stands out in European history as a time of great social and economic changes, albeit changes so scattered, both geographically and in time, that it is difficult for the historian to bring them together into a general picture of the age. The picture is further fragmented by the local character of social and economic life: until the industrial revolution, transport, both of people and of merchandise, communication and commerce were very much restricted. The economic and cultural horizons of the masses were defined by the tolling of the church bell, not by the throb of international commerce and financial exchange which pulsated through European economic centres such as Bruges, Antwerp, Venice or Amsterdam. Feats of long-distance navigation, great geographical discoveries – these were things which ploughed a slow and difficult furrow in the mentality of the time; they did not impinge on local, isolated life. For this reason the pace of evolution varied not only between whole countries, which would not enjoy economic cohesion until the expansion of their internal capitalist markets, but also from one region to another, according to specific natural and historical conditions. Nevertheless, with some concessions to simplicity, a general picture of the evolutionary tendencies of European societies can be drawn.

Indeed, given the diversity of conditions, the harmony which modern studies have been able to discern in the evolution of Europe at the time is astonishing. And despite the difficulties of research in the economic history of the period, statistical work on 'pre-statistical' data does provide some insight into the extent and direction of evolution, by establishing the relevant proportions and orders of magnitude. The movement of prices and wages provides some general information on production, trade and the labour market; historical demography is able to shed some light on the size and movement of populations; and, finally, data concerning the money flow and the relation between the quantity of precious metals and the size of the money market can often serve as a general indication – a sort of seismograph, to borrow Marc Bloch's term – of economic rhythms. The main objects of interest here, however, are the social consequences of economic development, the changes in social structure and the relations between wealth and poverty – in short, the social circumstances. For pre-industrial society, the indicators we have are neither uniform nor precise enough to enable us to trace the long-term tendencies, not to mention the short-term fluctuations, of these circumstances. We can, however, consider the problem of 'mass poverty' in the context of economic trends and those spasmodic events which marked the modern era – food crises.

In looking at price movements as indicators of tendencies in economic evolution, historians have found that, from the beginning of the twelfth century, which already provides ample documentation on prices, to the second quarter of the fourteenth century, prices rose, and this rise reflected economic expansion; in the first half of the fourteenth century they fell, reflecting a profound crisis in the European economy. There are a number of objections to be made to the drawing of such conclusions on the basis of price fluctuations alone. For example, and most importantly, our own everyday experience as well as historical and economic research shows that price increases are not necessarily signs of an economic boom. One could also question the extent to which these alleged consequences of price fluctuations affected an agrarian society, where the so-called natural economy was still dominant, with the market playing a much reduced role. These objections aside, however, the fact remains that all the other indicators of economic growth confirm this picture. The 'fourteenth-century crisis', as it is known, left so lasting and profound a mark on the economic life, both urban and rural, of so many Western countries and regions that it must be treated as a structural one.

Among the various interpretations of this crisis (a prominent object of study in recent historiography) the most popular has been the demographic theory. On this version, demographic growth, one of the factors of economic expansion in previous centuries, now began to exceed the limits of agrarian technology. As the land cultivated was less and less fertile, and the soil in fields which never lay fallow grew poor and exhausted through over-use and lack of fertilizer, farming became less and less profitable. Harvests remained at the same level while the population continued to grow; in the second half of the thirteenth century population growth in the most highly developed areas of Western Europe exceeded 10 per cent, and the exhausted agrarian economy could not cope with this additional burden. The rising prices of agricultural products at the end of the thirteenth century (in the Paris region the price of bread, for example, doubled between 1287 and 1303) was one effect of the 'overheating' of the economic mechanism through demographic pressure. The food crisis of 1315–17 and the series of fatal epidemics and famines over the same period were caused primarily by an unfavourable climate in Western and Northern Europe, but they were also striking testimony to the disparity which had formed between the size of the population on the one hand and the food reserves and agricultural yields on the other.

The demographic version, however, as its critics have pointed out, is more a description than an interpretation of events. Demographic pressure cannot explain the mechanisms of the fourteenth-century crisis, for the Black Death, which must have swept away about a third of the population of the West, failed to redress the balance. On the contrary, the great epidemic of 1348–51 and the subsequent series of 'plagues' laid bare in all their starkness the deficiencies of the economy. The demographic question should therefore be seen within the social context of the age and the internal structure of medieval population growth.

Demographic expansion in the first half of our millennium was at the root of the vast urban evolution that was taking place throughout Europe. In some major cities, such as Paris or the great cities of northern Italy, the increase in population began to exceed the limits of the food reserves. This excess was even more striking in the case of smaller, provincial towns, which often housed a population far greater than was warranted by the needs of the local market, while at the same time failing to develop an urban industry which would provide its inhabitants with jobs. Studies of the Rouergue region in the south of France have shown that small towns such as Millau, Rodez or Castres absorbed the demographic surplus of the countryside, and that their evolution, far from being a sign of economic prosperity, was a symptom of over-population and poverty in the region. The widespread agricultural activity in such towns made them largely self-sufficient in food; but feeding an ever-growing population was not the only problem. The small demand for labour and the rigidity of corporate structures resulted in a growing number of professionally unstable inhabitants who worked only occasionally and were at the mercy of circumstances for their continued survival. Cities, both large and small, were more resistant than the countryside to the crisis of a bad harvest: the demands of urban living had accustomed their inhabitants to stocking supplies. But they suffered in equal measure when unfavourable circumstances came together to affect production, commerce and agrarian exchange. The problem of over-population in late medieval Europe should be seen as relative: a widening gap had formed between demographic expansion and economic development and, while the former was dynamic, the latter remained stagnant, unable to create sufficient productivity to maintain an equilibrium between yields and a growing population. The demographic pressures on cities overrun with newcomers indicate that the problem is closely linked to the general development of the agrarian economy in medieval society.

Another consequence of demographic expansion was that more and more farms were parcelled up. The workings of the feudal economy in the fourteenth century were an obstacle to development: most farmers could not afford to invest properly in their land, or even to fertilize the soil, and the burden of taxes and seigniorial duties was sometimes so great that it threatened their survival. Once the market economy began to penetrate into the countryside, disparities in material wealth became more visible among the rural population; divisions between rich and poor made themselves felt. Most striking, however, was the proliferation of farms struggling at the limits of their resources, too weak to resist adversity of any kind. Increasing taxes and feudal duties further hastened the economic decline of such farms. The most eloquent signs of this decline were the dietary habits of the farmers and their families: the American historian N. J. G. Pounds considers that by the turn of the thirteenth century malnutrition had attained proportions vaster than Europe had ever seen. The root of the crisis, therefore, lay in the social realities of the feudal system and in its methods of dealing with a production surplus: very few peasants were rich enough to increase their yields and the efficiency of their labour by investing in the land, while the feudal lords, who held most of the production surplus, were nonetheless reluctant to invest it in agriculture.

By the first quarter of the sixteenth century, demographic expansion was visibly slowing. For this a high mortality rate seem chiefly to have been responsible. Studies of the peasant population of Winchester Abbey show that the coefficient of mortality between 1292 and 1347 was between 40 and 52 per cent, an extremely high rate. The gap between demographic and economic growth was therefore transitory. Population growth was checked by low agricultural yields; the biological reasons for the high mortality rate among the underfed peasant masses can thus be seen to have had their origins in the socio-economic structures.

At the end of the food crisis of 1315–17 the price of grain remained stable, then fell: for the economy in general this was a turning-point. At the same time the price of industrial products was on the rise, leading to what is known as a 'scissors' effect. Without going into the complexities of this price disparity (which Wilhelm Abel links to a fall in demand for agricultural products corresponding to the fall in population, and Guy Bois to production costs which were higher in the cities), we may say that it was an element of the structural crisis of feudal society and of the 'agrarian depression' of the fifteenth century.

The Black Death, although it exacerbated the social crisis of the age, failed to resolve any of its contradictions. One might have expected it to counter the effects of over-population and restore an equilibrium between the population and the food available, but nothing of the sort took place; the twin scourges of famine and epidemics continued their ravages unchecked throughout the second half of the fourteenth century. Ruggiero Romano has unearthed some astonishing remarks in the writings of the Italian chronicler Matteo Villani:

> It was thought that depopulation would bring with it an abundance of all the fruits of the earth, but it was not so; human ingratitude was such that there was a great lack of everything, and this lasted for a long time. In some parts, indeed (and we shall speak of this presently), there

was terrible and extraordinary famine. And it was thought also that there would be clothing in plenty, and an abundance of all the other things which, besides food, the human body has most need of; but again, this was not so, and these things were lacking for a long time. But payment for labour and the cost of such things as are wrought by craftsmen and artisans of all kinds more than doubled compared with their customary price.[2]

What is striking about these remarks is not only their perspicacity but their value as testimony: they show that people living at the time were very much aware of the changes which were taking place and asked questions analogous to those posed by modern historiographers studying the period.

The social changes taking place in the second half of the fourteenth century present a multidimensional picture, further complicated by the often vast disparities in development between particular regions. In Western Europe the evolution of the countryside was marked by the growing role of small family farms in the structure of rural life. The price of agricultural products being low, and labour expensive, great landowners tended to be discouraged from investing in technology for developing their land. The acreage of land which they cultivated diminished, and the peasants took advantage of this to expand their own farms through the cultivation of some of this land. The social and legal condition of the peasantry also improved: serfdom, for instance, disappeared almost entirely. The great majority of the peasants' seigniorial dues were exacted in the form of money, and since the amount was fixed (sharecropping existed only in France and in Italy) currency devaluation made these charges a relatively light burden. As a result of all this the divisions between rich and poor in rural communities were sharpened, for those who were most able to profit from the situation were above all, if not exclusively, wealthy farmers. Only they had the means to accumulate capital and to extend their farms by leasing or buying more land; they could afford to buy more cattle, invest in agricultural technology, embark on the cultivation of new crops, use hired labour when there was a profit to be made or breed the kind of livestock that does not require much work. Most peasants were unable to profit from the new situation, and became victims rather than beneficiaries of market mechanisms. The tax registers of the rural districts of Burgundy or the Netherlands, for instance, show that the number of peasants unable to maintain their economic independence was rising at a dizzying rate.

No less complex was the situation in the labour market. The series of epidemics in the fourteenth century, combined with a drop in the birth rate, had depleted the labour force, resulting in a steep rise in wages. Employers complained, and successfully insisted that local and state authorities take energetic steps to remedy the situation.

In France, John the Good, in his ordinance of 1351, issued a harsh condemnation of vagrants who refused to return to their past occupation (and past wages). A few years later, in November 1354, there was a new ordinance, which took up the problem of labourers and wages in the typical context of the cost of craftsmen's products; craftsmen justified their high prices by saying, 'labourers will not work if they are not paid the wages they demand; and the wages they ask are so high that we are forced to put up the price of our products.' When administrative measures were taken to fix the maximum wage for day-labourers, the labourers circumvented the restrictions by agreeing to work only on a fee basis for tasks accomplished or else refused to work altogether, sometimes even abandoning their homes and families to seek employment in a place where these laws were not enforced. They also demanded a variety of supplements to their wages, such as wine and meat and 'any other thing to which their status did not give them access'. Finally, there were complaints that many hired labourers were idle, loitering in taverns and boasting that their high wages allowed them to limit their work to two days a week. It is apparent from these descriptions that employers were attempting to protect their interests as a class, and that the royal edicts echoed their arguments. The resulting laws were explicit and unequivocal: all able-bodied persons who had in the past earned their living as hired labourers were to return to work immediately, on pain of the pillory, branding with a hot iron or banishment. This was, in effect, a measure which obliged them to accept work on the employer's terms, a form of non-economic intervention in the labour market. The series of royal and local decrees issued in the 1360s, 1380s and 1390s continued these policies against 'excessive wages' and vagrancy.

In England it was in 1349, in the reign of Edward III, that the 'Labourers' Ordinance' was issued, making work obligatory for all those who were able-bodied. Two years later Parliament issued another decree in a similar spirit. The English 'labourers' statutes' were a faithful and complete reflection of the doctrines underpinning social policies after the Black Death. The obligation to work, imposed on all the able-bodied up to the age of sixty, involved a further constraint:

that of being bound to accept wages which had been average in 1325. Employers were also forbidden to offer wages higher than those imposed by the statutes. Finally, severe restrictions were imposed on the mechanisms of the labour market: labourers were bound to remain at their jobs until their contracts were up and landowners were forbidden to hire the 'fugitives' who defied this rule. They also had first right of hire of their own villagers.

The kingdoms of the Iberian Peninsula also took measures to check the depletion of the labour market after the Black Death. In 1349 Peter II of Aragon set up a special commission to study the problem of labourers' wages. In 1349 and 1350 the Cortes of Aragon fixed the maximum wages for tailors, blacksmiths, tanners, carpenters, stonemasons, agricultural labourers, shepherds and domestic servants, hoping in this way to put an end to their excessive demands: it was claimed that they demanded wages four or five times greater than before the Black Death. In 1351 similar measures were adopted by the Cortes of Castille in Valladolid: maximum wages were set; all able-bodied people over the age of twelve were ordered to take up work immediately, and a complaint made under oath and confirmed by two witnesses was enough to condemn any recalcitrant labourer as a vagrant. In Portugal the new legislation was even more severe: a series of laws, beginning with the 1349 decree of Alphonse IV, not only set a strict ceiling for wages but obliged labourers to return to their old places of work on the same conditions as before the epidemic. Migrating workers were condemned as vagrants, and it became illegal to beg, or to move from one place to another, without special permission. In 1375 the *Lei dai Sesmarias* in Portugal imposed forced labour on vagrants, while in Castille a decree issued in 1381 allowed anyone who captured a vagrant to make him work without wages for a month.

Legislation of this type was enforced with varying degrees of severity in each European country, and its effects must have been limited. After all, one could not undo the Black Death, nor could any amount of laws restore the situation to what it had been before the crisis. But it does seem to have kept wages down, and to have blocked the normal supply-and-demand mechanisms of the labour market. The basic tendencies of late medieval legislation show up clearly in the context of labourers' wages, for which only an upper limit was set; the coercive measures introduced against labourers treated the refusal to work as a crime. One might say that these measures contain, in a much abbreviated form, the basic principles of modern social policies.

Social and economic life after the Black Death was undoubtedly marked by shrinking supply in the labour market, further depleted by a whole series of epidemics which continued to rage throughout the fourteenth century. It has been calculated that, while the Black Death destroyed 30 per cent of the rural population, the epidemics of 1357–74 were responsible for demographic losses of over 20 per cent. Normandy lost more than half of its rural population during this period. The human losses in cities were equally great. Our very fragmentary data on rates of mortality in different social classes show, not surprisingly, that they were higher among the poor. As a result the balance of supply and demand in the labour market favoured those offering their labour.

It was, in the view of some historians, precisely this situation that led to the 'golden age of hired labour'. Labourers' wages did go on rising well into the middle of the fifteenth century, and remained high even in the second half of that century. The curve which plots the long-term evolution of real wages, evaluated in terms of purchasing power, shows that by the middle of the fourteenth century they had reached a level not exceeded until the nineteenth century. The 'golden age' theory was propagated in the nineteenth century by the English economist Thorold Rogers, and more recently by the German economic historian Wilhelm Abel; contemporary studies, however, have cast doubt on its accuracy.

The first doubts arise when we come to look at the purchasing power of rural wage labourers. Their basic needs were not supplied through the market: they had their own allotments, cultivated by the whole family, and were often given a meal at work. Their real wages seem to rise because the price of grain was steadily falling; but the price of meat, fish or wine, which they also bought, was not falling in the same way, and industrial products were still very expensive.

The 'golden age' theory was based mainly on data concerning wage-earning craftsmen; Wilhelm Abel uses these data to argue that craftsmen were highly paid, both nominally and in real terms. More detailed monographic studies, however, suggest the contrary. Let us look at two examples: Bruges and Florence.

Fernand Braudel has reconstructed the hypothetical budget of a labourer's family. Allowing between two hundred and fifty and three hundred days to the working year, and between ten and twelve hours of work per day, he obtained a figure of around three thousand working hours per year. He also calculated that the average labourer's family of four people consumed about twelve hundredweight of grain in a year. In studies of real revenues it is generally assumed that if a hundredweight of grain is equivalent to more than a hundred hours of work, the family is very hard pressed indeed; if more than two hundred hours of work are required, its survival is threatened; more than three hundred means starvation. The Belgian scholar Jean-Pierre Sosson used these markers in evaluating the real revenues of three categories of building labourers in Bruges: master carpenters, carpenters' journeymen and unskilled aides. The difference in wages between these three categories is significant: a journeyman was paid half as much as a master, while an aide, who was an unskilled labourer with no professional guild, was generally paid about 20 per cent less than a journeyman. Tables drawn up for the period between 1360 and 1490 show that the salary of a master craftsman did not fall to the level of the first marker – over a hundred hours of work for a hundredweight of grain – until the food crises of 1437–9 and 1481–3. The salaries of labourers in the two remaining categories, however, fell below the second marker (over two hundred hours) during these years, and were habitually below the first. Of the period of a hundred and one years covered by the data, forty-six were so critical that labourers in these categories needed to work more than a hundred hours in order to earn the equivalent of a hundredweight of grain and sometimes approached the dangerous threshold of two hundred hours.

Studies of social relations in fourteenth-century Florence, where early forms of capitalism were particularly quick to develop, show that poverty was widespread among craftsmen. The gradual descent into poverty of large numbers of independent artisans, and the general disinclination, quite marked in the second half of the fourteenth century, to invest in craftsmen's products, lead us to suppose that there was a general crisis in Florentine crafts during that period. The group which felt it most keenly, however, were the wage labourers. When Charles de La Roncière studied the real value of their wages, he calculated it in terms of calories. Thus he evaluated a labourer's wage (assumed to feed an average family of four) in terms of the caloric value of the foods that could be bought with it, and in this way tried to reconstruct, with the aid of the account books of the Santa Maria Nuova hospital in Florence, the budgets of a gardener, an assistant mason and a mason. The average number of calories needed by each family member simply in order to survive is 2,200 (average because a manual labourer needs 3,500). The wages represented by this figure allow for a basic minimum of food necessary for survival, but not for any variety: the food is assumed to be limited to a single product. The cheapest such product, and the highest in calories, is of course bread; Charles de La Roncière accordingly bases his calculations on the price and caloric value of bread, and assumes that the entire wages are spent on it alone. Anything below this figure means malnutrition and hunger. However, if we include in the budget essential expenses such as rent, clothing and other kinds of food, more expensive per calorie, then we reach the figure of 3,500 calories per person as the basic minimum. When we compare the average daily wages of labourers in these three categories, it turns out that the master craftsmen are rarely in danger of hunger; it is only between 1340 and 1347 that their wages fall to the bare minimum, and for two decades after the Black Death they are comfortably off. Labourers in the remaining two categories, however, find it much more difficult to make ends meet, and it is only between 1360 and 1369 that they are able to maintain themselves above the danger level. It must also be remembered that these average wages conceal a great variety of individual cases. When we look at the minimum day wage registered in the accounts of the Santa Maria Nuova hospital, we see that the situation was much more precarious, for even in the decade after the Black Death – considered to be a particularly good one for wage labourers – the two lower categories are unable to rise above the bare minimum.

It turns out, then, that life was harsh for hired labourers in fourteenth-century Florence; the fear of hunger and dire poverty, the prospect of living as beggars, were constantly with them. Loans were a temporary measure, and in most cases they made things worse. The trials for debt heard by the Florentine Arte di Lana show the desperation to which many wage labourers were reduced: in 1387 a wool carder sued by a merchant draper for an unpaid debt of 26 lire saw his working tools confiscated, along with the few miserable furnishings of his house; in 1389 a draper demanded the arrest of a wool carder who owed him 30 lire and was, according to the plaintiff, 'a man of doubtful character, a fugitive and a vagabond'.[3]

One might, however, question the assumption that a labourer's wage was intended to feed an entire family. It is true that a considerable number of wage labourers were unmarried (Charles de La Roncière has in fact made similar calculations for unmarried labourers), and that some wives and children earned additional income, however meagre and sporadic. It is also likely that the low wages made labourers, especially the unskilled and lowest-paid among them, disinclined to marry and found a family early in life.

At the same time, however, one must remember that the situations described are cross-sections of long-term trends in economic evolution, and that they also tend to distort the picture, since they do not take account of short-term fluctuations. When we look at averages over a period of decades, we must not forget the sharp fluctuations in the price of food which took place over shorter periods. For example, the table drawn up for 1335 in Florence is based on data from 1326 to 1339, and reveals wages of very low calorie value (an average of 1,755 calories); but in 1329, when the price of grain rose just before the harvest, the daily wages of a gardener represented just five hundred to six hundred calories per family member — in other words, near-starvation. More important still, however, is the fact that the global picture fails to take account of unemployment, which was quite widespread at certain periods and for certain categories of labourers. Fewer than half the building labourers in Bruges, for example, worked longer than four weeks on any one site. Craftsmen and labourers in permanent positions were rare; alongside them was a whole contingent of 'reserve' labourers who took short-term jobs, which meant not only that they were constantly on the move but also that they were without work for varying periods of time. Unskilled labourers, the group which made up the majority of the urban poor and absorbed the influx of rural emigrants, were, in the words of J.-P. Sosson, the 'chronic unemployed'. Finally, the internal structures of industrial production as it developed in the late Middle Ages created social divisions and swelled the ranks of the proletariat. The activity of rural craftsmen, organized and controlled by merchants and entrepreneurs, had the effect of lowering labour costs, and was seen as a threat by incorporated craftsmen in the cities. As the Polish historian Marian Malowist has demonstrated, the crisis in traditional urban craftsmanship in Western Europe crushed the economic independence of a large number of previously stable craftsmen, forcing them into the proletariat. The urban guilds looked after the interests of a minority, an elite whose privileges derived from wealth, technological equipment, professional qualifications and investment possibilities. The overwhelming majority of craftsmen, however, did not enjoy these privileges of a stable life, and lacked the wherewithal either to profit from favourable market conditions or to weather the slumps.

Because we have been concerned chiefly with the way in which social evolution can generate poverty, we have put much stress on crises and misfortunes. But history does not consist solely of crises; they are followed by periods of prosperity, reconstruction and equilibrium. The fourteenth century owed such periods to the fall in population and the rise of agricultural yields (if only because the cultivation of poor and unfertile land was abandoned). But these more stable and prosperous times lend themselves to study only on a small time-scale; in the long term the most significant tendency, visible until the 1460s, is stagnation and falling prices in agriculture.

We have seen that the economic development of the fourteenth and fifteenth centuries created sharp social divisions both in the city and in the country. Most striking was the economic weakness of the great majority of manufacturers, whose survival was under constant threat. For wage labourers, on the other hand, the age was a good one, especially when compared with the one that followed: grain prices continued to fall throughout the fourteenth and fifteenth centuries, and to a large extent defined the social tendencies of the age.

This state of affairs changed considerably with what historians call the 'price revolution'. Sharp fluctuations took place not only in prices in general but also in the relative cost of different products, including the cost of labour. From the beginning of the sixteenth century all prices began to rise; in the 1520s they soared. Most affected by this change were grain, spices and farm products; the price of crafts and industrial goods rose less sharply, which led to vast discrepancies, favouring agricultural products. Wages failed utterly to keep up with the general increase, and remained stable for a long time; their rise, when it finally came, was slow and in no way compensated for the increased cost of living. Clearly, wage labourers in the cities were at a double disadvantage, for the comparatively lower prices of industrial products were reflected accordingly in their pay. The two curves which plot the rise in prices and the fall in the real value of wages are based on the example of building labourers, whose earning power is frequently cited in economic history as the most reliable indicator of fluctuations in the real value of wages in the pre-industrial era; the divergence between these two curves indicates a clear and constant deterioration in living standards for the working masses throughout the sixteenth century. The social result of this was that, as Fernand Braudel has pointed out, the rich became richer and the poor became poorer.

The interpretation of the origins and development of the 'price revolution' of the sixteenth century has spawned controversy no less heated and vigorous than that surrounding the crisis of the fourteenth century. On the social consequences of the price/wages relation, however, opinion is less divided. There is no doubt that the sharp rise in prices lowered the living standards of the masses, and of wage earners in the various professions in particular. Its suddenness and intensity fascinate historians, and studies of the history of prices and wages, which constitute, in modern historiography, the first chapter of 'cliometrics', or quantitative history, bring out all the drama of the period. It must be said, however, that modern historians succumb in large measure to the fascination which this rise in prices held for those who lived through it. It was commented on by sixteenth-century annalists, historians and political writers; it provided the material for the first attempts at modern economic analysis. But what made it so striking was the contrast it presented with the relative price stability of the previous age. In the sixteenth century the price of grain rose sixfold; it quadrupled in Poland and tripled in the Netherlands. This represented a rise of 4.3 per cent per year, or a cumulative annual rise of 1.5 per cent relative to each previous year. For people in the sixteenth century the persistence of this trend was astonishing; they saw that their standard of living had suddenly, inexplicably, plummeted, and they complained. Peasants and noblemen, townsmen and labourers, all spoke of it. People harked back nostalgically to the beginning of the century, when 'there was meat on the table every day, food was plentiful, and wine was drunk like water', while 'today [1513] a pound of mutton costs as much as a whole sheep was worth'.[4]

The simplest explanation that has been proposed attributes this sudden rise to a massive influx of silver from the newly discovered American continent and the disturbances which this entailed in the value and circulation of money. This is how people explained it at the time, and most modern historians concur with this theory. However, the chronology of events alone makes this unlikely. Studies of the evolution of nominal prices show that prices were already on an upward trend by 1460–70, well before the influx of precious metals from America; and the growth in silver yields from the mines of Central Europe at about the same time is not sufficient to explain this evolution. In fact the inflation in the sixteenth century arose from internal structural contradictions. Agriculture was stagnating; the spectacular development of farming on the estates of landed gentry in various regions of Europe, both East and West, was due to the increased prices of agricultural products, and did nothing to compensate for the simultaneous demise of peasant agriculture. A study of the evolution of the countryside in Normandy in the late Middle Ages shows that both agricultural yields and human productivity fell considerably after 1460; there was a similar fall in the profits from animal husbandry, which resulted in poorly fertilized soil and insufficient draught animals. At the same time demographic growth led to a dangerous imbalance between the population and the resources available, in the social and technological conditions of the time, to feed it. The relation between currency and precious metals is only one of a long list of factors contributing to inflation: the unequal pace of development in the city and the countryside, growing consumer expenditure on the part of the gentry, the accumulation of profits from trade and so on.

The inflation which spanned the sixteenth century was therefore the product of internal mechanisms. Among its social consequences was the sharpening of contrasts between rich and poor in the countryside. The parcelling out of farms continued at an increased rate; in addition, peasants saw their land taken over by landed gentry, by townsfolk and by rich farmers. Of country dwellers, only this last group was able to reap profits from the new market conditions. Feudal duties, paid in currency, were smaller in real terms, for their amount remained fixed; taxes, however, rose, and their additional burden impoverished the peasantry still further. Finally, the small farmers, who had to supplement their income by working as hired labourers, were hit by the fall in the real value of their wages, the central feature of sixteenth-century inflation.

Since labourers' wages rose much more slowly than the cost of living, their purchasing power went on diminishing. If we take the years 1571–80 as representing 100 on a scale, real wages in Spain were 127.8 in 1510, 91.35 in 1530, 97.6 in 1550, 105.66 in 1570 and 91.31 in 1600. In Hamburg the wages of masons increased by 150 per cent, those of weavers and carpenters doubled; women's pay rose by an average of only 40 per cent, while the price of grain increased by 380 per cent in the course of the century. The fall in real wages affected all categories of labourer, from those with no skills to guild artisans, although in differing degree; in some cases it could be balanced out by an offer of board, or payment in kind, as part of the wages.

Wilhelm Abel has traced the evolution of the real wages of a mason's assistant in Augsburg in the years 1501–1620. In doing so he adopted indicators slightly different from those to which we referred in describing the situation of wage labourers in the fourteenth century, and based his calculations on a family of five people. He took 3,500 calories as the basic daily minimum for a man, 2,400 for a woman and between 1,200 and 2,400 for the three children; the daily minimum for the whole family was therefore established at 11,200 calories, giving an average of 2,240 per person (which accords more or less with the figures adopted by Charles de la Roncière in his study of fourteenth-century Florence). From these calculations it emerges that a labourer's wages often fell below the daily minimum, and from 1540 to the end of the period studied remained consistently below it.

The picture becomes more complicated in the countryside, where three types of wages coexisted on a large scale: payment in kind, payment in currency and a mixture of the two. Studies have shown, however, that real wages diminished in all three cases. Emmanuel Le Roy Ladurie has shown this to be the case for sixteenth-century Languedoc, where the reapers' share of the harvest fell from 10 per cent to 6 per cent between 1500 and 1600; when payment was made in currency, it fell from 100 to 54 on a scale, and in the case of mixed wages, calculated in grain, from 31 to 16 hectolitres. Women were even worse off, for they generally received half of a man's pay for the same work. This principle is confirmed in account books in the Languedoc throughout the fourteenth and fifteenth centuries, and in the sixteenth century the situation is even worse: by the second half of the century women were sometimes rewarded with as little as a quarter of a man's pay for the same kind of work. Generally speaking, women earned at most 37 per cent of the pay of a casual farm labourer or mason's assistant. Between 1480 and 1562 child nurses saw no increase at all in their wages, whereas grain prices increased by 150 per cent over the same period; the increase they finally received in 1562 was far too small to catch up with the pace of inflation. It was the rule that women's wages were not only considerably lower than men's, but also that they increased much more slowly, so that the disproportion between their wages and prices was far greater than for men. Emmanuel Le Roy Ladurie concludes that 'women in particular were victims of poverty'[5] and stresses the gravity of their situation, especially in the second half of the sixteenth century.

The sixteenth century, therefore, an age of economic expansion, was also an age of falling living standards for the masses; it was they who suffered most from the prevailing set of circumstances and paid the price for the modernization of the social system.

The sixteenth century was a turning-point in long-term economic trends. The sudden price increases of the previous century gave way to a certain stability but, although the fluctuations diminished, the price of agricultural products remained very high in relation to labourers' wages. The nature of the social and economic changes of that time, both in the city and in the country, continues to be a subject of live debate among modern historians, with few conclusive results. The crisis of the first half of the seventeenth century, which some date at around 1620, others nearer to 1650, brought into sharp relief the limits of Europe's economic expansion in the fifteenth and sixteenth centuries: where the basic feudal structures of agrarian society remained unchanged, evolution was blocked. The subsequent problems in commerce and banking, in navigation, in the circulation of currency and in the financial management of cities and states resulted from the conservatism of the relations of production and the system of government. Industrial evolution and the adoption of a system of government privileging the bourgeoisie was the only way out of the crisis. It was adopted, a first step on the way to industrial revolution, by England and the United Provinces; other countries were to follow much later.

As for standards of living and the relation between wages and prices, the situation born of the aftermath of the fourteenth-century crisis persisted, and proceeded to worsen dramatically in the first quarter of the sixteenth century. Where priority was given to industrial evolution, on the other hand, the situation was reversed: wages increased tenfold, while grain prices merely doubled. But the general tendency of 'pre-industrial' Europe, best illustrated by a comparison of the movement of wages and prices in England and Germany, was depressing; even the slight increase in wages in cities during the first half of the eighteenth century did little to change this state of affairs. In the second half the situation changed once more, leading, finally, to a drastic fall in real wages at the turn of the nineteenth century.

2.2   Poverty and Economic Expansion

These very broad outlines of the social and economic trends in the period which concerns us here are of course very rough and schematic, owing to incomplete documentation as well as to the lack of solidly based research. Nor should they be seen as applying to all countries and regions of Europe: feudal agrarian societies had a number of different models, in which the use of 'commercial' indicators was not always appropriate; in the great majority of cases the economic life of these societies was not regulated by the circulation of money or the structures of trade and commerce – all precious sources of information for historians. It is precisely for this reason that the surprising aspect of the development of these societies lies not in their differences but in their similarities – from London to Constantinople, from Moscow to Lisbon – within an economic system which theorists call one of 'imperfect control'. Price movements in particular areas sometimes conflict with the general tendencies traced in research and paths of development can diverge, but regional studies on the whole confirm the general principles of development. Emmanuel Le Roy Ladurie distinguishes a period of depression in the fifteenth century, followed by one of expansion in the sixteenth and the beginning of the seventeenth centuries (when the wages of farm labourers nevertheless fell), then the period from 1630 to 1670, known as the 'time of unresolved tensions', and, finally, another phase of depression which lasted until 1740. The Dutch historian B. H. Slicher traces similar stages in Western Europe's agricultural development: an initial phase of expansion, followed by a slump when the area of cultivated land diminished, in the Middle Ages; the price revolution of the sixteenth century; and finally the hundred years' economic depression between 1650 and 1750.

In this picture of European development the problems and successive slumps of the fourteenth and seventeenth centuries have a particular significance. The British historian Perry Anderson rightly points out that it was recent research on the upheavals of those times which shed light on the dynamics of feudal methods of production. Without venturing into the details of the debate to which these crises have given rise among historiographers, it will be useful to look at the changes in socio-economic structures which they revealed.

The crisis of the sixteenth century was linked to a fall in feudal revenues, due to the smaller value of feudal duties. This single fact, regardless of its causes and ramifications, was what prompted the search for a solution to the problems of the feudal system. A choice then presented itself between two different paths of economic evolution. That choice would determine the future development of

Europe's agrarian system, and would have an enormous influence on the transformation of her socio-political system as a whole. The alternatives for the feudal lords were as follows: to enter into commercial relations with the peasants and to modernize the management of their estates, or to extend and intensify the cultivation of their land using a labour force bound to them in servitude. The first led to modernized farming methods and the development of animal husbandry and crops that were more profitable and better adapted to the needs of industry (in England in the sixteenth century sheep breeding was introduced at the expense of land cultivation, squeezing out small crop farmers and leading Sir Thomas More to write that 'sheep are devouring people'); the second resulted in an expansion of traditional farming which relied on the unpaid labour of peasants tied by feudal obligation. The servitude by which these peasants were bound to their feudal lords was the guarantee of their labour, and the reversion to these practices on a large scale is known as the 'second serfdom' of the peasantry.

The agrarian system of Europe thus evolved in two different directions, the line of demarcation between them being generally agreed by modern economic historians to lie along the Elbe. It was not until much later, however, and after a long process of evolution, that the regions thus divided could be distinguished and geographically defined in this way. In the fifteenth century, at the end of the crisis, the two models coexisted in particular countries and particular regions throughout Europe, offering a choice between two opposing ways of socio-economic evolution. The choice of one or the other, however, was not the result of individual decisions based on local relations between the peasantry and landowners, but emerged from more general concerns: the level of economic evolution, the state of the market, commercial relations between small producers, the relations of power between the peasantry and the feudal landowners and the role of cities and of the bourgeoisie. It was the interplay of all these elements that lent particular countries and regions their characteristic structure.

Variations in models and rates of evolution appeared everywhere, not only between North and South but also – a fact frequently overlooked – between East and West. At the risk of considerable simplification, one could say that the 'North' and the 'West' were economically the most highly developed regions in the modern and early modern history of Europe. Such a claim seems well founded when one compares extreme examples, such as England or Sweden on the one hand and Portugal or Sicily on the other – or France and Muscovy; but it becomes more doubtful when we look at intermediate cases, such as Bohemia and the German states. If we adopt the choice between modernization and 'refeudalization' of the agrarian system as our criterion we can, very roughly, divide Europe geographically into four economic zones. The first, the zone of modernization, includes England, the Netherlands, northern and Atlantic France and the southern German provinces; the second, representing classical 'refeudalization', contains the countries of Central and Eastern Europe; the third, in which both models coexist, covers the Iberian and Italian peninsulas. Finally, there is the South-West of Europe, whose particular traditions and political situation gave rise to a specific model based on the conservative agrarian system.

The second 'general crisis', that of the seventeenth century, crystallized and developed the separate evolutionary tendencies which had first begun to emerge in the fifteenth century, and the new type of 'economic concentration' which followed further defined and sharpened their outlines. The advanced level of evolution attained in England and Holland in the course of that century to a certain extent defined Europe's prospects of industrialization; but their example had little impact before the eighteenth century, and the extent of its social and economic influence should not be overestimated. The process of proto-industrialization unfolding in these two countries, interpreted by some historians as a 'minor' industrial revolution, changed little in Europe's essential socio-economic structures. Land remained the overwhelming basis of the European social order, and social conservatism, leading to the formation of an aristocratic system, remained the dominant tendency throughout the seventeenth century. A radical and large-scale transformation of the social and economic structures, leading to an industrial society, did not take place until the eighteenth century, on the eve of – and during – the industrial revolution.

Changes in population density were an important element in defining the overall socio-economic climate, and they merit particular attention. Already, among ordinary people as well as in the writings of those who were to become the precursors of modern social and economic thought, demography was frequently appealed to. Even before Malthus, people noticed that famines and poverty were the direct result of over-population.

Our information about Europe's demographic growth is too fragmentary to allow us to trace, with any degree of accuracy, the population curves for particular regions or for Europe as a whole; from what we do know, however, it seems that the basic tendencies correspond to the general patterns of economic growth. According to Helleiner, the hundred years between the beginning of the Black Death and the middle of the fifteenth century saw a marked fall in the population; this was followed, in most European countries, by a period of growth, which in turn gave way to another hundred years' demographic decline. While the demographic decline of 1340–1440 is not in any doubt, the decline alleged to have taken place in the seventeenth century is more problematic: some historians date it to between 1650 and 1740. There appears to be no sustained correlation of any sort between population growth and wages; the most that can be said is that population growth generally tended to cause wages to stagnate or fall.

An agrarian society which has not undergone fundamental changes in its traditional structures is unable to absorb a population excess, and colonization is the result. In the sixteenth century there was a great wave of colonization, both within particular regions and further afield, to less populated countries; another wave followed the Thirty Years' War in Germany, and yet another, on a large scale, in the eighteenth century; none of them, however, could do more than temporarily alleviate the sustained demographic pressure. The territorial expansion of the sixteenth century, in the form of military or exploratory expeditions, was another attempt to find solutions to a demographic excess which a feudal society was unable to absorb; Swedish expansion, expeditions to the New World and the colonization of Europe's eastern regions, of which the Polish colonizing thrust towards Muscovy was an example, all had their origins here.

This demographic increase also swelled the labour market, leading to greater unemployment and poverty. The demographic map of Europe reveals some correlations: in the Netherlands, England, France, northern Italy, southern Germany and Castille, where the population density was great, paupers were very numerous. It would be misleading, however, to place too much weight on this correlation: we should not take literally the claims of contemporary Malthusians who, approaching theory in the way that Monsieur Jourdain approached prose, pronounce that, if there is a large number of poor, it is because too many of them are being born. In Spain, in the sixteenth and seventeenth centuries, population growth was highest in Navarra and Catalonia; yet it was not here that the poor were most numerous, but in Castille, Valencia and Aragon, where the population was falling at the time.

What is certain, in any event, is that population density and demographic evolution must sooner or later confront the problem of production, and unemployment is the result. It can have one of two direct causes: an excess of supply in the labour market or a lack of demand on the part of employers. In the pre-industrial era, lack of demand from employers was the chief problem; the unemployed, for their part, were often restrained by socio-cultural barriers, unable or unwilling to seek work which would force them to adapt to new conditions and an alien socio-economic environment.

The French demographer Alfred Sauvy used a 'marginalist' theory to shed light on the complexity of the relation between population density and poverty. He claimed that, in a society where marginal production has been reduced to a minimum, the cost of hiring additional labour is so disproportionate to the slight production benefits which it brings that there is an incentive to limit the number of new jobs. The justification for this is that the resulting unemployed, although subsidized by the work of others, will consume less, whereas if they worked they would consume far more than they produced. In this situation a society will naturally aim to exclude women, children and a large number of men from productive work, accepting to subsidize them at a very basic minimum, lower than the standard labourers' wage. The labour force, too, will prefer to survive on the barest minimum rather than work, if working brings only a slight improvement in their standard of living. This is an interesting interpretation of a complex social phenomenon; the chief objection to it is the doubtful validity of applying 'marginalist' theory to a system of 'imperfect control'. In such a system, the urban, and therefore industrial, labour market absorbs only a small part of the surplus population from the country. Its population must be taught to adapt itself to urban society: it must learn to live to a different rhythm, to think in terms of money and profit and controls; it must also acquire be it only the barest rudiments of professional skills. But if work provides no more than the minimum needed for survival, then the incentive to be idle is very great.

Among the principal recurring themes in the social evolution of modern Europe, I have mentioned famines and those critical periods when famine, epidemics and bad harvests descended all at once on the population, as if by some 'infernal compression'. We may leave aside epidemics, treating them in this case as side-effects of malnutrition, which led to exhaustion and a lowered immunity. Famine was a permanent danger in a traditional agrarian system, where yields were scant, the number of crops limited, transport difficult, food stocks meagre and storage inadequate. A crop failure or an increase in the population was immediately followed by hunger, for even if grain was brought in from other regions, the inevitable price increases made it too expensive for most family budgets. In the Middle Ages the threat of famine was permanent; even at times of agricultural prosperity and increased grain production, the annals of the period abound in descriptions, frequently exaggerated, of famines. Most of these, however, remained local. One of the first in the series of 'fourteenth-century crises' was the great famine of 1315–17, which spread beyond the local level to a large area of Europe.

Harvests alternated periodically between good and bad, illustrating the biblical parable of the seven fat cows and the seven thin cows; the alternation is explained by agrarian economists in a large array of theories dealing with the cyclical nature of agricultural production, but the claims put forward in these theories are not confirmed by modern historical research. Nor have climatological interpretations found confirmation in the sources. Regardless of their periodic or cyclical nature, however, these great famines constantly perturbed the life of agrarian societies. We must therefore distinguish between long-term trends in the price of agricultural products and the short and sudden increases which followed a particularly bad harvest. But the small farmer suffered whatever happened: if the harvest was a good one, grain prices fell so much that his work was hardly worthwhile; if it was bad, higher prices did not compensate for the low level of production, and he had no reserves with which he might speculate in an attempt to regain his losses. Such speculation was rife whenever prices rose; the Polish historian Witold Kula has stressed the importance of terms of trade in traditional agricultural economies.

The 'old type' of crisis set in motion interconnected mechanisms which limited both purchasing power and the demand for labour. Thus the poor, at those times, had neither bread nor work. Food crises coincided with a dramatic increase in the numbers of beggars, vagrants and tramps in the city streets. The first in the series of such crises came in the 1520s, when the bad harvest of 1528–9 caused vast numbers of impoverished country-dwellers to make their way, in a mass exodus, towards the great cities of Paris, Lyons and Venice in search of bread and work. This crisis was particularly significant in that it revealed the full extent of the problem and brought an awareness of the need to provide assistance to the poor; but it was smaller in scale than the food crises which were to follow, in that century and in the centuries to come. Their intensity, and their devastating dimensions, did not lessen as they followed one upon the other, from the last quarter of the sixteenth century and the soaring prices of 1594–7, through the famine of 1659–62, to the years of famine between 1771 and 1774. Their consequences were socially well defined: the mass of common people were by far the worst affected. An Italian *avviso* – a kind of newspaper published in the form of a leaflet – from February 1558 contained the following information from Rome: 'nothing new here, except that the people are dying of hunger'.[6] Hunger was indeed a feature of the lives of the poor; it did not affect the rich. The victims of famine were those who even in normal times suffered from malnutrition. In Geneva, in a 'normal' year, a casual labourer's daily wage was worth five pounds of bread; in times of famine its real value fell to two and a half pounds; and two pounds of bread was considered to be the daily minimum per person. This means that in a 'normal' year a labourer's daily wage barely met his family's most basic needs, and in a hungry year failed to meet even those.

Poverty was endemic in the societies of that time, both in its material and in its sociological aspects. Large sections of the population, particularly in regions of industrial growth and, to a lesser extent, in areas which had been 'refeudalized', lived in a permanent state of near-starvation; the slightest fluctuation in the delicate balance between prices and wages, or between basic needs and harvest yields, was enough to fill the roads and city streets with crowds of paupers. Poverty was inherent in the structure of these societies; the existence of large groups of people permanently dependent on charity was accepted as normal, and it was the recognized aim of social policies and assistance programmes to alleviate the lot of the poor, regardless of the activities of charitable institutions, the intensity of repressive measures against vagrancy and the direction that reforms happened to be taking at the time. But the waves of poverty which swept Europe as a result of economic and food crises exceeded the scope of social policy; poverty on so vast a scale was met only with fear, threats and closed doors. Occasionally, however, it evoked individual and even collective bursts of compassion which could lead to the creation of new institutions providing aid to the poor.

Poverty in the Middle Ages would seem, from the historical sources, to be a product of fourteenth-century crises. Indeed, it is around 1350 that we begin to see the creation of numerous laws aimed at vagrants and rapidly increasing numbers of paupers and unemployed in most European countries. But the sources can be misleading on this point. The flurry of new legislation concerning vagrants does not necessarily indicate that the rising tide of poverty was the product of an unfavourable set of circumstances. Nor is it obvious that the beginning of this new tide coincided, or was causally connected, with the legislation.

In his work on labourers' wages, the French economist and sociologist François Simiand considers the relation of poverty to wage fluctuations. His findings indicate that the number of vagrants and beggars increased or remained stable at a high level when wages were falling or frozen at a low level; conversely, their numbers decreased when wages were high. The 'anti-vagrant' legislation of the fourteenth century does not bear out such a correlation; on the contrary, it seems to obey the opposite principle, increasing in volume and severity in periods when wages were high. This should not be surprising if one considers the fact that the chief motive behind such legislation was to protect the interests of employers, who sought to keep wages down and to counteract reductions in the labour market. Thus the high levels of poverty in the mid-fourteenth century were not due to the pressures of external circumstance: their causes were purely structural.

Studies of the demographic structure of late medieval cities indicate that beggars and paupers made up between 15 and 20 per cent of the population, and that this percentage was stable. In the sixteenth and seventeenth centuries, when it became possible to calculate estimates on a national scale, the poor — those dependent on public or private support — made up one-fifth of the population. This does not mean, however, that one can combine these two statistics to conclude that one-fifth of the population of pre-industrial societies formed the structural extent of poverty. In the late Middle Ages these statistics could only take account of the urban poor, beggars who were permanently dependent on private charity and on the aid of the city's charitable institutions. In the country there was no such permanence: the alms distributed by monasteries and parishes drew paupers, sometimes in their thousands, from various parts of the country. Only the city could provide such people with a permanent place of residence; in the country they were never in any one place for very long. And there was another kind of poverty in the country, harder to discern and integral to the structure of family and community life: the poverty of those who worked but could barely survive from their work. Such people formed an important and cheap source of labour in all sorts of professions, not only in agriculture but in rural crafts and industry; the textile industry, for example, recruited unskilled labourers as helpers from among the country poor.

Rural poverty acquires a different dimension when it is the result of attempts to modernize the agrarian structure and develop it on a capitalist model, one of the options at the end of the crisis of the fourteenth century. The new distribution of property which these transformations involved led to sharp social and economic divisions among the peasantry and resulted in the ruin of many small farmers, who were unable to maintain their economic independence in these new conditions. Fifteenth-century tax and property registers for Burgundy, Normandy and Tuscany, for instance, showed an increasing number of peasants exempt from tax and classed as 'indigents' or 'paupers'; they sometimes accounted for over half of the families on the registers. In most Western European countries there was a marked increase in rural poverty throughout the sixteenth century. This increase was a constant and regular process, but accelerated sharply at times of food crises. Peasants sometimes saw themselves expropriated, and small farmers cut off from their means of production, both in England, as a result of the Enclosure Acts, and in Normandy and Burgundy. This hastened the descent of the small farmers, economically the weakest among the peasantry, into the ranks of the proletariat.

Thus the trend towards increasing poverty in the sixteenth and seventeenth centuries was due to the transformations taking place in the agrarian system and the social structure of the countryside. Where traditional feudal structures were maintained or restored and social relations were governed by a variety of non-economic constraints intended to bind the peasant to the land or to his feudal master, vagrancy rather than poverty was the chief problem: vagrants were assimilated to fugitives and were therefore incompatible with a system based on dependence rather than personal liberty. Such societies clung to a model in which poverty played a structural role. Although it was endemic in the country, the peasants nevertheless managed, by performing casual labour of various kinds, to earn their living; in the city there were groups of professional beggars who relied on charity, sometimes organizing themselves into corporations, brotherhoods or 'beggars' guilds'.

2.3   The Dimensions of Poverty

The process of impoverishment is not, any more than that of enrichment, exclusive to any one social system or particular 'means of production'. What distinguished the social system of the late Middle Ages and the 'early modern era', however, was something more than simply poverty; it was a very clear poverty-increasing tendency. It was not merely the vast numerical extent of poverty at that time, nor its near-ubiquity, that lent it special importance, but its role in the formation of a new system: capitalism. The medieval perception of poverty had, as we have seen, involved a particular kind of functionalism, and in the ideology of that time poverty had had a specific role to play. Now, as the huge mass of beggars and unemployed began to impinge on the collective consciousness, poverty came to be perceived as harmful to the public good, and was divested of its previous function. At the same time, however, the impoverishment of small producers had a new role to play, for it was a condition of the development of capitalism and an integral part of the first accumulation of capital; this was true primarily of agrarian systems in the throes of transformation. Thus poverty retained an important function in society, but the nature of this function had changed.

Processes of accumulation, however, could also be found in traditional agrarian systems of the Middle Ages; moreover, as G. Bois has pointed out, they took place not among the great landowners, but rather on the level of peasant agriculture. The concentration of means of production, and particularly of land, naturally accompanied economic growth; when the balance between work yield and taxes was favourable, small farms prospered and expanded. Periods of low wages combined with high prices for agricultural products encouraged this process of concentration, but the depression which followed each phase of growth broke its continuity. Its progress was also hindered by the various social, economic and psychological barriers to accumulation inherent in the structure and mentality of medieval societies: technological conditions favoured small family farms; the dues which landowners received from the peasants discouraged them from expanding their own land; and the notion of profit was only very gradually seeping through to the economic consciousness of the time.

In the sixteenth century the process of accumulation in the country took on a different character. This was partly because the amount of land a peasant possessed, the number of his cattle, his technology and methods of farming now varied much more widely; but also because landowners were no longer interested in maintaining the economic independence of their peasants. Both of these changes exerted a strong influence on all aspects of Europe's future development, economic and political. In his account of the processes which opened the way for capitalism, Marx placed particular stress on their non-economic aspects, the social and political mechanisms of constraint. But it was at precisely this moment that the evolutionary tendencies which emerged from the crises of the fourteenth and fifteenth century were beginning to take on a more definite shape; it was here that the economic paths taken by Eastern and Western Europe began to diverge. The fall in revenues from feudal dues, together with profitable conditions for agriculture, discouraged landowners from continuing the system of sharecropping. They chose, instead, one of two opposing paths: either to 'refeudalize', by attaching the peasants to their own estates, or to evict the peasants from their land. The two can be seen to coexist in both evolutionary zones, albeit on different scales. Indeed, the Polish historian Jerzy Topolski claims to find far-reaching similarities between them, similarities which lay very generally in the various attempts made by the nobility to rationalize its economic policies.

In the most highly developed regions of Europe, the eviction of peasants from their land and the growing differences of wealth between them led to the accumulation of capital for some and to utter impoverishment for a large number of others. In the course of this 'degradation of the peasant world', as A. de Maddalena put it, landowners confiscated a third of the arable land, pasture and forests used by the peasants and considered, until then, to belong to the community, invoking *urgens et improvisa necessitas* ('urgent and unforeseen necessity') in order to dislodge the peasants from the land; and dealings in land increased greatly among the bourgeoisie. The number of people no longer able to provide for themselves and their families by cultivating the land continued to grow.

The parcelling out of peasant land was a process which had already left its mark in the late Middle Ages; but in the sixteenth century it assumed much greater proportions, leading to the impoverishment of part of the rural population. This is revealed both by the tax registers and by what we know of the evolution of the size of peasant farms. In the parish of Saint-Nicolas d'Aliermont, in eastern Normandy, peasants with less than six hectares of land represented 48 per cent of the population at the end of the fourteenth century; by 1477 this figure had fallen to 41 per cent; in 1527 it rose again to 51 per cent. The trend indicated by these statistics becomes clearer when we consider the demographic evolution of the parish: at the first census it numbered a hundred and thirty-five peasants; by 1477 their number had dwindled to a mere seventy-two, and by 1527 had again risen to a hundred and fifty-one. The conclusion is clear: in periods of economic depression, the first to go under were the smallest and therefore economically the most vulnerable farms, and the number of such farms increased with demographic growth. In this not very fertile region, a family found it hard to eke out a living from six hectares, but there were even smaller farms in the parish: at the end of the fourteenth century it contained twenty-two farms of less than two hectares; in 1477 there were eight such farms in the parish, and by 1527 their number had risen to thirty. By the sixteenth century these families could no longer survive on their farms and were forced to seek what work they could find as hired labourers. If they failed to find work they were reduced to a life of begging.

In most parts of sixteenth-century France this type of small family farm was predominant. In Cambrésis, in northern France, farms of this size accounted for 86 per cent of the total number of agricultural holdings at the end of the century, and this percentage was by no means unusual in the rural geography of France at the time. It is also important to remember that five to six hectares of land was the very minimum needed to allow an independent existence based on land cultivation alone, and that below this limit a family had constantly to fight for its survival, either by maintaining a very precarious independence, weathering bad periods as best they could and risking ruin at every turn for the worse, or by seeking work elsewhere and becoming smallholders, treating the cultivation of their own land as a source of additional income. In England at that time 37 per cent of peasant farms were smaller than two hectares; this implies that 37 per cent of all peasant families must have had other sources of income.

Tax registers from the fifteenth and sixteenth centuries are a good indication of the extent of impoverishment among the peasantry, and invaluable in providing a wide-scale overview. The 'indigent' are classed here as a separate category, because they were exempt from taxes, and on this basis one can attempt to calculate the number of poor in the various countries of Europe. Unfortunately these registers are of almost no use in any comparative analysis, for their definition of poverty for tax purposes varied from year to year and from country to country, so that it was possible for a man to be classed as taxable one year and exempt the next. The terminology also varied to such an extent that it is sometimes impossible to pin down the range of reference of certain terms. The registers for Burgundy, for example, distinguish between 'taxable', 'poor' and 'mendicant' families, or 'homesteads', while in Dauphiné the terms used are 'indigent', 'possessing nothing' (*habentes nihil*) and 'mendicant'; in the Netherlands some families were classed as poor but taxable at a very low rate, while others were not taxed at all. Thus the definition of poverty as a criterion for tax purposes was a rather fluid one, and a 'fiscal pauper' was not always, as Michel Mollat has said, a pauper at all. In addition, the various regional conventions imposed both on the terminology and on census methods cast further doubt on the reliability of these documents. Despite their failings, however, these documents are a source of some invaluable insights, statistical as well as social and psychological. Their statistical significance lies in what they reveal about the proportions of wealth and poverty within different communities, while their social and psychological interest lies in the insight they provide into attitudes towards the poor, which distinguished between beggars, paupers and the merely 'poor', and varied accordingly.

Norman tax registers (*fouages*) spanning the years 1480–1506 and encompassing about forty-five rural parishes class 15 per cent of 'homesteads' as 'poor and mendicant' (*povres et mendians*). A study of similar registers from the middle of the sixteenth century, encompassing the same number of parishes (although, owing to gaps in the documentation, not the same ones), reveals an increase to 24 per cent. An increase in the number of poor families is a general tendency throughout the sixteenth century, but in some parishes it seems to have been much more drastic: the parish of Bretheville-l'Orgueil-leuse, for instance, contained 6 per cent of poor homesteads in 1500, but 60 per cent in 1539 and 81 per cent in 1566; in Bailly-la-Rivière, during roughly the same period, the increase was from 11 per cent to 46 per cent to 36 per cent, while Aubusson leapt from 0 per cent to 19 per cent to 22 per cent.

Documents from the Netherlands show a similar tendency towards impoverishment. The tax registers for 1494 and 1514 in Holland, for instance, are particularly informative about the poor. In 1494 the village of Heyloo had a hundred and fifteen inhabitants, of whom fifteen lived from begging; in the village of Zoetermeer, eight or ten of the thirty-one inhabitants relied permanently on some form of charity. In 1514, forty of the hundred and twenty inhabitants of Huysse were judged incapable of paying tax, Alblasserdam counted forty or even fifty paupers among its seventy-two residents, and Rijnsbruch could boast of only twenty, out of a total of a hundred and ten, who earned their living without any assistance; the remaining ninety relied on charitable institutions (Tables du Saint-Esprit), alms distributions at the local monasteries and begging from door to door. The general picture which emerges from the 1514 registers is one of great contrasts from one district to another; in some the poor might account for as much as 34 per cent of the total population; in others they represented only 10 per cent. Generally speaking, however, the number of villagers classed as poor by the local administration appears to have represented between a third and a quarter of Holland's rural population. Brabant was a similar case: in 1526 the poor, according to the registers, represented 27 per cent of its population, and for the rural district of Louvain the figure was 41 per cent. In Wallonian Flanders in the middle of the fifteenth century, 27 per cent of the population, according to the registers, were paupers; by the end of the fifteenth century they were 30 per cent, and by the middle of the sixteenth, 40 per cent. In the case of Flanders one can also see, thanks to continuous documentation covering a long period of time, occasional fluctuations in the number of poor which appeared as dips in the poverty curve: between 1485 and 1498 the percentage of poor among tax-payers fell from 37 per cent to 30 per cent. These details concerning increasing poverty within the structure of the population as a whole serve only to bring out the significance of the tendency of the age: they do not mean that poverty increased continuously and relentlessly, nor do they imply that its intensity was everywhere the same.

The available data on small farms, and the lists of peasant families described as poor in the tax registers, do not define the limits of rural poverty in the sixteenth century; rather, they define its possibilities, for they concern principally those families which were most at risk. It was with reluctance, however, that such families left their villages;

they clung with all their strength to their old existence, however poor and wretched. For, at the same time as economic mechanisms were pushing small farmers out of agriculture, the peasantry was being dispossessed of its land. The process took place throughout Europe, although its intensity varied from one region to another, depending on such factors as the strength of the peasants' rights over their land (rights traditionally more deeply entrenched in France than in England), government policy (favourable in some German countries, as kings and princes had military and tax reasons for wanting to maintain peasant property) and, finally, the likelihood of strong resistance from the peasantry.

The English example, on which Marx built his theory about the role of mechanisms of coercion in the modern process of rebuilding agrarian systems, is no doubt the most familiar. Enclosures may not have been exclusive to the English countryside, for they could also be found on the continent, but it was in England that their brutality was most striking. The enclosure of common pasture and arable land began to take place in England in the middle of the fifteenth century. It was carried out by landowners and rich farmers without the consent of the community, depriving farmers, especially those with small holdings, of their livelihood. At the same time, the profits to be made from animal husbandry encouraged landowners to transform their arable land into pasture; this involved extending their estates, which could only be done by taking over tracts of peasant land. As this process continued, the overwhelming majority of English peasants – those whose land belonged to them by customary right – fell victim to expropriation. Landowners continually increased the dues to which peasants were liable when taking over a farm – when they inherited, for instance. The peasants complained of these abuses: 'They are taking away the roof over our heads, forcing us to sell our land, putting up our land rent, and demanding huge and unreasonable dues.' Sixteenth-century reports and petitions (those from the years 1517–1618 were published in 1897 in Isaac Saunders Leadam's book *The Domesday on Inclosures*) are good illustrations of the process, showing how small farms were gradually absorbed into the estates of great landowners, the peasants who had lived on them becoming just so much useless baggage. When Marx considered the social effects of enclosures in *Capital* he quoted Holinstred, the sixteenth-century chronicler who described, in moving detail, how the countryside was depopulated, peasant homesteads ruined by force or by poverty, small farms devastated, and even whole villages turned into pasture for sheep. The people of the sixteenth century saw the enclosure of open fields as the cause of their poverty and their inability to find work in the countryside; all the harmful social effects of the modernization of English agriculture were laid at its door. The Crown, also, was worried. In 1517 a commission was created to look into the problem, followed, in successive years, by other identical commissions, and the matter was a frequent subject of debate in Parliament. A variety of royal edicts was issued in an attempt to put a stop to enclosures. A decree forbidding the transformation of arable land into pasture was issued as early as 1489, in the reign of Henry VII. A decree issued in 1533 linked the question of enclosures to that of land concentration, making it illegal for one person to own two farms (or, more precisely, to own a second farm in a different parish) or more than 2,400 sheep. What is significant in these decrees is their assumption that farms were accumulated on the strength of profits from sheep raising. In 1595 landowners were enjoined to return to the plough all pasture which had been cultivated in the past for at least twelve years. Joan Thirsk has shown that enclosures were linked to land concentration and to the accumulation of farms not only in royal ordinances but also in the life of the English countryside. Land enclosure, both for specific crops and for pasture, increased efficiency of production and was a reaction to growing demographic pressure; moreover, it was used not only by the great landowners but also by peasants. Its social effects varied from region to region, depending on the relation between the number of people and the area of cultivated land in any given stretch of territory: they became truly horrendous when a dearth of land was combined with growing numbers of impoverished peasants. Any farmer attempting to enclose fields and to turn arable land into pasture was immediately seen as betraying, from base motives, the interests of the community. Enclosure was seen as the obvious cause of high grain prices, reduced demand for agricultural labour (animal husbandry required less work than land cultivation) and the growing number of paupers with no means of subsistence: it was the source of all ills. The reality, of course, was much more complex than this, but it remains true nevertheless that the sum of the measures undertaken to modernize English agriculture and diminish demographic pressure drove vast numbers of people from the countryside and rendered them useless.

The true dimensions of this process are still a subject of debate among historiographers. The descriptions provided by contemporaries are no doubt exaggerated: the figure quoted, half a million peasants allegedly deprived of their livelihood by enclosure, must be excessive. Enclosure was only one element in the process of transforming England's agrarian system, and this process as a whole was responsible for the ruin of a large section of the peasantry. By the end of the seventeenth century, close on three-quarters of all land was in the hands of landowners, who not only used it to expand their own crop cultivation and sheep farming with the aid of hired labour, but also leased it out on new conditions, without feudal charges. This encouraged both technological progress and investment in the land. Yields improved considerably as a result of the capitalist transformation of the countryside, so that England (unlike, for instance, France) was unaffected by the great food crises which marked the first centuries of the modern age. The cost and condition of this progress, however, was a lowered standard of living for the great majority of the rural population, and the expulsion of large numbers of peasants from their land: in both cases increased poverty was part of the evolution of capitalism. It was not merely its by-product, its social price, but one of its integral elements, for those who became impoverished were forced to seek work as hired labourers. The reserve contingent of hired labourers thus formed in the countryside, described by R. M. Tawney as the 'residual population', could choose between entering the labour market and remaining on the margins of society, where they lived from begging, or crime, or sometimes from both at once.

There is reason, however, to doubt the explanatory value of the English model. It is, after all, considered a classic example of agrarian transformation precisely because England, unlike almost all other countries of Europe, undertook the capitalist modernization of its countryside within a condensed period of time and with the support of the new government structures which resulted from this revolution. Elsewhere in Europe the process of transforming the agrarian system was much more spread out in time and much less consistent; the accumulation of property on the English model was also hampered by the persistence of the old power structure. As a result the peasantry had a double burden to bear: heavier feudal dues, which hampered technological progress and discouraged investment, and higher taxes imposed through the absolute power of the State.

The figures indicating an increase in the number of 'poor' and peasants with little land in the European countryside reflect two distinct factors: firstly, the structural transformation of the system, which deprived the poorest and most vulnerable peasants of their independence as farmers; and secondly, the consequences of policies implemented by landowners in order to increase their revenues, and the new relation which these entailed between demographic expansion and agricultural yields.

In England it was this search for increased revenues on the part of landowners that led to a thorough transformation of the system. In other Western countries the evolution towards capitalism may have been slower, but analogous tendencies towards expropriation of the peasantry could be seen. The number of villagers living only from hired labour increased enormously: in the canton of Zurich, half of the rural inhabitants were day-labourers, and in New Castille in 1575 the proportion was similar. In Poitou in the sixteenth century, increased agricultural activity on the part of landowners and the penetration of capital from the towns drove large numbers of peasants from their land, while the system of land tenure reduced many sharecropping peasants to the position of hired labourers. The lack of technological and structural progress in agriculture in sixteenth- and seventeenth-century Continental Europe regularly reduced the most economically vulnerable groups to extreme penury.

In pre-industrial society the countryside represented by far the largest area of inhabited land. City-dwellers, despite the intense efforts made towards urbanization in the Middle Ages, were still a relatively small category of the population, their numbers varying according to national and regional levels of development. In Muscovy city-dwellers were a mere 2.5 to 3 per cent of the population; in Germany they were 10 per cent, in France 16 per cent, in England 30 or even 40 per cent and in the Netherlands over 50 per cent. The average in Western and Central Europe at the end of the eighteenth century is assumed to have been from 20 to 25 per cent, but until the end of the sixteenth century city-dwellers are unlikely to have exceeded 10 per cent of Europe's population as a whole. The reality behind these figures, however, was much more complex: some urban centres were little different, in their professional structure and the way of life of their inhabitants, from large villages, while at the other extreme were huge cities of tens or even hundreds of thousands of inhabitants. These vast urban agglomerations flourished mostly because of their role as administrative centres of government and bureaucracy. Amsterdam had 30,000 inhabitants in 1530, 115,000 in 1630 and close to 200,000 by the end of the seventeenth century.

London grew to become the largest European city, the number of its inhabitants rising from 80,000 to 250,000 in the course of the sixteenth century and to 400,000 by the middle of the seventeenth century, and continuing to grow until the end of the eighteenth century. These metropolitan giants were centres for the development of specialized branches of industry, for the expansion of international commerce, banking and exchange, and above all for the production of luxury goods on a huge scale. These were aimed mostly at the great landowners, constituting a drain on their revenues, and at the same time opening up enormous possibilities for the development of the tertiary sector: the great cities teemed with services. The whole production structure in these cities was determined by the luxury goods market, as demand for such goods was great. This was not, of course, true of other urban centres, even those cities which we consider large; what distinguished a great metropolis from other cities was not merely its size and population density, but also its function and its internal structure. Large cities which did not function as national capitals did not benefit from the same influx of revenue from property and the State treasury.

All cities, however, had a particularly important social role to play in dealing with poverty and the poor. Unlike the countryside, with its rigid framework of 'functions' and 'posts' in which fluctuations took place only at times of great crisis, the city offered great possibilities for work of an unstable, temporary and casual nature; to those who had been driven from the countryside they seemed almost limitless. One could always find work, or at least alms, in the city; there were no dead seasons here, as there were in the country. The city expected and drew strength from the waves of migrants, and it encouraged migration, not only from country to city but from city to city as well. The population density had a specific effect on human relations, which were marked by growing anonymity; group solidarity could only be expressed within an institutional framework, either inherited from the old guilds and professional corporations or newly created for the purpose. This exposed, quite harshly, the realities of urban poverty: those without stable work and a regular income lived in constant fear of penury, and it was in cities that such people were most numerous.

Both rural and urban poverty had its roots in the disintegration of the medieval structures. The policy of municipal authorities and medieval professional organizations was to suppress competition by limiting market mechanisms or eliminating them entirely. This also applied to the labour market, on which the authorities sought to impose strict controls in order to prevent the 'overheating' of economic mechanisms caused by too great an imbalance between supply and demand. This policy was quite successful in the smaller, local centres of trade and industry, but failed in larger cities, where the range of activity was too wide to be brought under effective control: the sphere of uncontrolled activities continued to widen in these cities, as did the disparity between the interests of tradesmen and the traditional policies maintained and imposed by the craftsmen's guilds. As commercial capital penetrated into industry and entrepreneurs began to involve themselves in organizing production, the nature of social relations in crafts and industry changed profoundly. As the volume of production increased and industry developed more and more specialized branches, those workshops which failed to expand were integrated into a system of interdependence to become links in a production chain. This was true particularly of the cloth industry, one of the leading areas of medieval production. Craftsmen found it increasingly hard to maintain their independence, and hired labour came to play a more prominent role; master craftsmen as well as their aides and apprentices, who could no longer hope for professional independence, sank to the ranks of the proletariat, which also engulfed the growing numbers of unskilled labourers. In a context of mounting disparities of wealth, urban society from the late Middle Ages onwards saw a significant, and sometimes vast, increase in the number of its poor.

One of the aspects of social evolution stressed here has been the precarious existence of hired labourers. Labourers' wages in fourteenth-century Florence, calculated in calorie values, were a good indication of this, for the sample on which the statistics were based was a large one. Evidence based on tax registers is less reliable, for a number of reasons: the terminology here is often vague and imprecise, a fault also found in descriptions of rural wealth and poverty; criteria change from place to place and year to year, which makes it difficult to find a common denominator that would embrace them all and provide reliable results. More reliable is the picture which emerges of the hierarchy of urban wealth: the very fact that a section of the population was distinguished as a separate category and labelled as 'poor' is in itself indicative of the fundamental otherness, and weakness, of this group.

A study of German tax registers dating from the late Middle Ages, begun by Gustav Schmoller and continued by his students, reveals a widening gulf between extremes of poverty and wealth among the city population. In most cities, considerably more than half the population was composed of people whose revenues were estimated at less than a hundred florins; in Lübeck they were only 52 per cent, but in Augsburg 87 per cent and in Basle 68 per cent. The people in this category were not necessarily the very poorest, but they were permanently on the borderline of penury. A similar picture emerges of the social structure of French and northern Italian cities. The category of people under the description of 'poor' or 'possessing nothing' covered between a third and a half of the population. A comparison of graphs also reveals that the major part of a city's wealth was in the hands of a relatively small number of people, and that the gulf between rich and poor continued to widen: more and more wealth was concentrated in the hands of a few, while the number of those who possessed nothing or very little continued to grow. Florentine registers for the years 1427–9 show that 10 per cent of the inhabitants of Florence held 68 per cent of the city's wealth, while the poorest category, which represented 70 per cent of the inhabitants, held only 10 per cent. The distribution of wealth in other cities of Tuscany at that time was similar. The number of people too poor to pay taxes went on rising in a sharp curve.

These disparities, reflected in city registers of the fourteenth and fifteenth centuries, were further sharpened during the sixteenth century. At the bottom of the social hierarchy the only shifts which took place were in a downward direction; the ranks of the poor were swelled by people descending from their position a few rungs higher up. At the same time those at the top continued to accumulate wealth. This was particularly true of cities with a rapid pace of commercial and industrial evolution, whether they were large or small; in this case size alone was not a determining factor. In 1437 Brussels defined 10 per cent of its 'homesteads' as poor; in 1496, 17 per cent were so defined, and in 1526, 21 per cent. This progression was even sharper in the small towns in the Brussels region: in 1437 poor homesteads represented 9 per cent of the total; by the end of the century they already accounted for 30 per cent and by 1526 for over 34 per cent. But even these figures are not an accurate reflection of urban reality, for a certain number of families, particularly those who lived on the outskirts of cities, were not included in the tax registers;

such families, moreover, belonged to the poorest category of the population.

Estimates based on the amount of aid accorded by a city to its poor concur in a general way with these observations. Before dealing with them in detail, let us consider just one example. In 1522 the city of Nuremberg, which in the early sixteenth century must have had about 45,000 inhabitants, provided permanent aid to some five hundred people; if we include recipients of partial or occasional aid, this figure rises to five thousand. In addition, bread was distributed to a further thirteen to fifteen thousand people at times of poor harvests. Rudolf Endres added up these calculations and found that in this prosperous city a third of the population was either poor or in danger of poverty.

In order to understand the social transformations of the modern era in their entirety, one must constantly bear in mind the contrast between the city and the country. The country was the real source of poverty; even the city poor, those who lived within the walls, turn out, insofar as their origins can be documented, to be largely recent immigrants from the countryside. But the processes which create poverty were also at work within the city walls, set in motion by the mechanisms of urban evolution. Craftsmen gradually lost their independence, unable to compete with rural and urban industrial production organized by commercial capital, unable even to secure the raw materials or find a market for their goods. They were reduced to hired labourers, a position which from the point of view of the tax registers relegated them to the ranks of the poor. However, although statistics concerning, respectively, the urban and the rural poor might occasionally indicate a similarity of proportion, city and country poverty were fundamentally different. The country poor were created by the disintegration of the old structures: they made up that 'residual population' which, having lost its place in the country, migrated to the cities, where it was absorbed into the proletariat. In the city, on the other hand, poverty was less a product of the disintegration of traditional structures than the result of the formation of new ones. The city poor, at least those listed in the tax registers, represented the 'poverty of the working masses'.

Indeed it may be that the use of the word 'poverty' is an exaggeration in this context. These people, completely at the mercy of the labour market and without any guarantees of a stable existence, were nevertheless able, in the urban market, to find sufficiently regular sources of income to prevent any threat to their survival. It remains to be seen, however, whether the city could create, on a large enough scale, the social conditions necessary for the absorption of those whom the countryside had rejected.

The rapidity of urban and industrial evolution in the sixteenth century would indeed seem to indicate that, at the dawn of the modern era, such conditions were being created. The figures concerning urban population growth tend to confirm this assumption; it is further borne out by evidence of the development of new branches of industry, the growth of new lines of production and the rise in the number of hirings. Indeed the development of industry could be the chief, if not the only, factor in the growth of a city. This was demonstrated by Émile Coornaert on the example of the Flemish city of Hondshoote. The growth of this city, from 2,500 inhabitants in 1469 to 15,000 in 1560, was owing to the development of a new branch of the cloth trade and the production of a fabric which, although of poor quality, found a large demand on the European market. More established urban centres also experienced the effects of rapid industrial growth, some thanks to the development of a single leading branch of industry, others through a more diverse range of activity. In Venice there were 3,300 shipyard workers employed in the city's arsenal, 5,000 in the cloth industry and another 5,000 in the silk trade. There was also printing, the first modern European industry and one in which Venice led the field, but here no statistics are available. But the 13,000 employed in the other three branches constituted an astonishingly large number: with their families, they represented a third of Venice's 140,000 inhabitants. In Lyons, which from the end of the fifteenth century experienced a great demographic boom, with 60,000 inhabitants by 1531 and 70,000 by the middle of the century, industrial production on a large scale, intended for export, did not develop until the 1530s. Before that, at the turn of the century, the city owed its prosperity to its role as a commercial and banking centre. Printing also evolved in a vigorous way, introducing, as Henri Hauser pointed out a hundred years ago, a capitalist mode of production. But the number of people one could employ in the printing industry was limited, and the work demanded high professional skills. When the silk industry was introduced in 1536, it radically altered the city's social and economic structure. Dominated by a small group of entrepreneurs, who organized it on manufacturing principles, it provided employment for about 12,000 people – a fifth of the city's population – by the middle of the century.

Behind these impressive statistics, however, lay the more sombre picture of relations between the city and the country at the end of the Middle Ages and the beginning of the modern era. However rapid the development of industry and urban growth in the sixteenth century, it was still not proportional to the degree of real or potential poverty and unemployment in the country. This was the basis of the boom in rural industry at the time. Commercial capital began to be directed into the country, where labour was cheap and plentiful and there were no restrictions of the kind imposed by professional guilds and municipal authorities. Under these conditions the system of home production, organized by an entrepreneur who provided the raw materials and took charge of selling the finished product, flourished on a large scale. Fernand Braudel has even suggested that rural industry in the sixteenth century equalled urban production in the number of people it employed, if not in its quality and profits. This system succeeded, for a certain time, in providing a livelihood for the reserve labour force in the country, but its efficiency as a solution to the problem of unemployment was short-lived.

The period of growth for rural industry was also brief. Its brevity was characteristic of all industries before the industrial revolution, and was connected with the internal structure of investment, in which the amount of stable capital was relatively small. Commercial capitalism required that expenditure on durable means of production be kept at a minimum, so that capital was free to circulate between different cities, regions and branches of industry. As a consequence of this the growth curve of particular industrial centres is elliptical. The Flemish city of Hondshoote mentioned above produced eighty thousand lengths of fabric between 1560 and 1569, three times as much as it had produced in 1528; a hundred years on, however, it was producing only 8,000. Silk production in Venice fell by two-thirds in the course of the seventeenth century, and in Genoa by three-quarters between 1565 and 1675. In Milan, a third of the workers in the silk trade were unemployed in 1620, and in the textile industry the situation was even worse. At the same time other branches of industry were developing; this was a flourishing period for textile production in England and Holland. The population of Leiden rose from 12,000 in 1582 to 70,000 by the middle of the seventeenth century, and its cloth production attained 140,000 lengths by 1671. These sudden boom periods in proto-industrial development drained the countryside of its labour reserves, but the periods of crisis left a huge mass of labourers bereft of their livelihood.

It was not only poverty that drove the rural population towards the cities; they were also attracted by the hope of higher wages, and the motivation which this hope provided should not be underestimated. At the same time, however, low wages and poverty were the chief elements in the early stages of capitalist evolution, and this hampered the growth of some urban centres. Antwerp, after a flourishing period in the sixteenth century, saw its population reduced by two-thirds in the hundred years between the middle of the sixteenth and seventeenth centuries: its production fell and its role as a centre of trade and industry diminished. It has been shown that Antwerp's expansion took place in two stages, the first based on the low standard of living among the masses between 1470 and 1490, the next on the 'second great fast of the proletariat' during the years between 1520 and 1550. Hence the poverty of the working masses which so strongly characterized the early stages of industrial evolution. The rural immigrants hoped that in the city their situation would improve, and when they found work this hope was fulfilled, if only for a short time. For the majority, however, life remained precarious, their earnings only just allowing them to survive. A combination of bad harvests and bad luck easily drove them below the 'poverty threshold' to penury.

An interesting study undertaken by Richard Gascon attempts to define that 'poverty threshold', and with the aid of this definition to trace the social evolution of Lyons in the sixteenth century. He bases his calculations on that part of a day's wages which could be spent on bread, and estimates that a family of four needed about two and a half kilos of bread a day. Given that wages were paid, on average, five days a week (counting 260 working days a year), and that three-tenths of them must be spent on rent, heating, light, clothes and food other than bread, such as meat, oil and wine, the 'poverty threshold' turns out statistically to be a situation in which half of each day's wages are spent on bread. The results of this study reveal that a large section of the masses lives on or below the poverty threshold. In the course of the sixteenth century this threshold gradually progressed upwards in the social hierarchy, confronting increasing numbers of people. The lowest-paid labourers, a category known as the *gagne-denier* ('pittance earners'), fell below the poverty threshold for five years in the last quarter of the fifteenth century; in the first quarter of the sixteenth century there were twelve years in which they were below it, and in the second another twelve; in the third quarter they experienced twenty such years; finally, in the last quarter of the sixteenth century, there was not a single year in which they could maintain themselves above this threshold. There was even a year, in this final period, when journeymen fell below it, and for unskilled aides seventeen such years.

These figures, unlike others cited here, include expenditure on rent, clothing and food other than bread as an indispensable part of the budget. When the poverty threshold is reached, it is obviously these expenses which must be reduced in order to stave off hunger or malnutrition. But even these calculations do not take account of unemployment, the extent of which defies statistical analysis; and yet it was the unemployed who were nearest the poverty threshold. Harvests are another factor to take into account, for they influenced the labour market and the whole industry of Lyons: at times of poor harvests, labourers faced weeks or even months without work or prospects, and were forced to live on what reserves they had from previous earnings. Finally, sickness or accidents could make work difficult or impossible. And in the city it was precisely unemployment that caused people to slip below the poverty threshold.

Unemployment, however, was not only the result of the periodic crises to which whole industrial centres or particular branches of production fell victim, and which left the working masses, regardless of their status or qualifications, without a source of income. It also soared at times of food crisis in the countryside, when the cities saw a massive influx of rural labourers in search of work; this naturally created an excess of supply on the labour market, especially in the category of unskilled labour. In both cases the surge in unemployment was sharp and sudden, and in both cases it was perceived by the authorities and the propertied classes as a threat to social order. Chronic under-employment, on the other hand, a situation in which employment was incomplete or partial, was quite a different situation. It was advantageous for employers, for ample supply on the labour market, slightly above demand, kept wages down; and for the majority of urban labourers, particularly the unskilled, an existence somewhere mid-way between unemployment and work was the norm. It was a condition which prevailed both in highly developed countries, such as England and Holland, and in those where the capitalist economy evolved more slowly, with less vigour and fewer visible effects.

The first European attempts at statistical analysis were concerned primarily with estimating the number of poor. This concern was already apparent in works of Florentine chroniclers of urban life in the fourteenth century. Most important, however, were the attempts at demographic analysis undertaken in France and England at the end of the seventeenth century, in the context of what is known as 'political arithmetic'. Gregory King, in considering the income and expenditure of various professional and social groups, estimates that in England, around 1688, out of a population of five and a half million (about 1,350,000 families), 1,300,000 people (about 400,000 families) could be described as cottagers or paupers and 30,000 as vagrants; together they represented 24 per cent of the population. He also estimates that an enormous number (1,275,000 individuals, or about 364,000 families) of wage-labourers – 'labouring people' and 'out servants' – were unable to satisfy their basic daily needs from their wages.[7] The Marquis of Vauban, politician, statesman and high-ranking functionary in the royal administration, lacked Gregory King's ambitions in the area of statistical analysis; however, when he turned his attention to tax reform, proposing a better distribution of taxes, he drew up a table analysing the make-up of French society. According to this table, beggars represented 10 per cent of the total and a third of the population was on the borderline of beggary.[8] Thus in England, according to King, the poor represented 47 per cent of the population; in France, according to Vauban, 40 per cent. These figures do more than indicate the rough dimensions of poverty; they show that people living at the time, despite their lack of statistical information on a national scale, were aware of the huge extent and significance of poverty.

3

Reformation and Repression: the 1520s

The social development of Europe determined by the economic transformations of the sixteenth century defined the trend that would prevail for five centuries to come. The mechanisms of change which, despite their varying degrees of intensity and efficiency, so thoroughly transformed urban and agrarian life generated poverty on an unprecedented scale. This led to new attempts, not only by institutions but by society as a whole, to find solutions to this 'challenge of time'.

Research on the origins of capitalism and the initial stages of its expansion has revealed certain variations. Roughly speaking, three types of early capitalist system can be distinguished: 'agrarian', 'commercial' and 'industrial'. These are conventional labels, indicating only the domain in which the most rapid changes and the greatest accumulation of capital took place. In all three cases the low wages responsible for the great degree of poverty among the labouring masses were instrumental in the process, for they allowed the propertied classes to fulfil their ambition of maximizing profits. The fall in real wages was a general tendency in the sixteenth century, as Earl Hamilton has shown; the existence of exceptions such as the Netherlands, where, unless there was a food crisis, the fall in wages seems to have been neither so sharp nor so visible as in other countries, only confirms the rule. The resulting 'inflation of profits' became a driving force in the evolution of capitalism, and bears out the claim, further supported by the need for a free labour market, that poverty was inherent to early capitalist evolution. This explains the extent of poverty in sixteenth-century Europe. The urban movement to reform social aid was therefore an attempt to respond to the changes of which the cities were the principal arena. Its aim was to create propitious conditions for these changes and to defuse the social tensions which were their side-effect.

Sixteenth-century archives present poverty as a fact of urban life. The real roots of poverty lay in the country, in the changing agrarian structures; in light of what we have said, the fact that its impact was felt above all in the city is not really paradoxical. At the turn of the fifteenth century cities were not yet able to create the kind of 'adaptation structures' that could cope with the huge influx of people without professional skills or familiarity with city life. The old system of traditional corporate structures allowed new immigrants to adapt gradually to life in the city and a new profession; they became apprenticed to a master craftsman or learnt their work with a tradesman, and participated fully in the family life of a bourgeois household. With the huge scale of immigration which followed demographic expansion and growing poverty in the countryside, and with all the changes in urban production, these traditional mechanisms of gradual assimilation could no longer function as they had in the past.

We have already seen how the growth of poverty in Western Europe was determined by food crises. The first such crisis in the modern age took place in the last quarter of the fifteenth century; however, we know little of its effects. But the experience and observation of those times must have influenced such writers as Geiler von Keyserberg, Johannes Pauli or the Spanish humanist and theoretician of poverty Juan Luis Vivés in their awareness of poverty as a social problem and of the links between poverty and employment. They may also have influenced the reform of urban charitable institutions and the formulation of modern social policy. All these problems, a complex of issues in which politics and ideology, practice and doctrinal polemics, merge and intertwine, seem to have come to a head at the same moment: in the 1520s. In 1522 Nuremberg centralized its aid to the poor; Strasbourg followed a year later, and in 1525 Ypres adopted similar measures, which achieved such popularity that they were in turn copied by a number of other cities. In 1526 Vivés' *De Subventione Pauperum* was published, and a few years later, in 1531, an imperial edict was issued sanctioning these measures, laying down the principles of social policy and defining the lines along which institutional aid to the poor should be reorganized. It was just this chain of events which provoked such violent debate between Catholic and Protestant historiographers, each side claiming the credit for the innovations.

That all these things happened at the same time was not, of course, merely fortuitous, but more important than the question of who copied whom and who was the precursor of what is the fact that they happened at a critical moment in a time of social and economic crisis.

In 1521 and 1522 poor harvests affected most of Europe, and since the previous decade had already been a lean one their consequences were particularly harsh. In Languedoc the barren years of 1495–7 were followed by another lean period lasting from 1504 to 1508 and a similar one from 1513 to 1515; after this every other year was poor in yields, and the authorities were forced to forbid the export of wheat from the region, which was normally a leading exporter. Export was also forbidden in 1522 and 1524, and for another ten years from 1526 to 1535. During this cycle of barren years various measures were taken to alleviate the lot of the poor. At the end of the fifteenth century bread distribution and shelters for the poor were organized in the worst years; during the 1504–8 crisis parishes refused to provide further assistance to those who were able to work, expelling them from the village; and in the lean years from 1513 to 1515, in an attempt to cleanse the cities of their crowds of paupers, beggars and vagrants were punished by whipping. The final cycle of unfruitfulness, from 1526 to 1535, revealed the extent of the disparity between demographic growth and food supply; vagrancy assumed mass proportions and the wave of repressive legislation aimed at paupers intensified. The crisis, according to Emmanuel Le Roy Ladurie, was a profound one, for it had its roots in the internal contradictions and psychological structures of society; now, with a combination of famine, malnutrition and a particularly deadly epidemic in 1530, it was shaking that society to its biological foundations. It marked a turning-point after which it became impossible to live or to govern as before.

It was also a crisis on a pan-European scale, a definite signal that agriculture could no longer cope with demographic growth and that the social costs of its transformation would be great. Commerce and finance were also affected: the market for industrial products shrank considerably, and cities, far from providing a solution to the huge increase of supply on the labour market, could not even maintain previous employment levels. Unemployment and an excess of supply over demand existed on both labour markets, for skilled as well as unskilled labour; these markets were strictly separate and to a large degree autonomous.

England in the early modern era was spared the food crises which raged on the continent thanks to her radical reform of agriculture. The crises which she experienced in the sixteenth and seventeenth century were a combination of bad harvests, with the subsequent increases in the price of food, and fluctuations in international commerce, which led to diminished demand for English industrial products on both the foreign and the domestic market. The problem of the poor, however, became at such times no less pressing than on the continent. In 1527–8 it became imperative to organize some sort of aid to the poor, for the bad harvest of 1527 had led to higher wheat prices and a wave of food speculation; a commission was therefore established to combat such speculation and assess the level of food stocks. The results of this enquiry more than justified the initial concern: the commissioners found that in certain parts of Wiltshire only 3 to 5 per cent of the population had any reserves of wheat. In Essex and Suffolk they appealed to the wealthier sections of the population to buy reserves of wheat for the poor, but their appeal brought few results. At the same time efforts were stepped up to catch vagrants, and the punishment for those who were caught was severe. In 1528 the harvest was better and the situation improved. Throughout this time disturbances in the labour market added to the difficulty. At the beginning of 1528 England allied herself with France in a war against the emperor, and this led to the closure of the market for English cloth in the Netherlands. The closure was brief, but nevertheless provoked temporary unemployment, and the privy council put pressure on the cloth merchants to buy up stocks, despite the difficulty of finding a market for them, in order to prevent unemployment in what was a leading branch of English industry. It is significant that in both cases where the authorities intervened, whether to alleviate food shortages or to prevent unemployment in the cloth trade, they acted out of concern for preserving public order and fear of social unrest. Their concern was not unfounded, for both unemployment and high prices, the latter felt all the more keenly after a currency devaluation in 1527, did provoke popular unrest.

It is also worth remarking on the case of Spain, for this was one of the very few countries where beggary was not declared illegal in the sixteenth century. But even here, in the 1520s, such measures were attempted. The Castillian cortes expressed their concern at the growing number of beggars, and in 1523 the cortes of Valencia, appealing to a petition made on the matter in 1518, decreed that the poor could beg for alms only in their place of birth. In 1525, a year of poor harvests, the cortes of Toledo made it illegal to beg without a special licence, a measure also adopted in 1528 by the cortes of Madrid and renewed in 1534.

Another measure of the social crisis of that time were popular revolts: wars and peasant insurrections in Germany (1525–6) and Spain (1520–1 and 1525–6), and a series of both rural and urban disturbances in England, France and the Netherlands. It is estimated that uprisings in cities of the empire in the latter half of the fifteenth century took place on average once every two years, while by the 1530s their frequency had risen to 4.5 times per year, nine times that. Emmanuel Le Roy Ladurie points out in addition that the progress of the Reformation in Languedoc during the years of crisis from 1526 to 1535 was connected to this climate of mounting unrest.

In these difficult conditions the problem of the poor presented itself in two guises. On the one hand, cities had to deal with the masses of starving paupers who flocked in from the surrounding areas; even if they could not enter, they besieged the city by camping around its walls. On the other hand, some sort of organized aid to the poor, with well-defined principles regulating the activity of charitable institutions, was urgently needed. The situation within the cities demanded such measures, but they were also an attempt to do away with the attractive image of the city as a place where alms were plentiful and a beggar might always find generous support. At this point it is worth stopping to look in some detail at three different examples of urban reform, and to trace, albeit without attempting an exhaustive monographic study, the main difficulties faced by each city and the measures taken by the local authorities to solve them.

3.1 Paris: Moral Anxiety and Fear

Paris was in a particularly difficult and complex position because of its role as an example for other cities to follow. Its importance as the nation's capital, administrative centre and royal seat naturally influenced the actions of its local authorities, who, knowing themselves to be under constant scrutiny, were conscious of the need to obtain the approval of higher powers for their every move. The problem of the capital's poor was handled directly by the Parlement, and funds for social aid were provided from the royal treasury. Another factor which influenced the local authorities was the presence of the university, which maintained its prominent role in Christian tradition as the highest authority on matters of theology and doctrine. It was the doctrine and practice of the Church, however, that had the most direct influence on decisions concerning the poor. Finally, the task of the local authorities was made more difficult still by the expectations of other cities, which looked to Paris to set an example and provide practical guidance. And yet Paris, still one of the largest cities in Europe and an important commercial, financial and industrial centre specializing in luxury goods, was struggling, like all the other cities, with the disturbing increase of poverty on its streets, unsure of what measures to take.

Work and debate on reorganizing the hospital administration in Paris began at the start of the sixteenth century. From 1505 the Hôtel-Dieu was supervised by a commission of lay administrators – an important step in the secularization of the hospitals and a decisive moment in the conflict between the local authorities and the Notre-Dame chapter. Indeed the secularization of hospitals was progressing, gradually and at different rates, in all the cities of France. In 1520 Francis I entrusted the reform of the hospitals and royal hospices to his his Grand Almoner. He was to appoint, for each diocese, two overseers, one a layman and the other a clergyman, to supervise the reforms. But despite the almost revolutionary step of appointing lay administrators, the clergy and the authority of the Church continued to play a predominant role in the running of the hospitals.

The local authorities' decision to act in the matter of hospitals was sparked to a great extent by epidemics. Each wave of epidemics required immediate action, and it was the Paris Parlement, the highest judicial authority in the kingdom, endowed with a wide range of functions and prerogatives, that held the initiative. Assemblies and consultations of the Parlement were organized; they were attended by representatives of the Chamber of Accounts and of the Paris chapter, as well as by court officials and local government functionaries, for Paris was not a free city and its government was a two-tiered system of royal rule and local self-management, represented respectively by the royal provost and the head of the local governing body, the merchants' provost. Such consultations took place, for instance, in 1510, when a terrible epidemic of whooping cough broke out in August; it was decided then that a wisp of straw should be hung for two months, as a warning, from the window of every house in which the illness was present. A few years later, in 1515, at a special assembly of experts and local dignitaries, Jean Brissonet, president of the Chamber of Accounts and energetic organizer of charitable activity in Paris (he was to be one of the two overseers of hospital reform appointed for the Paris diocese by the Grand Almoner of Francis I), suggested the building of special wards in which contagious patients could be kept apart from the others. This project, however, was not favourably received either by the Faculty of Medicine or by the local authorities, and was not carried out.

Beggars and vagrants, on the other hand, were dealt with in 1516 by stringent measures, however short-lived their effect. In that year the Parlement decreed that all vagrants ('vacabons, oysifs, caymens, maraulx et belistres, puissans et sains de leurs membres')[1] must leave the city, on pain of capture and arrest by the authorities. If they failed to do so, their capture and arrest were to be followed by forced labour on the city's public works, such as fortifications or drains. The city magistrates further decided that four guards should be assigned to every group of twelve vagrants during the day, and two at night; at night, moreover, the vagrants were to be chained together in pairs. These decisions cannot have been widely applied, however, for there is only one example in the archives, of a group of twenty-four vagrants who were arrested and brought before the magistrates a month after the decree was issued. The measures were an *ad hoc* response to a situation which demanded urgent action, and their effect was brief; but the imposition of forced labour on vagrants who were sound of body and able to work constituted an important precedent for social policy in Paris.

In 1519 there was a new epidemic in Paris; in the interests of safety, public assemblies and theatrical performances were banned. In the summer of 1522 another epidemic descended on the city, and the fear of contagion bordered on mass psychosis: the doctors who visited the sick at home and in hospitals swathed themselves in protective garments of a bizarre and complicated nature, hoping in this way to ward off infection through contact with the patients. Nicolas Versoris, a Parisian lawyer, left a description of this epidemic in his journal:

> It should be noted that a plague reigned in Paris at this time, dangerous and wondrous strange, and so deadly that a hundred and twenty people died within three days, so it was said in the Hôtel-Dieu of this city. At the cemetery of the Holy Innocents more than forty were

buried in one day, and common burial was given each day to twenty-eight or thirty people, so that after two months there were dead in great number, not counting those buried in the cemeteries of other churches. It was said that death descended mainly on the poor, so that porters, the pittance-workers of Paris, of whom before there had been a great number, seven or eight hundred, perhaps, were reduced to a small handful after this disaster befell them. As for the Petits Champs quarter, it was quite cleansed of paupers, who had lived there in great number. In short, this year may be said to have been a time of great mortality, for there was death not only in Paris but in the whole kingdom of France, and this was so even in Normandy and the city of Rouen. May God the Creator have mercy on their souls![2]

What strikes one in this description is the link made between poverty and the spread of disease. Contemporary studies of food crises stress the connection between high mortality and high prices, even though documents from the pre-statistical era are too vague to enable us to define the precise moment at which malnutrition becomes the direct cause of death. But there is no doubt that malnutrition is at the very least favourable to the spread of epidemics. The decription in the diary of Nicolas Versoris mentions the Petits-Champs quarter, an area near the city's covered market, as a zone of particular poverty. There was a number of such zones, ghettoes of poverty in a sense, in the city's topography; they arose spontaneously and were particularly fertile ground for the spread of epidemics. One might expect to find indications that epidemics controlled demographic growth by reducing the number of poor in the city, but this was not so, for at times of epidemics, hunger and food crises masses of paupers from the surrounding countryside sought shelter and aid within the city walls.

Epidemics did, however, bring a heightened awareness of the danger which large numbers of poor represented for the community. *Ad hoc* legislation against beggars and vagrants, by now traditional at times of crisis, formed part of the arsenal of urgent measures taken to combat their spread, and contributed considerably to general fear of the poor. Thus the epidemic years which spanned the first few decades of the sixteenth century brought an awareness of the need to reorganize aid to the poor, and speeded reform; in the case of Paris, at least, all the evidence points to this conclusion, and yet, when the time came for concrete measures to be taken, progress was slow.

In the spring of 1525 the Paris Parlement once again took up the debate on the subject of the poor. Animated discussions took place between, on the one hand, the merchants' provost and the city magistrates, and, on the other, the presidents of the Parlement and of the Chamber of Accounts, the highest tax authority in the kingdom; for 'poverty is so great, and the number of poor higher than ever before.' On 15 May 1525 the first president of the Parlement said in his speech at an assembly that he felt it was his 'duty to speak of the poor, who are now present in the city in great and surprising number. There are many people of good will who give alms, and it would be a great, a very great blessing from God if we could put some order into their charity and ensure that the poor had enough to eat, for alms are not being properly distributed.' To this end, he continued, every parish should make a list of all its deserving poor and take charge of distributing alms. He went on, significantly, to cite the example of Amiens, which had decided to drive out all the 'alien poor' and to ensure proper support for the remainder. It is significant that the speaker, in citing the example of Amiens, referred to this particular decree, with its suggestion of expelling all paupers alien to the city; but he did not go on to develop this theme in his speech.

Three weeks later, however, the merchants' provost, the leading representative of the city's local government, stood before the Parlement to speak of the poor. He began by saying that providing aid to the poor was a Christian duty, and was clearly hostile to any suggestion of expelling beggars who were foreign to the city. He dismissed the example of cities in Normandy and Picardy as irrelevant to the argument, claiming that these cities had been forced to expel their alien poor because of their particular situation as border towns, and rejected the suggestion that beggars and paupers be isolated from the rest of the population in designated areas within the city. For, he said, if five hundred of them were gathered together in this way, they would be six thousand within a week, and this would present a danger. His solution, therefore, was to employ them, and to pay them for their work, although he conceded that their wages should be set at the lowest level.

This was a polemical speech, unlikely to have been inspired by any genuine desire to defend the poor from repressive measures. Perhaps the local self-governing body was trying, by this means, to avert changes of which it would have to assume the financial and administrative burden. But the rhetoric of the speech, whatever the purpose which lay behind it, does indicate a degree of moral unease with the repressive measures that accompanied the reform of charity, and this ambivalence pervaded the debates and decisions of the period.

The fear of the consequences if large numbers of poor were concentrated in one place found frequent expression in these debates. In an earlier debate on the state of the city's fortifications, Jean Brissonet suggested employing the poor at public works. Many beggars would like to earn their living, he said, and begged only because they could not find work. Similarly, those who gave alms would prefer to help people who were working for the public good rather than subsidize idlers. But such a project gave rise to fears that, 'if a large number of poor are gathered together, there will be riots. And even if only six or seven hundred people are put to work in this way, after two days there will be more than two thousand; they will revolt and sack the city.' This argument echoes the doubts expressed by the merchants' provost, and shows the extent to which fear of social revolt contributed to general distrust of the poor. The argument that an offer of work would draw crowds crops up time and again. The fact that the prospect of work, however badly paid, was so attractive indicates clearly that a shortage of jobs was the cause of the increased number of beggars on the streets of Paris. This situation did indeed present a risk to social order and a threat to the propertied classes.

The debates were endless, but slowly some sort of plan began to emerge. It was finally decided that the city should be closed to 'alien poor', that work should be found for the unemployed and a permanent fund set up for the purpose. A special indirect tax was imposed to raise the necessary funds, despite objections from some officers of the Crown that 'we propose to feed some five hundred vagrants, instead of driving them out, until the price of meat rises so much that a revolt breaks out.' Matters did not seem to have improved, however, and the Parlement received complaints that the local authorities were employing whomsoever they liked at the public works, regardless of the fact that these were financed by the 'tax for the poor'. The merchants' provost, summoned before the Parlement to reply to these complaints, explained that the local authorities, in selecting candidates for employment, had to choose between two categories: on the one hand there were the 'shamefaced poor', such as unemployed craftsmen's, printers', tailors' and furriers' journeymen, who needed to support themselves and their families and could not find other work, and on the other there were the idlers and vagrants who went begging from door to door. Between a hundred and a hundred and twenty people could be employed at these works from among the 'shamefaced poor', on a modest wage paid from the funds raised through the 'tax for the poor', and there were not enough funds to employ everyone; the suggestion that vagrants be paid a lower wage than the others was dangerous, for such a step could lead to conflicts and riots.

These solutions were clearly far too feeble for the scale of the problem. The number of poor on the streets of Paris was not getting any smaller; women with children begging for bread were a common sight, and the influx of paupers into the city continued, on an even greater scale, it seemed, than before. Records of the meetings of the local government body show that public works employing the poor, and limited distributions of alms to those who were unable to work, continued to be organized in the succeeding years; and it seems that alms as well as jobs were in short supply in Paris, for there were complaints that on distribution days many of those who were employed at the public works feigned sickness or disability in order to receive alms, and these distribution days were the only times they were absent from work.

Thus the hospital reforms undertaken at the beginning of the sixteenth century, which gave secular authorities a greater say in the running of hospitals, were followed by a gradual reorganization of aid to the poor in Paris. In addition to limiting the influx of the poor into the city, the local authorities employed them at public works and distributed aid to those who were unable to work. The introduction of the 'tax for the poor' in the spring of 1525 was the most important step in carrying out a social policy based on the principle that the city should feed 'its' poor in an organized way. It also paved the way for the eventual creation of a special institution to oversee aid to the poor, the 'Aumône Générale'. A decree issued on 7 November 1544 entrusted all aspects of aid to the poor to the city magistrates; only repressive measures against vagrants remained the preserve of the Parlement. A week after this decree was issued, every parish was urged to draw up a list of its poor, and by the beginning of 1545 regular alms distribution had been organized, limited to those who were unable to work. In this way the Great Bureau of the Poor began its activity in Paris. Some documents suggest, however, that it was founded as early as 1530: a small treatise about aid to the poor in Paris, probably written between 1555 and 1557, dates the creation of the Paris Aumône to 1530, and proponents of social reform in Lyons were invoking it as an example as early as 1531.

The precise date at which this institution formally came into being, however, is of secondary importance. The principles of social policy which the city was to adopt emerged in 1525, when the financial basis of aid to the poor, as well as the powers and duties of the city magistrates in this regard, were debated and defined. The debates also revealed how central to these policies was the fear inspired by the swelling crowds of paupers in the city streets, next door to the royal palace.

3.2   Venice: Social Hygiene and Repression

Venice in the first half of the sixteenth century was a flourishing city. Her population grew at a steady pace, and she developed a stable structure of production in which, alongside her traditional shipbuilding industry, textiles began to play an increasing role. She took advantage of the great demand for textiles on Levantine markets to develop her own textile industry, gradually abandoning her old position as intermediary in the export of Flemish, English and Catalonian fabrics; and she was aided in this by a crisis in the textile industry in Tuscany and Lombardy. Indeed profits from textiles are considered, along with investments in land, to have been the main source of Venetian wealth. The extent of this wealth was staggering to anyone from outside. From the middle of the fifteenth century Venice did not cease to build and to grow in splendour; her patrician palaces dazzled with their imposing architecture and the sumptuousness of their interiors. Her elite flaunted their wealth and social position by making spectacular gifts of charity; and a well-developed and efficient administration ensured that the city's external appearance and the social order which reigned on her streets reflected the power, wealth and prestige of the 'Queen of the Adriatic'. In the 1520s, however, disaster struck this city of opulence and plenty: the *gran fame*, the great famine of 1527–9. It affected mostly immigrants from the surrounding areas, but the spectacle of poverty which it brought into the streets and squares of Venice inspired pity and fear.

Famine, plagues and wars devastated northern and central Italy. Bad harvests and epidemics, linked in a cyclical pattern, returned in the years 1527–9 with a renewed intensity. Military operations and marauding pillagers left whole provinces in ruins and obstructed or even destroyed transport routes. Venice found it increasingly difficult to obtain grain from her usual sources. Grain prices rose everywhere to double, triple, even quadruple what they had been before 1527. Famine drove country people towards the cities, since only the cities had any organized system of stocking food. Venice had wealth and she had food, and crowds of starving peasants thronged to her gates.

The Venetian chronicler Marino Sanudo described in detail the progression of events in those years:[3] in the winter of 1527–8, the cost of living was crippling, and 'every evening on the Piazza San Marco, on the Rialto, in all the city streets, crowds of children would cry out to passers-by: "Give us bread! We're dying of hunger and cold." It was terrible to behold. And in the morning there were corpses under the palace porticoes.' That was December 1527, less than a week before Christmas. Then, in the first days of February, during the Carnival, 'the city was celebrating, there were many masquerades, and at the same time a huge crowd of paupers, day and night, all over the city; because of the famine many wandering beggars had decided to come to the city with their families in search of food.' At the end of February he writes:

> I must set down here something to serve as a reminder that there is still great famine in the city. In addition to the Venetian poor who can be seen wailing in the streets, there are also the poor from Burano, with their scarves wrapped around their heads and their children in their arms, begging for alms. Many also come from as far as Vincenza and Brescia, which is surprising. Impossible to listen to mass in peace, for at least a dozen beggars will surround you; impossible to open your purse without an immediate plea for money. They are still there late in the evening, knocking on doors and crying, 'I'm dying of hunger!'

If the poor came to Venice all the way from Vincenza, it was because in Vincenza the situation was even worse. This is how it was described by a local observer in March 1528:[4] 'If you give alms to two hundred paupers, you will immediately be surrounded by two hundred more; if you walk down the street, or cross a square, or enter a church, a crowd of beggars will rush at you. Hunger is written on their faces; their eyes are like empty holes and their bodies seem to be no more than bones covered with skin.' The governor of Vincenza mentions in his proclamation that the impoverished peasants and their families lived like animals, feeding on grass and water. These were perfect conditions for an epidemic. And indeed, in March 1528 an epidemic did break out in Vincenza, with strange symptoms which no one could identify; it was attributed to the poor peasants who had swarmed into the city.

When the number of poor increased, especially after an influx from outside, indeed when any kind of migration involving the poor took place, people perceived the threat of an epidemic. Here, as in Paris, the element of fear was central to the authorities' decision to intervene; at any rate it was a recurring theme in any argument in favour of organized measures to help the poor.

In Venice such measures were suggested at a Senate assembly in March 1528. By then the epidemic had spread to a number of Italian cities. Descriptions of the symptoms are very vague, but they seem to indicate that, in addition to the plague, typhus was involved, spread by malnutrition, lack of hygiene and migrating populations. The Senate feared that the steady increase of beggars in the city and the constant influx of paupers from outside might bring the epidemic as well as famine into the city. In December 1527 a weekly distribution of bread had been organized in every parish, and the threat of an epidemic now seemed to require measures to isolate the poor.

This type of measure was not new to the Venetian authorities. The *provveditori alla sanità*, the commissioners responsible for hygiene, had been keeping a close watch on immigration to the city since the end of the fifteenth century, when the local authorities restricted alms distribution to those who had a special licence from their parish, and sentenced those caught begging without such a licence to imprisonment and whipping – further proof that the distinction between different kinds of poor was defined and applied in the Middle Ages. In 1528, faced with an epidemic, the Venetian authorities decided to apply similar measures, but on a much wider scale. On 13 March 1528, after much debate, they finally made their decision. In accordance with the proposals of a special commission which had been set up to examine the problem, three or four temporary hospices were to be built where the poor might find shelter and a bed of straw for the night. All the poor were to gather at these shelters, for begging on the streets and from door to door was punishable by imprisonment, flogging and expulsion from the city. The boatmen were to inform all their passengers that begging was forbidden in the city. In future, moreover, the new shelters would accept only the city's local poor, but the 'alien'/'local' distinction was not applied to those already in the city. A special tax was introduced to fund these shelters, collected in parishes by the curate and two lay overseers, and passed on to the *provveditori alla sanità*; the names of all those who were late in paying were to be read out at mass during holy days. The local authorities accepted responsibility for feeding the poor until June, the time of the next harvest. After this date the poor were to be taken from the shelters and transported back to terra firma, with the strict injunction to go home; they were told that if they were ever caught begging in Venice again, they would be flogged all along the way from San Marco to the Rialto.

These measures, which may be considered Venice's first 'law on the poor', were clearly temporary, an *ad hoc* response to a specific problem; it was stressed that the new provisions in no way altered the existing system of social aid provided by every parish to its 'shamefaced poor' and impoverished residents. Thus each parish continued to be responsible for its poor; this principle was embedded into the new laws, and further confirmed by the mixed make-up of the commissions whose task it was to collect the new tax. The genuinely new element, therefore, was not the secularization of social aid, which in any case was not uniform or consistent, but the authorities' assumption of responsibility for elaborating and carrying out a programme of aid to the poor.

By the beginning of April four hospices for the poor had been built. The poor, however, fearful of such isolation, were reluctant to fill them: there were acts of violence against the hospice guards, and beggars still roamed the streets of Venice. But by the middle of April about a thousand of them were living in the hospices and receiving their rations of bread, soup and wine. Overcrowding must have become a problem, because the authorities decided that henceforth they would admit only the sick; the able-bodied poor would be expelled from the city.

Mortality in these hospices was high: between March and May, two hundred and ninety-three people died in one hospice alone. In the spring of 1528 mortality was already high in Venice as a whole; in the summer, because of the epidemic, it rose to an even higher level, where it remained, with some intervals, until the following summer. The *provveditori alla sanità* recorded about 1,850 cases of illness between April 1528 and November 1529; the British historian Brian Pullan remarks that deaths from hunger and illness in 1528 did not exceed 4 per cent of Venice's permanent population, which was relatively little compared with the ravages of the Black Death in the fourteenth century and with the great epidemic of 1575–7, for instance, or that of 1630–1. But this epidemic had been preceded by a long period of stability, and its suddenness shocked the authorities into rethinking their social policy.

In April 1529, a year after the first 'law on the poor' was issued, Venice passed another law, this time of a more permanent nature. The Senate's decree began by setting down the main aims of the authorities: to provide aid for the poor and the sick and bread for the hungry, without at the same time encouraging in their idleness those who were capable of earning their own living. These principles, and the means used to put them into effect, contained the outline of the modern doctrine of charity.

By the specific provisions of this law, 'alien' beggars were banned from the city; intruders were to be sent home with a letter entrusting them to the care of their local authorities. Of the *terrieri*, the local poor, the able-bodied were put to work in the fleet; captains of ships were urged to take on as many beggars as they could, and to give them the same rations as the rest of the crew but only half the pay. Guilds and parish commissions were also enjoined to place women and children in service or in apprenticeships. The sick and disabled, on the other hand, were to receive permanent aid from the parish at home; the homeless were to be placed in hospitals and shelters.

The law contained no provisions, however, for a reform of Venice's charitable institutions. Monasteries, hospitals and brotherhoods were to go on distributing charity as usual. It was up to the parishes to organize aid to the poor: as well as distributing alms to the poor at home, they were responsible for the financial management of the brotherhoods and the collection of alms from parishioners. Once a year, at the election of their two lay helpers, the parish priests were to appeal to the faithful to vote a voluntary tax for the poor; and in their sermons they were urged to appeal for individual donations to the church collection box, the contents of which would be distributed by the parish commissioners.

In neither of her laws did Venice attempt to centralize aid to the poor in a systematic way. No central institution to oversee such aid was created, nor was there any effort to amass funds for such a project. The tax of 1528 was a provisional measure; the principle was that donations should be voluntary. The clergy retained a strong presence in the administration of charity: the Archbishop of Venice and the *provveditori alla sanità* were together responsible for seeing to it that priests did their duty in appealing to parishioners for donations. It is significant, however, that the local authorities entrusted the administration of aid to the health and hygiene officials: concern for public health and hygiene remained central to Venice's social policy. Clearly, the most important aspect of the Venetian authorities' interventions during the crisis of 1527–9 was not charity but repression: begging was forbidden, the poor were expelled or, if they were not local, isolated in special shelters, and the obligation to work amounted almost to forced labour, since the poor received only half the usual pay.

Once the crisis was past the Venetian laws on the poor were no longer rigorously enforced. They had been drafted to meet the need of the moment, and when the series of bad harvests came to an end and the wave of immigrants returned to the countryside there was no more need of urgent measures. They were renewed in successive years whenever the need arose: in 1537–9, 1544–5, 1575–7 and 1590–5, when hunger and epidemics threatened. Demographic pressure, however, created tensions on the Venetian labour market and, if the economic climate was particularly unfavourable, the city's existing structures could not cope with the strain; when this happened the social situation took a dramatic turn. More and more beggars and vagrants were being sent to the galleys. In 1545 a commission was set up to examine the question of the poor; of its six members, three were clergymen. But funds were still not forthcoming, either in the form of a regular budget or through a permanent tax. It was not until the end of the century, with plans for a central hospice for the poor, that Venice began to centralize its social policy in any systematic way.

Attitudes towards the poor, however, had changed radically during the crisis of 1527–9, so that it became possible, without in any way deforming the traditional doctrine of Christian charity, with its emphasis on voluntary and spontaneous acts of compassion, to implement a series of repressive measures aimed at the poor.

3.3 Ypres: Urban Poverty and Reform

Ypres was not a capital city like Paris or Venice, nor did it have the population density of a great metropolis. Nevertheless, the reforms of charitable institutions which it undertook in 1525 exerted a profound influence on the progress of such reforms in Europe as a whole.

By the beginning of the sixteenth century Ypres seemed long to have forgotten its medieval splendour; it was no longer among the leading industrial centres of Europe. In Flanders, however, it was still an important city, partaking largely of the benefits when the Netherlands prospered and feeling the effects of crises in equal measure. During the Middle Ages it had developed into a specialized industrial centre with a social structure characteristic of such cities. Its well-developed textile industry was known for its high quality and intended mainly for foreign markets. The production process involved a great degree of specialization, close cooperation between particular work-shops and injections of commercial capital, invested in the industry by the groups of entrepreneurs which were beginning to form in the city. The demand for labour was accordingly high. The recession came when, with a growing population, the market had to respond to new needs, and demand for luxury fabrics dropped. The competition with urban crafts was too strong, and the flourishing textile industry of Brabant had achieved such renown that by the start of the sixteenth century it was putting all other Flemish centres of cloth production in the shade. The decline of Ypres ground on slowly but inexorably: in 1510 there had been between three and four hundred workshops in the city; by 1545 barely a hundred were left. At the height of the city's prosperity there had been over a thousand. By the end of the sixteenth century nothing remained of the textile industry in Ypres. The city did not even attempt to switch to the production of fine fabrics. A few minor crafts, their products limited to the local market, were all that remained of its economy. But in the 1620s Ypres could still, in spite of all this, be considered a proto-industrial city.

In the Middle Ages institutions of charity in Ypres were well developed. During the period of its expansion entrepreneurs and local dignitaries had been concerned primarily with providing support for those who were temporarily unemployed in order to maintain a reserve of labour and prevent social unrest. In the fifteenth and early sixteenth centuries, however, the policy towards the poor was one of strict control and repression. There are no statistics to show how far this policy was successful in Ypres, but the tax registers for 1431 indicate that one-fifth of the total population was classed as poor, and this was roughly the same proportion as in other cities at the time. In the castellany of Ypres, however – the countryside surrounding the city – the proportion of 'tax paupers' was 9.6 per cent, a low figure compared with the 40 per cent in the castellany of Dendermonde or the 22.6 per cent in Cassel: Ypres was not threatened by an influx of unemployed peasants.

The third decade of the sixteenth century was a difficult time eco-nomically for the Netherlands as a whole. The military and political conflict which broke out between France and the Habsburg monarchy after the imperial election of 1519 hampered, even (according to the Belgian historian H. Van der Wee) paralysed, international trade. The crisis on Antwerp's currency and finance market reflected a general mood of economic uncertainty and unease. The main source of tensions, however, was the countryside. Food shortages, which grew more acute as the population continued to increase, were aggravated by difficulties in importing wheat from northern France and the Baltic regions. By 1521–2 there was famine. Rising prices and the collapse of international trade lowered the demand for craftsmen's products. Unemployment was spreading, and the high price of wheat, together with an over-supply of labour, caused real wages to fall.

Their fall was so rapid that wage labourers soon found they could barely subsist on their earnings. Studies of the purchasing power of wage labourers in Malines show that between 1521 and 1525 the wages of agricultural labourers remained below the basic subsistence level throughout the whole of this five-year period; moreover, the calculations were based on a working year of two hundred and seventy days, and did not take account of unemployment. Masons' and carpenters' assistants saw their wages fall below this level in four of those years. The wages of carpenters' journeymen, on the other hand, remained consistently above it. In the quarter-century which followed, there was not a single year in which agricultural labourers and carpenters' assistants earned enough to provide themselves and their families with even the barest essentials of life. Thus all categories of labourers below journeymen, whose wages fell below the basic subsistence level only in one year during the first half of the century, were impoverished on a mass scale.

Skilled labourers and artisans also saw their standard of living deteriorate, and although their survival was not threatened, they, too, became gradually impoverished. In 1510 the city of Lierre, near Antwerp, had 12 per cent of its families on the register of poor in need of support; in 1520 only 9 per cent of the city's families were registered as being in need of support, but in 1521 their number began to rise again, reaching 12 per cent in 1526 and a peak of 16 per cent in 1533, thereafter declining gradually to 7 per cent in 1553. It can reasonably be supposed that the increase reflected the gradual impoverishment of this group. Studies of the real wages of artisans and skilled labourers in Antwerp and Lierre show a downward tendency from 1520 onwards, both for skilled masons (in Brussels the wages of weavers exhibit a similar downward trend) and for masons' assistants; these latter were reduced to extreme penury, unable to subsist on their wages. In Lierre, which was a small city, their sufferings were particularly acute, for, except for a few years, the wages of masons' assistants remained below the basic subsistence level until the end of the century. Skilled labourers fared somewhat better, but since the preceding period had been a relatively prosperous one for them, they, too, now felt the contrast keenly, their frustration and anxiety about the future ready to erupt into active protest.

During the famine of 1521–2 there were riots in the cities. In Louvain, Malines and Vilvoorde women broke into the grain stores of monasteries and townsfolk; in Antwerp the peasants who brought the grain to market were attacked and robbed. The central authorities reacted in various ways, sometimes sending the army to quell the revolts, sometimes, as in the case of Gent, buying grain and reselling it to the poor at a lower price. They also stopped all export of wheat and took measures to prevent speculation on the wheat market and fraud by bakers.

The 1520s were a time of trial for cities throughout the Netherlands. In places like Ypres, a combination of natural disasters, famine and epidemics contributed to rising unemployment and poverty among craftsmen, making a bleak situation even bleaker. Hospitals and charitable institutions, inherited from medieval times, provided a framework for the distribution of aid to the poor, but administrative reform was needed. The first attempts at such reform, in 1515, had little effect. In September 1525, however, the municipal council undertook a general reform of charitable institutions; laws were promulgated defining the principles of reform and ordering its immediate execution. In December of that year another law introduced severe punishments for beggary; and in the course of the following year a number of laws, modelled on measures adopted by other Flemish cities and similar in spirit to the treatise of Vivés, supplemented the city statutes.

The social policies introduced in Ypres in 1525 reposed on the by now familiar principles of banning public beggary, organizing aid for the 'genuine poor', combating vagrancy and creating a fund to cover administrative costs. The essential thing, however, was that the city assumed all responsibility for organizing aid to the poor. Special officials, four to each parish, were designated for this purpose; they were to be 'as parents to the poor', distributing aid, regularly checking health and living conditions and keeping a discreet eye on the poor in their care. It was also their task to collect alms from the parishioners and to manage the money donated through the collecting boxes which were displayed in every church, for there were no plans in Ypres to introduce a special 'poor tax'. In addition, they were to provide shelter for the pilgrims and travellers who passed through Ypres, making sure, however, that these duly departed after a brief stay. 'Able-bodied beggars' – in other words, vagrants of all kinds – were to be treated in the same way. The problem of local unemployment was not addressed in any systematic way; on the other hand, emphasis was placed on extending charity to the poor in the educational domain, as 'it is better', it was said, 'to be well-taught than well-born'.

Within a few years, however, the new social policy implemented in Ypres was coming under fierce attack. The opposition came, in the autumn of 1530, from the Franciscans, the Dominicans, the Carmelites and the Augustinians, who together branded the reforms as heretical, and claimed that they would lead to persecution of the poor. The strength of this opposition, and the vehemence of the accusations, showed that the conflict was a profound one. The mendicant orders, whose revenues and whole way of life were threatened by the reforms, were deaf to the arguments of the municipal authorities. These latter responded by citing figures which testified to their efficiency: in 1530 alone, and with a few months still to go until the end of the year, between 1,600 and 1,800 poor had received aid. But the controversy was primarily a doctrinal one, and theologians and lawyers on both sides lost no time in continuing the battle on an ideological plane.

The principal issue around which this conflict revolved was the correct interpretation of the Christian's duty to help the poor. The municipal authorities prepared a complex series of arguments, drawn both from the Scriptures and from ancient literature, intended to demonstrate that their reforms did not in any way conflict with religious teaching. They ranged over the entire theological canon on poverty: from the life of St Alexis, described in the gospels, to hagiographical examples, to the writings of the Church Fathers. But times have changed, said the municipal authorities. This was their main argument. People no longer voluntarily embraced poverty as the way to Christian perfection, nor, if poverty was their lot, did they accept it with humility, as a condition imposed on them by the divine will; all that was past. Now, the poor were arrogant and dishonest, preferring lives of parasitical leisure to work, and flagrantly flouting the precepts of Christian life. These were the poor at whom the city's repressive measures were aimed.

Fearing accusations of heresy (which, in 1530, meant Lutheran sympathies, a very serious charge), the municipal council appealed to the theologians in Paris to resolve the conflict. The verdict of the Sorbonne was in their favour: the measures against the poor were severe but just, and did not conflict with Evangelical teaching. It was pointed out, however, that the interests of the poor must be safeguarded above all; accordingly, public beggary must be permitted, the Sorbonne declared, if the poor, whether local or 'alien', were in extreme need, and if the resources to support them were lacking from the central fund set up for the purpose. In addition, the poor from neighbouring villages should not be refused aid if they were unable to work for a living, nor should individuals be punished for giving alms directly to the poor. Finally, concluded the Paris theologians, the revenues and wealth of the Church were on no account to be depleted on the pretext of providing aid to the poor, for such a course 'would rather befit Godless heretics, Wycliffists, Lutherans and Waldensians, than faithful Catholics.'[5] Furthermore, the law banning beggary was not applicable to the mendicant orders, for their activities had the approval of the Church and were in accordance with ecclesiastical doctrine.

Thus the municipal reforms obtained their certificate of conformity with Catholic doctrine, although the restrictions imposed by the Paris theologians, especially those which concerned 'alien poor', were something of a hindrance to their plans. In practice, however, the municipal authorities both in Ypres and in other cities found that implementing the reforms entailed taking repressive measures which exceeded, and sometimes simply defied, the restrictions imposed by the Sorbonne. But even the Paris theologians were flexible in this regard, for their verdict included the recommendation that the system of social aid be constantly revised and updated in accordance with the needs of the moment. An awareness of the need to confront and adapt to a changing reality was fundamental to the processes which so radically transformed both institutional policies and the collective social conscience during the second decade of the sixteenth century.

4

The Reform of Charity

The reforms of the 1520s may be seen as the starting-point for a new social policy. Neither their efficiency nor their longevity, however, should be overestimated: in their complex meanderings it was difficult to trace the outline of a coherent and systematic policy. We have tried to place the first of these reforms in their social and economic context. We shall now go on to sketch the administrative measures and practical steps taken to centralize social aid in the cities.

In the reforms discussed above, local policies play the primary role; indeed, the bulk of sixteenth-century social reform took place on the municipal level. The State, however, intervened constantly, and many decisions concerning the scope of reforms rested ultimately with the central authorities. In the case of Venice, for example, the new social policy was equally the work of the State and the municipality, since in a city-state these were indistinguishable. In Paris, during the debates, royal representatives were constantly intervening to define the tasks and the powers of the municipal authorities. The complexities of combining social reform with repressive measures required intervention from the State; it was also up to the State to endow municipal authorities with the executive powers necessary to carry out their programme of reform.

The imperial edict of 1531 was a classic instance of state intervention in the domain of social aid; it was also influential in defining the principles of reform. It was issued after an initial study of the subject had been carried out by experts, who examined both previous legislation and doctrinal arguments concerning the poor. The emperor obtained from Flemish cities the texts of their laws on beggary, and it is likely that the ordinances issued in Ypres and Mons, at least, and similar laws promulgated in German cities, played a considerable role in the drawing up of the edict.

Already in 1530, in Augsburg, Charles V had issued a decree defining the principles of policy with regard to the poor. It ordered that the municipality impose strict controls on beggars and vagrants, and that permission to beg be accorded only to those who were sick or infirm. The children of beggars were to become apprenticed to a trade or enter domestic service, lest for them, too, begging become a habit. At the same time it was decreed that all cities provide food and shelter for their poor, and begging outside one's home town was forbidden. Those who defied this ordinance, the so-called *starke Bettler* or strong beggars – the term probably referred not to those who were able-bodied, but to professionals – were to be apprehended and severely punished as an example to others. If a town had more beggars than it could cope with, it could transfer some of them to another locality with a letter of recommendation. Local authorities were also given control of the hospitals and enjoined to see that admittance to them was restricted to the genuinely needy. Thus the decree laid down new principles of social aid and defined the chief duties of local authorities with regard to their poor. Among these the control of hospitals was particularly significant, for it was a new element, and an important step towards their secularization. The repressive measures, on the other hand, were simply extensions of previous legislation pertaining to beggars. The suggestion that towns transfer some of their beggars to other localities, although unrealistic and liable to lead to arbitrary decisions, is an interesting indication of the scale of the problem; and the recommendation that a place in society be found for the children of beggars was an important element in the modernization of social aid.

The edict concerning the Netherlands, proclaimed by Charles V on 6 October 1531, during his stay there, was much more elaborate and far-reaching than the Augsburg decree. This may have been owing to the influence of legislation which had already been promulgated in various cities in the Netherlands but of which the imperial chancellery had been unaware at the time of the Augsburg decree. Article IX of the 1531 edict presents the reasons for the new legislation. The first and most important of these was the vast number of beggars who were invading the country on an unprecedented scale. The others were presented in the form of a brief discourse on social philosophy:

... experience shows that if begging for alms is permitted to everyone *indiscriminately* [my italics], many errors and abuses will result; for they will fall into idleness, which is the beginning of all evils; they and their children will abandon their trade or occupation, from which they could have made a living, for a wicked and contemptible life, and condemn their daughters to poverty and unhappiness, and all manner of wickedness and vice; and even though they be young, and strong, and able-bodied, they will perfidiously and deceitfully wrest for themselves that which should be distributed to the old, the sick and the infirm, and to those in great need ...

The emperor therefore decided that before leaving the Netherlands he would remedy all these ills. However, to make his intentions clear, immediately after the above passage he added:

... but above all in order that those who are poor and sick, and other indigents unable to earn a living, might receive food and sustenance, to the glory of God, our Saviour, and according to His will, from true love and charity we have ordered and decreed what follows ...[1]

This introductory discourse should not be dismissed as mere rhetoric traditional to such preambles; judicial formulas often enunciate just those principles which, once expressed, come to seem self-evident. The discourse which forms the introduction to this edict strongly emphasizes two principles on which legislation should be based: the need to regulate beggary, a problem which had assumed such proportions that it threatened the public interest, and the continuation of traditional Christian charity.

The imperial edict unequivocally prohibited public begging in streets, squares and churches, and from house to house. The punishment for a first offence was a prison sentence; further offences were subject to whatever punishment the judges and local authorities saw fit to impose. Collecting alms for lepers, prisoners and mendicant orders was exempt from this prohibition. Pilgrims were permitted to spend one night in a hospice if they presented the appropriate documents to those in charge. At the same time the edict ensured that the genuinely sick and needy received the support they required by ordering all institutions of charity to pool their resources and create a *bourse commune*, a central fund managed by a committee appointed for the purpose. A collecting box was to be displayed in every parish church for individual donations for the poor; a committee which included, in addition to the curate, distinguished members of the community and representatives of the local authorities, was appointed to distribute the funds thus collected. The members of this committee also collected funds for the poor from the parishioners under the supervision of the local authorities, and drew up lists of the poor in each parish, noting their profession, their revenues and the number of their children, and indicating the amount of support they deemed appropriate for each. Such details were to be scrupulously checked during the weekly alms distributions, in order to prevent drunkards, vagrants and idlers from claiming a share. Able-bodied paupers were to be made to work and support their families. Significantly, only one thing could keep them from defying this injunction: the threat of being taken off the register of the poor. In other words, it was assumed in advance that their earnings would not in any case suffice to support them and their families. As for their children, who had lived as beggars and vagrants before the edict was issued, they were to be sent to school or into domestic service, or apprenticed to a trade.

The final clause of the edict was addressed to the parish clergy, to preachers and confessors, urging them to persuade their parishioners to make out their wills in favour of the fund for the poor. It would be of no particular interest were it not for the injunction which follows:

> . . . and if the poor supported through this fund come to complain to these curates, preachers and others, they should not be readily believed, but consoled with kind words and sent to the charity commissioners, who will consider what is the appropriate course to take.[2]

The imperial edict lent a large measure of autonomy to aid for the urban poor. Its text echoes some of the controversies surrounding Church teaching on such matters as the repression of beggars and the extent to which religious doctrine permits secular control over the distribution of alms. Alongside doctrinal concerns such as these, the experience of the first urban reforms is no less manifest as an influence in the shaping of the document: the appeal to the clergy not to intervene in complaints made by the poor is clearly made in the light of such experience. The transition from clerical to secular control of social aid inevitably provoked a certain amount of tension. The imperial edict is firm on this point: aid to the poor is to be fully centralized, controlled by a specially appointed commission and financed from a central fund created for the purpose. Thus the edict of 1531 may be considered a clearly articulated programme of secularization of social aid which nevertheless takes care to provide the clergy with a well-defined role in the reforms and seeks neither to question the traditional prerogatives of the Church nor to lay claim to any part of its wealth. The decrees regarding the poor which Charles V was to promulgate in the years following were conceived in the same spirit.

The laws against vagrancy issued by the French government were harsh: vagrancy became a crime, to be combated by repression: those caught were sent to the galleys or sentenced to forced labour in the city. With regard to social aid, on the other hand, the legislation remained vague. Its effects were evident chiefly in the administration of hospitals, which, as in the case of Paris mentioned earlier, passed gradually into secular hands. But even these reforms were inspired less by ideology than by financial constraints: hospital budgets and management were in a deplorable state, and many small hospitals were no more than farms in which one or two rooms were set aside for pilgrims and wandering beggars. When the Grand Almoner, in accordance with the edict of 1519, took over control of the hospitals, the situation improved somewhat; at the same time, however, pressure was being exerted by the royal authorities to transfer the administration of hospitals into secular hands. This was the demand made by representatives of the Third Estate when the Estates General assembled in Orléans in 1560, and it was met in a royal ordinance the following year. This ordinance cannot have had much effect, however, for the issue continued to resurface at successive assemblies of the Estates General. It also met with some opposition from the clergy, spurred to a burst of renewed activity by the decisions of the Council of Trent.

The French laws against vagrancy effectively banned all public begging and obliged every town to provide sustenance for its poor. The law punished not only vagrants found wandering outside their place of residence, or simply begging in a public place, whether in their home town or outside it, but also those who gave alms to beggars. On 5 February 1535 the Paris Parlement adopted a series of measures dealing with beggars in the capital; viewed as a whole, this legislation contains the outlines of a definite social policy:

1 All able-bodied beggars born in Paris or resident in the city for at least two years must, on pain of death, present themselves for employment at public works;

2 Those in the above category for whom the city can find no employment in public works are to present themselves for work as masons' assistants [it is significant that masonry was the profession with the largest capacity for unskilled labour]; the wage in both cases is set at 20 deniers per day, lower than any labourer's wage in the city;

3 All able-bodied beggars not born in Paris or resident in the city for less than two years must, on pain of death, leave the city within three days;

4 Beggars who feign illness or disability are liable to be flogged and banished; if they are recidivists, the judges may deal with them as they see fit;

5 No resident, whatever his status, may give alms in the street or in a church, on pain of a fine.

The threat of the death penalty, which appears twice, sets the tone for these laws. But their severity, even as it testifies to the breakdown of certain traditional psychological barriers with regard to beggars, is also a measure of the helplessness of the authorities. A series of similar laws passed by the Parlement in successive years further reveals the ineffectiveness of such measures.

Although the legislation against beggars applied only to Paris, it naturally influenced the decisions of judges and police authorities throughout the kingdom. The organization of aid to the poor, however, was left entirely to the discretion of local authorities. The principle whereby each town assumes responsibility for its own poor was an integral part of the doctrine that it is not the duty of the State to organize social aid. In 1586 the king, responding to a request made in one of the 'books of complaints' that funds from the royal treasury be made available to feed the poor, wrote that no funds would be given for this purpose, since 'this is a matter which depends on the charity and piety that good citizens ought, as good Christians, to show towards their brethren.'[3] When the king did intervene in matters of social aid it was only in emergencies, as in January 1545, when he recommended that the Paris municipal authorities organize public works in order to provide employment for the large numbers of poor arriving in the capital from Picardy and Champagne. Only the principle that aid was to be provided to the poor in their place of residence was enshrined in a royal decree – in the Moulins ordinance of February 1566, for example. But it was up to the individual cities to put this principle into effect, and indeed it was the municipal authorities who centralized social aid, creating a central bureau of the poor, financed by a special tax levied on the residents.

4.1   France: Grenoble, Rouen and Lyons

Generally speaking, the efforts of central authorities in Europe to reform social aid were not significant. In all the examples considered here the initiative came from local authorities, and reforms were carried out on the local scale. The reorganization of hospitals and institutional aid for the poor took place gradually city by city, when bad harvests and economic fluctuations made action necessary. All of these reactions on the part of individual cities, whether conceived as temporary emergency measures or as more permanent provisions, left something of themselves behind: experience was accumulated, new methods became familiar, psychological barriers to new social structures fell gradually away. This general picture of the process of reform is confirmed by the minutes of municipal council meetings in French towns, and it will be useful to consider a few examples of these.

An interesting case is that of Grenoble, an average sort of city of no special importance. Not specializing in any particular branch of industry, it attracted neither wealth nor labour. At the same time the proportion of poor peasants in the surrounding countryside – families economically so unstable that they constantly risked being swallowed up by the proletariat – was very great, and the tide of rural poor which periodically swept the city at times of crisis and bad harvests created strong social tensions.

In the mid-nineteenth century Berriat-Saint-Prix wrote a critique of Adam Smith's argument connecting the growth of poverty in England to the Dissolution of the Monasteries; in it he remarked that minutes of municipal council meetings show a similar growth of poverty in French towns of the same period. In the sixteenth-century registers for Paris and Grenoble he finds endless complaints about the large number of poor in these cities, and a record of the various measures taken to remedy the situation: a census of all beggars, the expulsion of able-bodied 'alien' poor, alms distributions among the 'passing poor', the hiring of menial officials to pursue and arrest vagrants, the introduction of forced labour on public works for local able-bodied poor, the identification of beggars by a system of visible signs and the 'distribution' of beggars to be supported among the city's inhabitants. All these measures were applied in various ways in Grenoble.

The Grenoble authorities began to act in the winter of 1513; in addition to expelling beggars from the city, a measure they renewed in 1515, they organized bread collections among the city's residents – a first step towards institutionalized public aid for the poor. In 1520, no doubt through fear of an epidemic, the bishop was ordered to distribute alms outside the city walls, and by the end of that year it had been decided to place sick beggars in hospitals and put the rest to work on river projects. These were certainly temporary measures, for the problem of beggars continued as a subject of debate in following years (1523, 1526), and it was finally decided to expel from the city all able-bodied beggars unwilling to work. In the years 1530–3 this decision was several times renewed, until the fear of an epidemic in 1538 forced the authorities to approach the problem in a more organized way. They decided to place all the city's beggars, who numbered about three hundred, in a special hospice, where they would be provided with food collected from among the inhabitants. Then came a plan to fuse the city's four hospitals into one central organism, followed swiftly by a new monthly tax on the inhabitants, introduced in 1544. In 1544–5, with the danger of an epidemic once again in sight, new measures followed in rapid succession. Indeed the situation was now critical: the Hôpital de l'Île housed nine hundred beggars, and it was unlikely that the authorities of neighbouring towns would respond to the appeal to take back 'their' poor. The attempt to expel alien poor from the city also seemed a hopeless enterprise, despite the three *chasse-coquins* appointed for the task, and the forced labour on the riverworks for the able-bodied was hardly more successful. At the end of 1545, however, the plan to combine the wealth of the hospitals and the brotherhoods was finally realized: the first step towards a centralized social aid had been taken.

Thus the reform of charity was preceded, in the first half of the sixteenth century, by a long experience of misery; it was this experience – the periodic pressures of famine, poverty and epidemics – which finally broke through the reluctance and inertia of the authorities, both secular and ecclesiastic, and forced them to adapt to real needs. In the years after 1545 the theory and practice of the new office of the poor created in Grenoble gradually emerged and began to assume a more definite form. Officials appointed by the municipal council inspected hospitals, remarked on the presence of many poor who had no right to be there, decided to create registers of the poor 'pour estre tenuz comme ung tresor', and, in May 1548, drew up a list of 'shamefaced poor'. In August 1548 a further, more general list of the poor was made, to include those who begged for alms as well. The census-taking proceeded methodically, street by street, and when it was over each official decided who, of those living in the particular street to which he had been assigned, deserved support, and who should be expelled. The able-bodied beggars who were allowed, as long-time residents, to remain in the city were to be employed at public works, and appropriate tools and wheelbarrows were bought for them. In drawing up the new regulations concerning the poor the authorities also made use of the Paris statute, which reached them in 1551; the reform of charity in the sixteenth century developed at a pace which varied little from one city to another, for its rhythm depended not only on social and economic fluctuations but also on a constant exchange of practical experience, a sort of collaboration between different urban centres. Thus the registers of the poor drawn up in Grenoble, for example, also served the effort to combat vagrancy on the scale of the whole kingdom, for they were used by the royal courts to identify the genuine vagrants, or *coquins*.

Finding suitable work for beggars continued to pose problems. Road and river works, for which public workshops had to be built, had proved too expensive, and every such scheme had ended in failure. The newly appointed social aid officials tried to provide a future for the children of the poor by apprenticing boys from the age of twelve and finding domestic posts for the girls. In 1560, seeing that the number of beggars obtaining support was steadily increasing, the social aid administrators suggested placing them all together in one hospice and organizing workshops where they might be profitably employed in some of the surrounding houses. But this plan, too, came to nothing.

The product of a succession of social crises, public social aid continued to function, despite endless obstacles, over the following decades. In normal, economically stable times it was able to deal competently with the problem of beggars; systematic censuses were taken, registers drawn up and kept up to date and regular alms distributions organized. Donations and collections generally covered essential expenses, even though the authorities sometimes found themselves obliged to exert pressure on those who refused to contribute, or who did not contribute enough, by sending beggars to their doors in person to ask for alms. At times of economic crisis, however, of which there were plenty in the last quarter of the sixteenth century, these measures proved insufficient, and as events remembered from the first half of the century began to repeat themselves, with hordes of paupers fleeing bad harvests and famine flocking into Grenoble from the countryside, and the danger of an epidemic loomed once again, the authorities were helpless. The city gates had to be closed, vagrants and 'alien' beggars expelled and emergency measures taken to provide additional forms of charity. In 1574 it was decided to allocate beggars to every resident, and plans were made to employ the able-bodied in the textile industry. During a census of 1576, one hundred and thirty-three people presented themselves to be registered, and their number was growing. By 1586 bread distribution was extended not only to beggars but to all those who found themselves unemployed – 'excluds de tout travail et negosse' – as a result of the epidemic which was raging through the city: in August the amount of bread distributed daily to each beggar was eight quintals, but by November, with granaries almost entirely depleted, and the epidemic in any case receding, this was cut down to five. Only the poorest, 'le plus petit et tout pauvre peuple', had remained in the city throughout the epidemic, and the disease had decimated their numbers. The houses left abandoned by the other residents in their flight were a temptation for burglars, and efforts were accordingly stepped up to drive all vagrants and 'alien' beggars out of the city. In 1587 the authorities, fearing a recurrence of the epidemic, made a serious attempt to weed out 'alien' beggars from the others by a system of identifying marks. To this end a veritable police raid was organized, with two or three officials posted in the streets to keep an eye on groups of beggars and prevent them from running from one street to another to escape the sweep. In 1588 an order was issued forbidding ferrymen from carrying beggars into the city; in 1589 the *chasse-coquins* were ordered to escort 'alien' beggars out of the city in the presence of local officials: the sick were placed in St Anthony's hospital and the healthy received a *viaticum*. In 1592–3, despite these measures, the problem returned with undiminished force, to find the authorities and charitable institutions once again helpless and no nearer to a solution that they had been before.

A different example was the city of Rouen, an important commercial and industrial centre, and from the sixteenth century also known for its textile production. In the autumn of 1510 there was an epidemic in the city, and in order to prevent its spread the authorities began to consider, among other things, possible measures to deal with the increasing number of beggars. They were everywhere, in streets and churches and even in private houses whenever they found an open door. And yet no concrete measures were decided on at that time. Nor were any steps taken in 1525, when the situation in Rouen was so serious that news of it reached as far as Paris: the number of unemployed was huge, and at the same time waves of peasants from the surrounding countryside were flooding the city. In the spring of 1525 five hundred people were put to work on repairing the city's fortifications, but the authorities soon ran out of funds to continue this project. Although the people thus employed were paid very little for their labour, and by the end there was not even enough bread for their daily ration so that they had to be divided into two groups, receiving their rations on alternate days, still crowds continued to form in front of the fortifications, looking for work. These shortages, however, were temporary, and had no lasting effects.

In 1534 the Rouen authorities proceeded with a thorough reorganization of hospitals and institutions of social aid. In December the problem of paupers and vagrants was the subject of a specially convened meeting of state and local authorities as well as hospital administrators, Church dignitaries and local notables. The opening speech at this meeting was made by the president of the Rouen Parlement, Robert Billy, who cited the interests of public safety and the threat to public order as the main arguments in favour of taking action against beggars. He also claimed that amid the genuinely poor were many common criminals and vagabonds who, in addition to begging, made their living as robbers and brigands, and simply preferred a parasitic life to honest work, of which they were quite capable. These people took the bread from the mouths of the genuinely sick and needy whom every society had a duty to support. This was his second argument in favour of vigorous action: the 'natural, civil and divine duty of every Christian to come to the aid of his neighbour when he is in need, for he is a member of the same body' ('l'obligation naturelle, civille et divine par laquelle chacun chrétien est tenu subvenir à la necessité de son prochain, somme membre d'un mesme corps').[4] Finally, he invoked the measures that Paris, Lyons and other cities had already taken against beggars. The dignitaries and government representatives at the meeting needed no persuading. The clergy and lay authorities were also in agreement as to the programme of reform; indeed, the suggestion that all the able-bodied be forced to work came from the representative of the chapter, thus laying to rest fears of opposition from the Church. It was also Billy who went on to propose the setting up of workshops in which the poor might be employed in manufacturing products which could then be sold, thus providing additional funds for those who could not work. At the end of the meeting a municipal poor law was voted. It began with a preamble in praise of charity, 'the greatest and most important of virtues', and went on, in its more detailed provisions, to limit rather than extend the traditional practice of the virtue in question. The essential points of this law were as follows.

1 All those capable of work who have no trade or other source of income and lead lives of idleness and vagrancy are to leave the city within eight days, or find themselves a master;
2 At the end of this eight-day period, the bailiff will order the arrest of all vagrants remaining in the city; these, when caught, will be chained in pairs and handed over to the local authorities, who will put them to work on sites within the city and provide their food;
3 Beggary is henceforth forbidden, on pain of flogging, even if the beggar is sick or infirm;
4 For each parish a list will be made of the poor in need of support, and a treasurer appointed by the authorities will be responsible for the management and distribution of funds.

This law is clearly more firm and unequivocal in its repressive measures than in its provisions for a reorganization of social aid. Once put into practice, moreover, these measures were to prove expensive, and funds were soon lacking.

At the beginning of 1535 the authorities considered the results of their census-taking. Seven thousand 'impuissants' – genuine paupers and those in need of permanent support – were found to be living in the city, as well as five hundred and thirty-two beggars, two hundred and thirty-five of them children. The former category would appear to correspond to the 'shamefaced poor', those who had a place of their own to live and did not beg in the streets, but were unable to earn their own living. Social morality and collective solidarity demanded that this group should be the first to receive support. But the city lacked the resources to support everyone at once, and, in order for the law against public begging to have the desired effect, priority should be given above all to the group of professional beggars. Whom, then, to choose?

The municipal council could not make up its mind. And there were practical decisions to be made: should the support take the form of money or food? How great should it be? Could one really begin arresting vagrants when there were still no resources to feed them? In the end only one thing was decided: that public begging was henceforth forbidden.

As a result all the measures relating to the poor taken after 1534 were almost entirely without effect: the administration of social aid comprised barely a hundred and fifty people, while the number of beggars and vagrants, this latter being the official term for the unemployed, continued to swell. The council continued its deliberations. During one of the debates a daring proposal was made, similar to the one put forward in 1534 by the representative of the chapter: it was suggested, namely, that the example of Lille, in Flanders, be followed, where 'there is a law about the poor whereby they are made to stay in the house where they are working, and may not go out of it, and are fed from the alms that have been collected' ('il y a eu ordonnance faicte pour le faict des povrez, par laquelle ils sont tenuz en une maison ou ilz besognent pour ung chacun sans pouvoir ressortir dud lieu et sont nourriz des denyers de l'omosne').[5] Such a law acts as a deterrent because the poor prefer to look for work themselves rather than risk being locked up.

But still the deliberations continued and no decision was made. They were rich in opportunities both for exchanging ideas and for exhibiting high rhetorical skills. Here are some of the suggestions advanced during a meeting in January 1542:

—— Those who are unwilling to work should indeed be expelled from the city, but those who are simply unable to find work should not be treated thus; instead, they should be put to work on sites in the city in exchange for food until such time as they succeed in finding work in their trade;

—— Idleness is harmful to the public good, and should not be tolerated; idlers should not be considered as poor;

—— People used to working in a particular trade find it difficult to adapt to another, and it would be unjust to reproach them for this; they should therefore be warned in advance of impending measures, so that they have time to find suitable work;

—— It would be best to expel from the city all those not born in Rouen, whether sick or sound of body;

—— A political body should take care of all its members, but this is a principle which should apply only to citizens;

—— It would be excessively severe to expel all those who are able to work; we should look to the example set by the ancient Romans, who engaged in military expeditions in order to provide an occupation for the young;

—— Before expelling the poor from the city we must consider whether our defensive capacity would not suffer from such a measure, for after all it is the people, and not the judges and councillors, who will fight if the need arises.

It is striking in this debate to see how closely the problem of the poor and the state of the labour market are intertwined, and how often those who are reproached with idleness or vagrancy are simply unemployed.

Nevertheless the policy of repression and aid regarding the poor did gradually acquire a more definite shape. An order went forth to nail the lists of the poor to the church doors in each parish, and the poor were told to wear a special sign, or a yellow cross on their sleeve, in order that they might easily be distinguished. In 1551 a municipal Bureau of the Poor was finally created, charged among other things with finding work for the poor, providing dowries for the daughters of poor men and sending their younger children to school or to be apprenticed to a trade. Raw materials such as linen, wool and hemp were bought for the poor to work with, and profits from the sale of their products went to the Bureau. Public works were still the mainstay as far as employment was concerned; in 1557 between seven and eight thousand poor men were put to work repairing the city's fortifications in exchange for a ration of bread and a small amount of money. But no decision was made to introduce a permanent tax for the benefit of the poor.

Nevertheless, poverty was a source of constant worry in Rouen. In 1566 the bailiff issued an ordinance concerning the danger which the poor represented to public order, warning 'all poor people of the said city and its environs, as well as all others, whatever their situation in life, against cursing, insulting, rebelling against or attacking, in word or deed, any councillors of the said city, or any citizens appointed by them to distribute alms and find work for the poor' ('Et si est tres expressement inhibé et deffendu à tous les pauvres de ladicte ville et banlieu, et autres de quelque qualité qu'ilz soyent, qu'ilz n'ayent à eux eslever, n'y s'esmouvoir, injurier, ny soy attacher en faict ny en dict aux conseillers de ladicte ville, ny aux bourgeoys par eulx depputez, ayans charge de leur faire ladicte distribution et les faire besogner, sur peine de fouet, pour la première fois, et d'estre penduz et estranglez, pour la seconde').[6] The threatened punishments – flogging for a first offence, hanging for a second – were extremely severe. In order to impress more firmly on the mind the warning contained in this ordinance, four gibbets were erected in those places where alms were habitually distributed and beggars and vagrants employed.

These extreme measures were neither exceptional nor temporary. The gibbet henceforth found a place in the permanent repertoire of measures intended to ensure the proper functioning of social aid in Rouen. Twenty years later, in June 1586, when the poor employed at public works were daily casting insults at the commissioners and showing signs of violent rebellion, for instance by fighting for bread during distributions, the gibbets once again took up their strategic positions wherever such works were in progress.

The Rouen gibbets were above all proof of the importance of repression in organizing the new system of social aid, and testimony to the tension created by huge gatherings of paupers, forced to work for a pittance, in one place. But they also showed how swift was the transition, among the social elite, from moral vacillation and doctrinal scruples to outright, unequivocal threats.

The examples of Grenoble and Rouen are just two of many, all noted down with conscientious monotony in the registers of various French towns throughout the sixteenth century. The same pattern, with some regional differences, was followed everywhere: the same human misery, the same attempts to deal with the situation, the same helplessness in the face of recurring crises. Local reforms, regardless of the extent of their proven success or permanence, always involved the same measures: taking a census of paupers, expelling as many of them as possible from the city, distinguishing those qualifying for support by various identifying signs, centralizing the administration of hospitals and social aid and providing, mostly through taxes, the resources for their continued activity. The similarity and repetitiveness of these reactions to crises can also be seen in long-term provisions and structural changes: the social tensions and changes provoked by particular short-term fluctuations were symptomatic of a structural crisis.

For French cities Paris and Lyons were the models to follow. The fact that Paris was seen as an example to emulate is hardly surprising: it was, after all, the royal seat, the country's capital, and an important centre of legal and theological thought. Paris was the first city to create a Bureau of the Poor, and reformers in other cities built upon its experience. The Paris Bureau's origins are less well documented than those of the Bureau later founded in Lyons: the first descriptions of its structure and work date back only to the second half of the sixteenth century. It is clear from these, however, that it was organized along much the same lines as the Lyons Bureau, which was also looked to as a model – partly because of its fame, which spread rapidly, and partly because a special study describing its work was published at that time and drew the attention of many experts in the field. A brief look at the structure and basic principles of this institution therefore seems indicated.

The Lyons Bureau of the Poor awakened the interest of a number of historians. Soon after its creation it was described by the humanist and lawyer Jean de Vauzelle and by the historian Guillaume Paradin, both from Lyons. In modern historiography it has been the subject of numerous regional studies at the turn of the century, and more recently of a series of monographs by Natalie Zemon Davis and Jean-Pierre Gutton. These studies revealed its creation to have been owing to the activities of a very particular type of local coalition. During the first quarter of the sixteenth century there was much tension in Lyons. In 1529 the soaring cost of living led to a popular uprising, the Grande Rebeyne: labourers, women, young people – all took to the streets to demand lower prices and an end to grain speculation; they plundered the city's granaries, the nearby Franciscan convent and even the houses of the wealthier residents. Stern measures were taken to quell the uprising, but in 1530 the protests began anew. That same year saw the first wave of an epidemic which raged through the city, and by 1531 the ravages of the plague combined with a poor harvest to produce the usual, familiar result: Lyons was invaded by swarms of paupers; half-starved peasants flocked in from all around – Burgundy, the Beaujolais, the Dauphine – and another uprising was feared. It was at this critical moment that a new organization called the 'Aumône Générale' was created to provide temporary relief. It was reactivated in 1532, still only as a provisional emergency measure. But its activities, together with the experience of those years, led to the formation of a 'pressure group' which insisted on the need for a permanent institution of social aid and for a radical restructuring of the hospital system. This group, as Natalie Zemon Davis has shown, consisted of Christian humanists and the city's dignitaries, both Catholic and Protestant. Its energetic efforts succeeded in spurring the city authorities to action: in January 1534 they decided to establish a permanent Aumône Générale on the model of the Paris Bureau, and to this end procured for themselves copies of legislation passed in Paris in the matter of aid for the poor. A prohibition on begging, a guarantee of institutional support for the poor, the obligation to work and taxes (theoretically voluntary) imposed on the clergy and the burgeoisie for the benefit of the poor comprised the basic principles of the subsequent reforms in Lyons, and the work of the city's Aumône continued to evolve around them.

The main task of the Aumône was to organize bread distribution; the old who could not eat bread were given money instead, while the 'shamefaced poor' had bread and money brought to them at home. The rest of the poor also sometimes received a small amount of money together with their bread ration. The distributions were strictly controlled: only those who had been resident in Lyons for at least seven years and were genuinely unable to work were eligible, and systematic checks were made to prevent cheating and fraud. The total number of those who received such support is difficult to estimate; in normal times, not counting critical periods such as 1531 (when eight thousand paupers received aid) or 1596–7 (when their number rose to ten thousand), the Aumône must have looked after about three thousand people. These three thousand represented 5 per cent of the city's population. Most of them were hired labourers: the registers for the years 1534–9 show that 41 per cent were day-labourers and the rest artisans, mostly in the textile industry. For many of them the distributions were probably no more than a temporary and provisional form of aid, to fall back upon when seasonal work was scarce or market demand for their products fell. The distributions were well regulated: they took place once a week, in the presence of guards and officials who maintained order and made sure that all those who came up to receive their share were on the list of eligible poor. A 1539 woodcut which illustrates a brochure about the work of the Lyons Aumône depicts one such distribution: the rectors of the Aumône are seated at a table, one of them checking off names on his list; flunkeys are distributing bread and money, while a crowd of beggars – cripples, paupers in rags, women carrying children – form an orderly queue, each waiting his turn.

The Lyons Aumône also tried to find an efficient solution to the problem of orphans and foundlings. In theory it was supposed to adopt them, send them to school and make sure they were taught a trade. In practice, however, it did its best to apprentice them to a trade or send them into domestic service as soon as it could. The principle of 'support through work' which lay at the centre of the new social policy was thus put into practice. Its implementation was made much easier in 1536, with the arrival in Lyons of the silk manufacturing industry; it was here that the Aumône sought to place the children in its care, and the Italian experts in the field who were brought in to teach this trade were told that their primary task was to train the poor. Many of those who launched new branches of industry in Lyons were also proponents of social reform and rectors of the Aumône.

In addition to this, the Aumône was also obliged to act as an organ of repression, and to do its best to enforce the law against public begging. Most of its efforts in this area, however, were in vain. It was also to combat vagrancy and idleness and control the influx of alien paupers into the city. For this purpose it was allotted first four and later six *chasse-coquins*, whose task it was to maintain order during the alms distributions and arrest those who accosted individuals to beg for alms. They were also posted at the city gates to prevent alien paupers from entering. As an additional measure, boats on the Saône and the Rhône were forbidden from transporting beggars into the city. But the frequency with which orders for alien beggars to leave the city were renewed testify to the inefficacy of all these measures.

In order to enforce these laws, the Aumône was endowed with judiciary and police powers, and it could count on the support of the authorities whenever repressive measures had to be taken against vagrants and recalcitrant beggars. Forced labour – paupers employed at public works in Lyons were not paid, only given food – was a common form of punishment and re-education for vagrants, who worked in chains. A sixteenth-century Lyons historian writes that, 'in order to maintain order and make efficient use of the police of the Aumône Générale, coercion and terror were necessary to curb certain beggars who were inclined to be turbulent and recalcitrant and refused to obey the rectors' ('*pour la conservation de l'ordre et police de ceste aumosne tant generale, il a esté besoing d'une coercion et terreur, pour tenir en cervelle et en bride aucuns des povres qui sont turbulens et refractaires, et qui ne veulent prester obeissance aux recteurs*').[7] The authorities placed at the Aumône's disposal one of the towers in the city walls, for use as dungeons: thus it also had its own prison for beggars. Imprisonment was of course a practical way of maintaining order, but it was also symbolic of the need for terror and coercion in implementing the new social policy. The repressive aspect of the Aumône's activities met with disapproval in some circles, especially among ordinary working people, who felt a certain solidarity with paupers and the unemployed and condemned their persecution. There were even some riots and skirmishes with the police, when crowds would set upon the guards of a pauper who had been arrested and try to wrest him from their grasp. While the social and intellectual elite may have accepted the new social policy and the new doctrine of charity, the rest of the population did not immediately follow suit.

4.2   Spain: Valladolid

In most European countries central legislation on social aid evolved in much the same way as it did in France, the Netherlands and England. Only Scotland took a slightly different line: the Scottish Poor Law of 1535 limited itself to recommendations of a general nature, appealing, for example, to the able-bodied poor to seek work and forbidding them to beg or solicit aid. At the same time, however, it permitted the old and infirm to beg within their own parishes, in other words in their place of birth.

In Spain, on the other hand, the problem of beggary and vagrancy remained the province of local authorities. There was no central government initiative to reform the system of social aid, nor were any measures taken to curb beggary and impose limits, either *de facto* or *de jure*, on the traditional system of individual alms-giving. On the contrary, the royal court tended rather to disapprove, on doctrinal grounds, of the efforts of the local authorities; some of the bitter polemics against the new system of social aid that one comes across in seventeenth-century literature echo this disapproval, and indeed seem, at times, to have drawn their inspiration from the royal court. And yet Spain was a country in which poverty was increasing at a dramatic rate and public order was being seriously threatened by vagrancy on a scale comparable with, if not greater than, that in other European countries – a curious and interesting case of so intransigent an attachment to ideological principles on the part of a state as to produce complete indifference to the country's real and urgent needs.

In the sixteenth century Valladolid was a wealthy city. Because of its wealth it was also, according to the historian Bartolomé Bennassar, a haven for the poor, for alms were distributed there more lavishly than in any other city of Old Castille. The sixteenth-century poet

Dámaso de Frías claimed that there were many poor in Valladolid because of the large number of charitable institutions to be found there; in years of bad harvests the poor would flock into Valladolid from Galicia, Asturia and the mountains, secure in the knowledge that here they would find support instead of being expelled after two or three days, as would happen in any other city. Valladolid also had its own poor, who received permanent and regular support; the registers for 1561 show six hundred and thirty-three poor families, about 9.5 per cent of the population. It is significant that, of these, only eighty were working families, the rest seeming to depend entirely on charity. The poor in Valladolid were in fact much more numerous than would at first appear, for the 1561 registers did not include poor people in the city's many hospitals and shelters, nor did they take account of abandoned children in the care of charitable institutions. Indeed the sixteenth-century reformists might well have cited the example of Valladolid to support their claim that the rate of poverty was high wherever alms were generous, were it not for the fact that in other cities the poor made up a much larger percentage of the population. In Segovia, a prominent centre of the textile industry, the poor made up 15.7 per cent of the population (although it must be said that most of them worked). Things were far worse in the little towns of Estremadura: registers from 1557 show 1,900 poor of a population of 7,400 in Cáceres, and 3,500 by 1595, when the town counted only 8,300 inhabitants; in Trujillo, in 1597, the poor made up half of the population, estimated at 9,560. As in previous cases, however, we must keep in mind that the criteria of wealth and poverty established for the purpose of these registers were largely arbitrary and constantly in flux; these statistics, no less than others mentioned earlier, must therefore be approached with a degree of circumspection.

The remark made by Dámaso de Frías, to the effect that other cities expelled victims of rural poverty, indicates that Spanish cities adopted the usual European policy of defence against hordes of 'alien beggars'. Valladolid, too, had occasional recourse to such measures – in 1517, for example, and also in 1575 – but hospice registers tend rather to confirm its generosity. In 1579 only thirty-one out of fifty-seven children in the Valladolid children's hospice were native to the town, and in 1589 only thirty out of a total of seventy-four; the rest had all come from elsewhere, sometimes from very distant provinces. Nevertheless, some efforts to limit vagrancy were made, by methods similar to those used in other cities. The municipal authorities appointed an *alguazil*, a paid official, to deal with the problem. In 1597 a census of the poor was taken, from which it emerged that only three hundred and ten of them were eligible for permanent support, and these were given certificates to that effect.

The Valladolid census was only part of a much larger operation, carried out on a nationwide scale and set in motion by the government. A similar census was taken in the same year in Seville, where all the city's beggars were ordered to assemble at the de la Sangre hospital in order to obtain their certificates. A Seville chronicler describes a crowd of two thousand people, men and women, healthy and sick, young and old, able-bodied and infirm, who gathered there. The sick were placed in hospitals, the infirm provided with certificates and the healthy ordered to find employment of some kind within three days, on pain of flogging and expulsion. This was not the first time that such measures were applied on the Iberian Peninsula; we have seen the authorities taking similar steps both in the middle of the fourteenth century and in the 1520s.

In 1540 the Castillian cities of Valladolid, Zamora and Salamanca decided to subject beggars to a degree of administrative control. In the same year Charles V issued an edict on social aid, in which he decreed that there would henceforth be no more than one hospital for every town – clearly a step towards centralization – and demanded that the administration of social aid be tightened and put in order, so that the genuine poor might be assured of permanent support and prevented from begging in the streets. In cities the poor were to be placed in the hospital while collections were made on their behalf by persons designated for the task. However, this decree, similar in spirit to the imperial edict of 1531, met with opposition from theologians and, after a flurry of controversy, died a silent death. With the reign of Philip II, such a conception of social reform was definitively ruled out.

The problem of vagrancy, however, remained; the Cortes returned again and again to the debate on the best way of forcing the idle to work. Among other measures it was proposed that an official, a *padre de pobres*, be appointed for each parish to find work for the able-bodied poor, so that they might no longer use their inability to find work as an excuse for idleness. The fight against vagrancy, considered necessary to the maintenance of public order, drew its support from the condemnation of idleness inherent in Christian doctrine and elaborated in early Spanish economic thought. For the extirpation of beggary, however, there was no such justification; nor was there any doctrinal support for reforming the system of social aid. Indeed, the unequivocal praise of individual charity inherent in the decisions of the Council of Trent left little room for reconciling Christian orthodoxy with any kind of reform of social aid. The urgent needs of the moment, however, inevitably led to some changes. The royal ordinance of 1565, Trindentine in spirit, recommended that all parishes look after their poor, especially the 'shamefaced poor'. At the end of the century the situation began to deteriorate rapidly: Cristóbal Pérez de Herrera speaks in a memoir of a hundred and fifty thousand beggars in Spain; in 1608 he mentions half a million, and by 1617 a million. These figures, while of doubtful statistical value, do at least indicate the scale of the problem and an awareness of it. The growing social and economic problems that Spain experienced in the 1590s explain the proliferation of measures against beggars, measures which many cities now found themselves having to introduce; they explain, too, the frequent allusions to poverty to be found in the literature of the period, and the new vigour with which the theme was treated. Throughout the sixteenth century poverty nonetheless continued, in Spain, to be seen primarily as an ideological problem, a doctrinal issue in polemics about the reform of social aid and the orthodox view of charity. It is no doubt for this reason that the authorities were reluctant to interfere in what the Church and the theologians considered to be their own domain, and it was this fear of controversy which slowed the process of reform.

4.3 England: the Edicts of Henry VIII and Elizabethan Poor Law

While Charles V's edict for the Netherlands set out the basic principles of reform, which had then only to be put into practice, the royal ordinances concerning France left the choice of suitable measures entirely up to the municipal authorities in each town. In both cases the extirpation of beggary was the dominant preoccupation, with the emphasis on prohibiting public begging. In England, where the problem was equally acute, edicts outlawing public beggary were only the prelude to a much broader reorganization of social aid.

The historian E. M. Leonard distinguishes three stages in the development of social aid in England in the sixteenth century: the years from 1514 to 1568, when reforms were initiated mainly by individual cities; those from 1569 to 1597, when legislation began to play a larger role; and, finally, the period after 1597, when the problem was dealt with by the Privy Council, whose decisions were handed down to local courts. It was only in this last stage, she argues, that the programme of restructuring aid to the poor in England was carried out successfully and efficiently. Nevertheless, in the course of the sixteenth century the king made a number of attempts to deal with the problem. Most of these took the form of laws against vagrancy, involving punishments much more cruel and severe than those on the continent. In order to make these measures effective it was necessary to set up a general system of control over the poor and restrict public begging, or even forbid it entirely.

The edict of 1531 proclaimed by Henry VIII (22, Henry VIII, cap. 12) ordered justices of the peace in the countryside, and bailiffs and mayors in towns, to take a census of the poor in their area and draw up a list of those who were genuinely unable to work as a result of age, sickness or infirmity; these were to receive a certificate enabling them to beg in a specified area. Those caught begging without a certificate or outside their designated area were subject to arrest. But the main burden of helping the truly indigent rested above all on the community and the framework of neighbourly relations. Beggars who were sound of body, on the other hand, were to be flogged, while those who gave them alms were subject to fines. A few years later, in 1535, Henry VIII proclaimed a further edict (27, Henry VIII, cap. 25) ordering local and county authorities to provide support for the poor and infirm and work for those who were capable of it. The children of beggars, all those between the ages of five and fourteen, were to be sent, by force if necessary, to be apprenticed with craftsmen. The residents of each town were to create, through the 'voluntary and charitable giving of alms', a fund for the care of the needy. Alms were not to be given directly to individual beggars; they were to be collected by officials designated for this task and put into the central fund. Only monasteries and the nobility were permitted to distribute alms individually; everyone else might do so only in certain well-defined cases, limited to fellow parishioners, the blind and ship-wrecked sailors.

There are two things to be noted about this edict: it did not forbid beggary, but rather subjected it to strict controls; and it stressed that the financing of social aid was to be based on voluntary contributions.

In his decrees and recommendations the king appealed to both lay and clerical authorities, and the commissions appointed to collect funds were similarly mixed. Later royal edicts gradually began to place increasing emphasis on the collection of funds: Edward VI and Mary urged the authorities to impress upon the populace the importance of charitable contributions, and by the time of Elizabeth's reign such contributions had become obligatory. In English historiography the dissolution of the monasteries in 1536 and 1539 is traditionally seen as being central to the growth of poverty and the deterioration of living conditions among the poor in England, and indeed alms distributions fell sharply at that time, while the secularization of Church property served only to enrich the king and the court elite.

We have seen that there was a clear link, in the 1520s in England, between poverty and unemployment. Manipulation of the labour market in order to reduce poverty was a constant feature of English social policy throughout the sixteenth century, reflected both in legislation against vagrants and in the organization of social aid. The most important document in this regard was the 'statute on artisans' of 1563. It defined the conditions on which labourers might be hired – for example, by imposing, for some groups of craftsmen, a minimum contract of one year; but above all it made work obligatory: by this law all bachelors and those under thirty years of age who could not find work in their profession had to agree to some other kind of work, in another branch and at wages fixed by the justice of the peace. In addition, all men between the ages of twenty and sixty who had no profession and were unable to find work were to be placed, at the same wage, as servants in the households of landed gentry.

A decisive measure in the development of legislation in Elizabethan England was the 'poor law' which came into existence at the turn of the sixteenth century.

During the period from 1594 to 1597 England witnessed a succession of particularly poor harvests, with grain prices fourfold or even fivefold what they had been in previous years. This led to a series of revolts. On 5 November 1597, during a Commons debate on a law against grain speculation, Francis Bacon spoke critically of the Enclosure Acts: 'For Inclosure of grounds brings depopulation [of the countryside], which brings first idleness; secondly, decay of tillage; thirdly, subversion of houses, and decay of charity and charges to the poor; fourthly, impoverishing the state of the realm'. The Commons appointed a commission to look into the matter of enclosures; this done, it was to apply itself to the problem of poverty. Animated debates went on in both Houses about a variety of proposed laws dealing with reformatories and houses of correction, the collection of funds for the poor, the organization of hospitals, parish aid for the blind and the aged, the 'extirpation of beggary', and so forth. The result of these studies and discussions was a series of measures dealing with different aspects of poverty and vagrancy.

With this legislation the central role in all aspects of social aid was entrusted to so-called overseers of the poor, appointed annually by justices of the peace. They were responsible, together with parish representatives, for sending children of the poor to be apprenticed to a trade, finding work for the unemployed (to which end they were provided with a permanent supply of raw materials) and looking after the crippled and infirm, for whom they were also to supervise the building of shelters and hospices. Funds for the care of the poor were to be provided through a special tax. Begging was permitted only in the beggar's own parish, and only for food. Alms might also be given to soldiers and sailors returning home; and justices of the peace were required to find them work or support of some kind in their home towns.

All these measures in fact introduced little that was new to the situation of the preceding years: the basic principles of social aid had already been set down in earlier legislation. The office of 'overseer of the poor', for example, had been in existence since 1536. The structure of social aid debated by Parliament emerged gradually from practice, shaped by the experiences of particular towns. London was, of course, the most important model; much of the subsequent legislation was based on what took place there. The legislation of 1597–8, however, was particularly significant in that it codified all these experiences and presented them as official government policy. Initially intended, when drawn up, to apply only for a year, these laws became the basis of government policy for many years to come, and in 1601 they were given their final formulation. The 1601 version differed only slightly from that of 1597–8. It specified in greater detail the principles on which aid to the poor and the methods of financing it through special taxes were to be administered; and it did away with a number of proposed measures which were no doubt thought to be unrealistic. One measure abandoned in this way was a clause whereby anyone found begging publicly for any form of alms other than food was to be considered a vagrant. Such a measure would have gone against the traditions of individual charity, a system that Parliament wanted to maintain, seeing it as a parallel form of aid which could exist alongside public charitable institutions; later parliamentary legislation was to confirm this conservative tendency. From this point on, however, three basic principles formed the doctrine behind the new social policy: institutional aid to the poor, job creation (alongside complementary measures imposing work on the able-bodied) and the repression of vagrants; these three principles were reflected both in royal decrees and in local practice. The law of 1601 (or, more strictly, of 1597–1601) was known as the Poor Law of the Elizabethan age; its permanence as law was confirmed in 1640 – the 1601 legislation having been intended as a provisional measure enforceable only for a year – and it remained the legal basis for the system of social aid in England until the great reform of 1834.

4.4 The Organization of English Social Aid

In England new policies were implemented in stages, and even though reform sometimes seemed slow in comparison with the continent, by the end of the sixteenth century it had more than caught up, and seemed more successful than in France. The more coherent and systematic nature of royal legislation in England is sometimes invoked to explain the divergence, but, as we have seen, other events which took place in the course of the sixteenth century make this unlikely. Equally unlikely as an explanation is the often stressed efficiency of English local authorities in implementing reform, although England's efforts to reform her administrative structures, more advanced than in other countries, certainly played a role in the successful implementation of the new social policies. The essential difference lies in the fact that the transformation of the agrarian system and of city economies in England was much further advanced than elsewhere. This fact had a specific effect on the structure of social aid in England before the Elizabethan Poor Law and during its application.

Already in the course of the first half of the sixteenth century a few cities followed London's example in taking precautionary measures. Bristol, for example, in 1522, and then Canterbury in 1552, bought up stocks of grain which could, if necessary, be sold to the poor in order to prevent speculation and price rises. In Lincoln in 1543 the local authorities ordered all the poor to present themselves before a court, where their eligibility for support was assessed. Those who qualified were given special markers to wear as a sign of their right to beg, and it was forbidden to give alms to any beggar not wearing such a sign. In 1547 the authorities of Lincoln took additional measures intended to force beggars to work, and in particular to find them places as domestic servants. In 1551 young 'idlers' were placed with drapers for a period of eight to nine years, during which time they were to work only for their food, without pay, on pain of expulsion from the city. In Ipswich in 1551 special commissioners were appointed to draw up lists of the poor in each parish. A tax for the benefit of the poor was levied, beggars were forced to wear distinguishing signs, and a municipal hospital was built to serve as a refuge for children and for the old.

The 1570s saw growing pressure to root out public begging, and plans were afoot to organize a permanent system of support for the 'genuine poor', funded through a special tax levied on all parishioners. The London law of 1579 made the parish 'controllers' of the poor responsible for providing aid to the sick and infirm, while the municipal authorities were charged with making sure that work was found for vagrants. Parish officials were to maintain up to date the registers of their poor and exercise strict control, sometimes to the extent of daily visits to the houses of some poor, to make sure that no one who was capable of it shirked work. In 1547 a fund for the poor was established in London, using money from special levies imposed for the purpose, and in 1572 the Poor Statute extended this type of obligatory tax to all towns in England. In all cases, however, both in London and in provincial cities, there were complaints of bad financial management or insufficient resources. Against this background the town of Norwich, in the east of England, appears as a particularly interesting example of how social aid was organized in the country in the 1570s.

In 1565 the Norwich municipal authorities took over from the local chapter the running of St Paul's hospice, at once a refuge for 'alien poor', a correctional institution for vagrants and an alms distribution centre. In previous years Norwich had not run into particular difficulties in providing aid to the poor, but growing social tensions in the city and its environs made the authorities and the propertied classes uneasy. Their feelings of foreboding were justified, for in 1549 large sections of the local population took part in the Cade uprising. In 1570 the Mayor of Norwich complained of the intolerable plague of vagrants in the city. This last, however, is not confirmed by historical sources, according to which only twenty-five or thirty vagrants at most were arrested each year, a small number compared with other places. But the authorities lived in permanent fear of revolt among the city's poor, and were anxious to contain the explosion by taking preventive measures in good time.

A census was taken and revealed that, of the city's 13,000 inhabitants, 2,342 were paupers, 1,335 of them adults. Only two hundred and seventy-two of these, or 18 per cent of adult paupers, were receiving some form of permanent support. Many of those whose names figured on the list gave some sort of profession, but in fact most of them lived by begging in the streets and from house to house. The city's authorities offered a typical explanation of this, namely that the citizens of Norwich were so generous in their alms-giving that the poor saw no advantage in seeking work. The municipal decree which installed a new system of social aid even described beggars as well-fed swindlers who pretended to be starving in order to collect alms: in fact, the decree said, they gorged themselves on huge amounts of food, and threw away what they could not eat. Because they never changed their clothes, they were carriers of disease; and if they spent their nights under church porticos, cellars and attics, this was only because they could not be bothered to find somewhere decent to sleep. This diatribe against vagrants was not, however, aimed at the city's registered poor, for the lists did not include the homeless.

As a result of the census a few paupers — a very small number — were expelled from the city, while the remainder was divided into three categories: the 'able-bodied', the 'infirm' and the 'indifferent', this last category probably applying to borderline cases where it was difficult to decide one way or the other. It is significant that, of these categories, the first was by far the largest: in one area only fourteen out of eighty-four men, thirteen out of a hundred and thirty-four women, and sixty-nine out of a hundred and seventy-nine children were found to be incapable of work and classified as such. The registers regularly listed children as young as seven as working. Those incapable of work and classified as 'infirm' were to receive regular support, the amount of which was strictly determined; some of them might also, from time to time, be given small jobs to do. Incorrigible 'idlers' were to be subjected to forced labour in a correctional institution run by the mayor, twelve at a time for a period of three weeks; they were to work from dawn to dusk, and those who refused to work would go without food. For women and children the city hired special female guardians who, besides making sure that everyone worked, were also responsible for teaching the children to read and write; each was in charge of six to twelve people. Those able to procure tools and raw materials were authorized to sell the products of their work, while the rest had to be content with a wage set by their guards, who were also empowered to administer the lash where necessary. The city regularly bought stocks of raw materials to provide work for those among the poor who were capable of it, and two hospitals were to feed and take care of the sick.

The introduction of this system was accompanied by a total ban on begging, on pain of flogging; conversely, anyone caught giving alms directly to a beggar was subject to a fine. The system as a whole was funded through taxes; individual parishes were no longer responsible for 'their' poor, so that the wealthier parishes might pass on some of their collected funds to the poorer ones, thus ensuring a uniform system of aid throughout the city.

The Norwich reforms were accepted, and took root; both the repressive measures and the system of social aid were efficient and successful. At the end of a year the balance was positive: after much detailed calculation, the authorities of Norwich concluded that the city, far from being financially overburdened, was making a profit, insofar as it was saving money by forcing idlers to work. The annual profits from the new system of aid were calculated at 2,818 pounds, one shilling and fourpence. It is extremely revealing that the advantages accruing from these reforms should have been calculated in financial terms, as an item in the city's collective book-keeping. The example of Norwich brings out forcefully the extent to which the element of rationality, the economic and bourgeois view of charitable activity and the evaluation of charity in monetary terms played a role in the successful development of the new social policy.

The 1570 census also provides a more detailed glimpse into the lives of those whom the city authorities classified as poor. Of the four hundred or so men listed, a hundred and eleven, or 22 per cent, were unemployed and, of these latter, forty-two were not skilled in any trade. This proportion was typical of the structure of unemployment. Most of the poor on the list had been trained for some sort of trade; more than half of them said they were artisans, and a quarter confessed to being day-labourers. But even of those who claimed to be artisans the majority were probably journeymen and hired labourers who had worked for artisans in some branch of production; only a very few can have been artisans themselves. In many cases, if the head of the household was unemployed, the women, children and other members of the family did work of various kinds. Of the local poor, and thus not counting immigrants and wandering beggars, most were able to find occasional or seasonal work. In 1570 18 per cent of the adults in the census were receiving permanent support; five years later they represented 30 per cent. This means that between 70 and 80 per cent of the adult poor in the Norwich census could be defined as proletarian: for them, for their wives and for their children, hired labour was the sole source of income, often insufficient even for basic needs.

The situation in Norwich seems to have been a case of 'taming poverty', making it a part of the daily lives of the city's residents. The reforms were initially inspired by fear of social unrest in the face of growing poverty. Did the new social policy succeed in laying those fears to rest? It is difficult to say. Certainly it integrated the poor into the community, and provided aid which, modest though it was, did give some stability to their lives. It reinforced the work ethic by keeping this support to a bare minimum and creating jobs for the unemployed. The threat of repressive measures ensured the system's continued functioning: punishment was swift and severe, based in theory on the royal legislation against vagrants but in practice dependent on the local apparatus of control, of which the special female guards for women and children are an example. The workhouse was a central element in this system of repressive measures: its prison regulations and its large turnover (although its capacity at any one time was small, over two hundred inmates passed annually through its doors) were strong deterrents. The problem of children had a central place in the programme. They represented over 40 per cent of the poor on the list, but for the most part continued to live with their families. An effort was made to train them and find them work in the appropriate trade. The same was done for orphans and foundlings, and for the girls a dowry was provided so that they might be able to found a family. Such attempts at education were a way of dealing with demographic growth. They were also a way of exploiting minors as a labour force, a form of exploitation developed by early capitalism. The combination of all this – the stabilizing of the labour market, the rigorous policy of repression and an organized system of aid – could

indeed 'tame' poverty and integrate it into the life of society. It is in
this respect that the system introduced in Norwich may be considered
a model one, for it enabled the city to control even the explosive
situation of the last, critical years of the sixteenth century.

The Poor Law of 1597–1601 did not bring with it any great
changes, apart from codifying the social policy and translating local
experiences into law. It also became the main point of reference for
English cities considering any sort of reform. Here, as in French cities,
new principles and institutions were established gradually, through
successive experiments. The reforms undertaken by the local authorities in Salisbury are a good illustration of this process.

For Salisbury, as for other English cities, the last years of the
sixteenth century were years of crisis. Bad harvests caused prices to
spiral, disease and malnutrition were rife among the poor, and the
growing plague of beggars awakened fears that the epidemic would
spread. Vagrants came to Salisbury in droves: in 1598 nearly a hundred were caught and flogged, most of them impoverished peasants
from the surrounding countryside. Half of them were women, which
is significant, for in normal years almost the only vagrants seen were
men without families. The epidemic continued for several years, and
the authorities were forced to increase aid for poor families in quaran-
tine. During the period from May 1604 to May 1605 one-fifth of the
city's population is thought to have received aid because of the
epidemic.

The epidemic died out, but the city was still in difficulties. The
textile industry in particular was feeling the effects of the economic
depression: the market was in a slump and demand was low. Unemployment was growing, and more and more people were in need of
support. In the 1620s the local authorities estimated that almost half
the city's population had been pauperized; the number of poor was
close to three thousand. It must be said, however, that this figure was
brought out mainly to impress upon central government the gravity
of Salisbury's plight: its total population was about six and a half
thousand. In 1625 a census of the poor was taken: the resulting list
contained two hundred and sixty-three names. Of these one hundred
and forty-one were unemployed, and they were to be placed with
master artisans. Forty-one were children – these were apprenticed.
The remaining eighty-one were incapable of work, and were entirely
dependent on whatever support the authorities could provide. This
census, however, encompassed only those poor who qualified for sup-

port by virtue of their condition: widows, children, the infirm. And indeed, of the adults in the census the overwhelming majority were widows. In the census as a whole, children and adolescents formed the largest group: one hundred and thirty-three children under the age of fourteen, and a further twenty between fifteen and nineteen. Only four of them were classified as unable to work; of the rest, ninety-two in the under-fourteen age group – including one child not yet five years old – were found places with master artisans and twenty were apprenticed.

Despite the new social policy, however, the criteria applied to the narrowly defined groups of poor included in the 1625 census were still firmly anchored in the old conception of poverty. Many things had changed: the city as a whole took over the administration of aid; professional training was provided and jobs created in order to integrate the poor into society. And yet the traditional view of poverty and the poor remained immutable. It was not until the critical years of the first quarter of the seventeenth century, when bad harvests, disease and a depressed market led to mass pauperization, that the traditional image of poverty was laid to rest.

As the English historian Paul Slack has shown, the old image of poverty began to dissolve in the 1620s. A census of the poor taken in Salisbury in 1635 already reveals a huge numerical disproportion between, on the one hand, the poor who received support, and fitted the traditional image, and, on the other, a great mass of equally genuine poor who received no support because they did not fit in with the traditional doctrine of charity; this census showed how limited and inadequate was the traditionally accepted definition of poverty in the face of pauperization on a huge scale. The parish of St Martin, with about 1,650 inhabitants, supported sixty-five poor, or 3.6 per cent of its population; this was more or less the same proportion as in Salisbury in 1625. At the same time, however, still in 1635, and in this same parish, the census-takers discovered that five hundred and ninety-five people, or 33 per cent of the population, belonged in this category. The criteria applied to obtain this new figure were clearly different: the new definition of poverty now encompassed the slum-dwellers on the outskirts of Salisbury, who worked for a living sporadically whenever work was to be had. The old distiction between the vagrant and the 'legitimate' pauper, who had a right to support because of his condition – age, sickness or infirmity – was being blurred. 'Vagrants' were no longer perceived as another category of poor people: they were dangerous criminals belonging to the margins of society, and were mercilessly hunted down, in Salisbury as everywhere else. Working families, pauperized by low wages and unemployment, now became the primary concern. They were townpeople, integrated into the community and prepared to work hard; they were unemployed because no work was to be had, and the community of which they were a part saw the need to provide them with support. By the 1590s Salisbury had made considerable progress in modernizing its system of social aid: charitable institutions had been centralized; commissions for the poor, composed of church men and lay overseers, had been established; a correctional institution and workhouse was created, with a capacity, in 1602, for six men and six women. The financial groundwork for the running of the new system was laid. But the problem of unemployment remained, and much broader political horizons were required, together with greater funds and more flexible methods, before it could be solved.

This state of affairs led to the gradual formation of a pressure group composed of Salisbury's Puritanical elite. Combining rigour and religious fervour with an eagerness to restore some measure of social equilibrium through a programme of reform, and guided by their experiences in local government, the members of this group set about putting into practice a policy on unemployment, long established in theory but not yet implemented. In accordance with this policy, the city hired women to train the poor for a trade; the scheme covered the costs of two years of training for a few dozen poor youths, undertook a detailed survey among artisans to determine how many of them could provide work for the poor, and decreed that the workhouse, in addition to its role as a correctional institution, should henceforth make room for a number of children, who would learn a trade within its walls.

Salisbury also launched itself into an entirely new enterprise in this domain, with the creation of a brewery; the profits from this were to go to the poor, for the revenue from the poor tax alone had proved insufficient to cover the costs of the new programme. This was somewhat paradoxical as a solution: already the Puritans among the local politicians were scandalized at the scale of alcoholism in the city, especially among the poor. 'Many beggars', wrote one observer, 'do not hesitate to spend all they have in inns; the poor drink to excess to forget their troubles, and also because they have nothing more to lose.'[8] Inns had mushroomed in the city: there was one per sixty-five inhabitants. All efforts to reduce them to a more reasonable number proved utterly in vain. Thus it was that the city, seeing that it could not win against alcoholism, decided, while continuing to condemn it, that it might at least be turned to some profit. This ingenious solution was soon adopted by other English cities. The authorities also decided to place collection boxes for the poor in a prominent position outside each inn, and to post two beggars permanently beside them, the better to remind passers-by of their charitable duties and elicit their compassion.

Finally, a step forward was taken in the traditional domain of stocking provisions. A warehouse was built for storing bread, butter, cheese, beer and fuel, to be sold to the poor at cost price in the event of a crisis; for the poor, who had no stocks of food, were always hardest hit by speculation and the resulting price increases. Those who depended on permanent support were now given special coupons which, presented at the warehouse, could be exchanged for food and fuel. This method also had the advantage of giving the authorities some control over the way in which the poor disposed of their alms.

Despite its efficiency, the new programme of reform soon became an object of conflict, both on a local and on a state level. A sustained and uncompromising battle was fought against it by the local brewers, a powerful and influential group in the city who saw the new policy as a threat to their interests. The new policy was also attacked by the clergy and the local chapter, who were opposed to the increased burden of obligatory contributions in aid of the poor, and alleged that social aid had been better organized before 1612, when it was in the power of the bishop.

But it was above all when faced with practical realities that the new policy proved unequal to the task it had set itself. The funds available to the charitable institutions of Salisbury were sufficient to support only a very limited number of people, and the stocks in the warehouse could feed no more than sixty or seventy. If the number of poor in need of support rose, the city was helpless. Moreover, the authorities were constantly having to deal with various expressions of popular discontent, riots and uprisings among the poor. Even the seclusion of the poor in fever-hospitals and pest-houses provoked rebellion. In 1627 a crowd flung curses at the mayor; one woman shouted, 'Were you born of woman or of beast, that your treatment of people of this condition [i.e., the poor] should be so bloody?' The textile industry of Salisbury was still foundering; bad harvests succeeded one another with monotonous regularity; the plague returned. The reform of social aid could do nothing to assuage these ills, and poverty remained vast and threatening.

Every few years a crisis would come, identical to the last, and every year the authorities resorted to the same methods of dealing with it. This cycle of crises revealed the limitations of a reform which aimed to eliminate the symptoms without going to the root of the evil. In this sense, in Salisbury and elsewhere, the reform of social policy was not, as R. H. Tawney put it, 'a cure for poverty, merely a palliative'.[9]

The role of the Puritans in developing the programme of reform involves social questions of broader significance, and deserves to be looked at more closely. English historiography has traditionally stressed the unusually severe social policies developed during the period of Puritan influence, and in particular the Puritan dislike of municipal charitable institutions and their activities. Monographic studies of what went on in particular cities and regions do not support this position. The crisis which shook the English system of social aid during the years of revolution was owing not to the influence of Puritan ideology but to a combination of nationwide discontent, a depressed industry and changes in the ruling administration. It is true that the Puritans looked with great distaste upon beggary as a phenomenon, seeing public begging as contrary to the divine order of things and inimical to the organization of a Christian community. But such a view was hardly unknown in the modern era: efforts to eliminate public begging entirely were made, at one time or another, almost everywhere, albeit, it must be said, to very little effect. What is unusual in the Puritans is rather the rigour and determination with which they acted, their will to succeed and the zeal with which they sought to carry out their aims – features characteristic of the modern mentality which, according to Max Weber, favoured or perhaps even largely determined the evolution of capitalism. The group which came to power after 1540 was indeed fired by a spirit of 'political activism' and by a desire to impose a rational order on the administration of the country: hence their strict imposition of the work ethic and their insistence on rigorous adherence to its principles. But there is nothing to suggest that the Puritan aversion to begging as a phenomenon was accompanied by a similar dislike of beggars themselves.

Indeed, quite the opposite: William K. Jordan's studies of English philanthropy in the modern era show that the Puritans, far from being incapable of feeling pity for beggars and exhibiting compassion in the face of human misery, actively tried to better the lot of the poor by individual acts of charity, such as donations and legacies to charitable institutions. Individual legacies began to decline sharply during the decade preceding the revolution; during the revolutionary decade, between 1641 and 1650, they amounted to half of what they had been between 1621 and 1630. Between 1651 and 1660, when the Puritans were in power, philanthropy was once again on the rise; the sums bequeathed during this period already surpassed, in real terms, the legacies of the pre-revolutionary decade. Thus there is nothing to support the claim which ascribes the decline of individual charity to the Puritans, nor the broader claim which holds them responsible for reducing the role of charity in social policy and similarly influencing social attitudes towards the poor.

This brief outline of the changes which took place in the organization of social aid in the modern era has made no mention of individual acts of charity which continued the Christian tradition. The tradition of individual charity endured throughout Europe in the sixteenth century, both in Catholic and in Protestant countries. William K. Jordan has shown how great a role it played in modern England. Public acts of charity remained an essential element of ritual attitudes towards life and death; they had their place in funerals and celebrations. They were also, of course, expressions of wealth, power and prestige. Thus they still had their place in social life, although they were no longer the dominant form of social aid.

The wills drawn up in the late Middle Ages often read like detailed accounts, calculated on the principle that money can buy salvation. Atonement for sins was measured in terms of the numbers of masses said, services celebrated and beggars supported. In modern times this same type of economic reasoning was applied to social aid, the sole difference being the nature of the investment: the aim was to be as effective as possible in distributing aid. Accordingly, in the evolution of the concept of charity itself one can discern the same type of social, political and psychological changes as in the municipal reforms of social aid. These reforms, which took place in sixty or seventy European cities, were the expression of a profound dissatisfaction with the traditional doctrine of charity. They were among the enormous changes which ultimately led to the formation of modern society.

5

Charitable Polemics: Local Politics and Reasons of State

Social policy was a subject of controversy, conflict and alliance between society and the various pressure groups within it, between lay institutions and the Church, between local administrations and central government. Its origins lay in acute socio-economic crises and in the radical transformations taking place in the social structure. Institutional reform of charity was accompanied by profound changes in collective attitudes; these changes were slow, gradual and not always consistent in their direction. Reform, regardless of its scope and degree of efficiency in particular towns, regions and countries, was far from being unanimously accepted by local populations; attitudes towards poverty and work were varied, and the concept of public interest was differently interpreted in different circles. Reform and attitudes towards it were both subjects of contention and controversy, arising either from divergent interests or from differences in attitudes and perspective. Conflicts of interest arose because the wealthy were opposed to taxation for the benefit of the poor, and because the Church, wanting to defend its traditional prerogatives, as well as its wealth, was opposed to total or even partial secularization of charitable institutions and hospitals. Differences in attitude arose because the popular strata of local society felt a measure of solidarity with beggars and vagrants and were opposed to their persecution, and because the laws against public begging and distributing alms denied expression to human and Christian feelings of solidarity with others, stifled the natural human instincts of charity and compassion, and made it impossible to affirm one's wealth and social status and demonstrate one's beneficence by giving alms. Such conflicts were played out both on the national level, in government debates, and locally, where they were a constant impediment to the progress of reforms. They also had an important place in the vast ideological and polemical literature on the subject of social theory.

There is a certain historiographical tradition which treats these discussions of social theory as a separate and autonomous subject of study, detached from the surrounding social context. Indeed, this tradition views the theories as more significant than their social context: they are considered as the driving force behind the new social policy and structure of social aid, and the writers and thinkers who developed them as the inventors of the 'modern reform of charity' and of the 'new philanthropy' – although this latter term did not come into being until the eighteenth century. One cannot reject these claims entirely. Even admitting, as we have tried to show, that pauperization on an unprecedented scale lay at the root of the new social policy and the change in attitudes towards poverty, it nevertheless remains true that ideological controversies concerning poverty and charity in the sixteenth century had an enormous role to play. They should be seen above all as attempts, on the part of contemporary observers, to articulate their awareness of the social problems besetting their era.

Attitudes towards the poor were a particularly prominent subject of debate during the Reformation. Criticism of the medieval doctrine of charity figured largely in arguments against the Catholic model of piety; in addition to its role in attacking the Catholic interpretation of 'good deeds' and the theory of predestination, it often surfaced in broader debates about Christian attitudes to social life and the proper organization of God's community on earth. It would be out of place here to embark on a detailed analysis of the social doctrine of the Reformation and of the complex relations between the Protestant ethic and the birth of capitalism; Max Weber's treatment of these issues is still a subject of controversy among historians. One aspect of the problem does, however, require some mention here, and that is Martin Luther's attitude towards the poor. An important point to remember about Luther's thought in this domain is that it was based above all on the experience of German countries, zones where the traditional agrarian structures had been maintained.

5.1 Luther's Attitude towards the Poor

The doctrine that a man's duties as a Christian and a member of the
human community are defined according to two laws – the divine law
of the gospels, which rules the kingdom of Christ, and natural law,
which governs man's kingdom on earth – was, as Ernst Troeltsch has
demonstrated, the cornerstone of Luther's social teaching. According
to this doctrine, lay authorities and legislators possess a peculiar sort
of autonomy in their running of man's kingdom, where natural law
prevails. This had important consequences for the Protestant programme of aid for the poor. In the main document laying out his
political programme, the August 1520 appeal 'To the Christian Nobility of the German Nation Concerning the Reformation of Christianity', Luther included a special section devoted to the problem of
beggars. His position was clear: 'It is of the highest importance to
extirpate beggary entirely from the Christian world. No Christian
should beg for alms.' The prohibition of begging was accompanied by
a properly organized system of aid for those poor unable to earn their
own living. The fundamental principle of this system was that each
city should assume responsibility for the care of its own beggars and
deny entry to 'alien' poor. It should not be forgotten, however, that
only the genuine poor, those who were incapable of earning a living
and had no other resources, were deserving of such solicitude. Neither
vagrants nor criminals, therefore, who merely simulate poverty,
should benefit from any extension of this aid to them. The local
authorities in each town should appoint special commissioners who,
in consultation with the parish priest and the local council, would be
responsible for organizing aid to the poor. Thus on the question of
who was to administer hospitals and charitable institutions Luther
settled for a compromise: he avoided altogether the question of the
secularization of these institutions, although it was among the most
prominent distinguishing features of the reform of municipal social
aid.

This document contains another element essential to Luther's programme, namely the recommendation that aid for the poor should be
kept within reasonable limits: 'It is enough that they do not die of
hunger or of cold.' The support provided should therefore not exceed
the bare minimum required for survival. The reasoning behind this

suggestion is clearly connected with the work ethic and the condemnation of idleness contained in the Scriptures. But it also seems to reflect a certain spirit of calculation proper to the bourgeois mentality, a spirit not without its influence on the course taken by the Reformation: it would be unjust, Luther declared, to allow some to live in idleness while others work, and to profit, and even enrich themselves, from that work, by the alms they receive.

This criticism of beggary, to which Luther returned often in his writings, had an obvious target within the Church, namely the mendicant orders; in this sense it is a prolongation of the anti-mendicant polemics of past centuries. But his main concern in the appeal 'To the Christian Nobility' was the common beggar, and this can be seen from his programme of reform of charitable institutions. His revulsion against beggary, on the grounds that it disturbed the harmony of the Christian community, went hand in hand with his detailed programme for the reform of municipal social aid.

This programme was followed up with a number of practical measures. In 1522, before his break with Luther, Andreas Karlstadt argued that begging should not be tolerated in Christian society. That same year in Wittenberg, in Luther's absence, he set about, in collaboration with the municipal council, drafting a new statute for the town. In this statute the problem of beggars received detailed treatment, and the practical measures introduced were in the spirit of Luther's recommendations. It was here, in Wittenberg, that the first 'common fund' was created for the administration of the city's hospitals and charitable institutions; it was to collect individual donations for the poor, and was the repository for the assets of secularized convents. Luther fully approved of these measures, and the following year he drafted a very similar law (*Ordnung eines gemeinen Kastens*) on the creation of a 'poor fund' in the small town of Leisnig, in Saxony. This law prescribed in great detail how aid for the poor should be administered by a Christian community. A commission, appointed and controlled by the town council, was responsible for managing the 'poor fund', keeping the accounts, which should include the amounts donated and the names of the donors, organizing alms distributions for the poor and according interest-free loans to members of the community who had fallen on hard times. Indeed the 'poor fund' was not limited to helping the poor; its aims were much broader, for it was conceived as a common fund for the use of a Christian community, which could draw on it for such expenses as were in the collective interest – for the support of the pastor, for example, or for the building of churches and schools. Initially, however, it was to serve as the financial basis for the effective enforcement of the prohibition of begging and for the organization of a system of aid to the poor.

Luther had the Leisnig statute printed and distributed, with a preface in which he urged all other towns to follow the example of Leisnig. Indeed, the establishment of 'common funds' on a large scale was one sign of the advance of Protestantism in German cities. In practice, however, such funds did not ensure the efficient functioning of social aid, for they were generally managed by the local authorities, who tended to use them for what they considered to be more pressing needs. Luther often complained of this, invoking the duty of Christian charity. In the following years it was Bugenhagen who took over the reorganization of social aid, but still in the spirit of the Master's teachings; the regulations he set out were part of a much greater task in which he was engaged, a kind of codification of the Church's provisions for the organization of Protestantism. Luther himself once more set out his ideas on begging in his preface to the German edition of the *Liber Vagatorum*, a famous tract against beggars; this was published in 1528. He wrote that princes, landed gentry and town councils would do well to heed the tract's descriptions of the ruses and swindles commonly perpetrated by beggars, for this would equip them better to recognize idlers, swindlers and vagabonds wanting to profit from the bounty of others; he therefore recommended that each town draw up a list of its poor, and ensure that support was accorded only to those with appropriate certificates authorizing them to receive alms. He added that vagrants would be weeded out if aid was limited to members of the local community.

Luther's ideas about beggars and poverty were rooted in the medieval tradition; they arose from a mixture of medieval theological doctrine and legislative practice. A number of antecedents to his programme may be found in the literature and preaching of the late Middle Ages; in addition to polemics against the mendicant orders, this literature also deals with the problem of public begging. Of Luther's precursors in this domain the most important was the Strasbourg preacher Geiler von Kayserberg, whose appeals to the municipal authorities and to the local inhabitants insisted on the need to reform social aid. He saw himself as the champion of the poor against the rich, warning the latter that the use of force was a legitimate means of survival to which the poor might resort if nothing was done for them; he even encouraged the poor to take up their axes and launch an assault upon rich men's granaries. But he was equally passionate in his condemnation of the 'bad poor', those who, despite being capable of work, preferred to extort alms by dishonest practices. The Strasbourg authorities introduced severe measures against vagrants quite early, in the second half of the fifteenth century, but these measures were not accompanied by any organized system of aid for the poor. Geiler naturally considered that the authorities had a duty to care for their poor, both by forcing idlers to work and by organizing aid for those genuinely in need. Similarly Jean Maire, a professor at the Sorbonne, wrote a commentary at the beginning of the sixteenth century on Pierre Lombard's *Sentences*, in which he grants princes and local authorities the right to outlaw public begging on condition that they also organize a system of aid for those in need.

The Leisnig programme and the appeal 'To the Christian Nobility' were also indebted to the practical experiences of late medieval towns: their attempts at elaborating a system combining both repressive measures and social aid in response to growing poverty and vagrancy were the practical models for Luther's programme.

Another source reflected in Luther's teaching is the *Liber Vagatorum*, in which he took a great interest. Together with Teseo Pini's *Mirror of Charlatans* and Sebastian Brant's *Ship of Fools*, it belonged to a popular strain of satirical literature which ruthlessly denounced and exposed the swindles perpetrated by beggars who took advantage of the medieval apotheosis of poverty, of the natural instinct towards charity, or simply of human naïvety to wheedle alms out of the unsuspecting. Monks, or beggars disguised as monks, figured prominently in this type of writing. Johannes Pauli drew upon some of its themes for his sermons in the early sixteenth century, and Luther, in his passionate denunciation of the mendicant orders and of the superficial nature of traditional piety, found its anecdotal style well suited to his aims. The social aspects of the lives of beggars which these writings described were of interest to Luther only insofar as they could be instrumental in developing his plans for a reform of ecclesiastical life and his model of Christian behaviour.

But the ancient dispute involving rival Catholic and Protestant claims to have pioneered the reform of social aid is not a proper subject of analysis here. Both Catholics and Protestants made efforts to meet the needs of their times; indeed it is the wide-ranging nature of the movement for reform that should be stressed, rather than claims on the part of particular groups, for it showed how pervasive was the sense, in all social and religious circles, of the contradictions inherent in the Christian doctrine and practice of charity. The fact that both reformers and defenders of orthodoxy took such an interest in the problem of social aid is proof more of their awareness of the growing scale of poverty than of any desire on their part for a confrontation between two religious doctrines; the polemics surrounding the subject went far beyond the bounds of a purely theological dispute.

5.2 The Influence of Erasmus, Vivés and other Individual Theorists

The internal tensions in the Christian attitude towards the poor are apparent in the writings of Erasmus, who strongly opposed the conventional forms of piety. Instead he praised the idea of *caritas* – a form of charity expressed not in frequent church-going, nor in regular devotions and recitals of prayers, but in the treatment of 'all fellow men as members of one body'. In his *Enchiridion* he explains how he understands the idea of Christian love, which should be the guiding principle of our behaviour: 'To reach out with a helping hand, gently to reprove those who have strayed and set them right, to instruct the ignorant, to raise up the fallen, to comfort the sad, to support the suffering and to succour those in need.' The true Christian, therefore, will help the poor and feel solidarity with the needy; a wasteful and frivolous life is an offence against the commandment to love one's neighbour. 'What is this? Will you feast on partridge while a member of the same body as you grits his teeth from hunger? Will your brother go naked and trembling with cold while your own clothes gather dust and decay from moths and mould?' True Christian love commands the rich man to treat his possessions as a common good of which he is merely the dispenser. For we would be in error if we assumed that the command to renounce worldly goods and to live in poverty applies only to monks; it applies to all Christians.

In Erasmus' writings the praise of work is accompanied by the condemnation of avarice. What Erasmus objects to is not so much the possession of riches as the desire for wealth; he praises not poverty itself but contempt for riches. Thus his violent criticism, in the

Moriae Encomium, of mendicant monks who 'sell their filthy beggar's poverty dear' is quite in keeping with the rest of his views. This criticism is developed in his *Colloquia*, one of which is devoted to the Franciscans. But in the *Colloquia*, which reflected living trends and debates – so much so that each new edition contained a discussion of current themes and events – Erasmus also took up the problem of ordinary beggars.

The *Convivium Religiosum*, which first appeared in the 1522 edition of the *Colloquia*, contains a polemical digression on the subject of beggars and alms-giving. Here, as in the *Enchiridion*, the problem of attitudes towards the poor is treated within a wider discussion of the principles of Christian life, surfacing in the context of Erasmus' condemnation of external and superficial forms of piety. While approving of discreet forms of aid to those 'in urgent need', Erasmus takes a dim view of the more ostentatious rites surrounding traditional forms of charity. His criticism is directed not only against monasteries and convents which exact contributions from the faithful, but also against excessive support of 'public beggars'. A city, he writes, should be responsible for feeding its own poor; it should not tolerate vagrancy, and above all it should not allow begging by the able-bodied, for they 'should be given work rather than money'. Alms should be given above all to people of proven moral worth of whose situation something is known.

The problem of beggars was a pressing one, and must, since Erasmus devotes a whole colloquium to it, have been a recurring theme in the intellectual debates of the time. The September 1524 edition of the *Colloquia* was supplemented by a dialogque between two beggars, Irides and Misoponus. This dialogue, full of rich descriptions of the swindles and tricks resorted to by professional beggars, also contains a rather curious passage in praise of poverty. Poverty, according to Irides, is a glorious condition, better than a king's. For beggars, like kings, may do as they please, without any of the worries and obligations of power. They also command universal respect, as if they were blessed messengers of God. Misoponus, who has renounced beggary and now practises alchemy for a living, replies that beggars will not be able to enjoy their freedom for much longer; for cities have announced that they will soon prohibit public begging and organize support only for those who are sick or infirm; the rest will be forced to work. When Irides asks the reason for such a plan. Misoponus explains that it is because 'they have seen great abuses of the law committed by beggars. And then, the harm that has been done by this corporation of yours!'

The tone of this text is firmer, more menacing than that of the preceding colloquium: in addition to the project of reform, Erasmus now mentions forced labour, an idea he had formulated some years previously. The principle of forced labour first appeared in European legislation in the middle of the fourteenth century; it was then conceived as an exceptional measure at a time of social crisis. By the sixteenth century, however, it had become an integral part of the programme of social reform intended to rid cities of their plagues of beggars.

It was also closely connected with a changing work ethic. This can be seen clearly in Sir Thomas More's *Utopia*. More was a friend of Erasmus, and in the imaginary land he described during his stay in Flanders in 1515 work was a universal duty, while the main function of the authorities was to weed out idleness. Everyone had to work for a living, and no one was permitted to be idle. For this reason there were no 'strong and healthy beggars concealing their sloth behind apparents signs of sickness' in Utopia. In another passage More recommends the general and wide-scale use of forced labour as a punishment for thieves and vagrants, and insists on the suppression of beggars and mendicant orders, at whom he aims a number of scathing and scornful remarks.

Praise of work, and even its glorification, was a dominant strain in sixteenth-century social thought. In spite of this, manual labour and the category of those known as *mechanici* were occasionally objects of scorn; Erasmus' intellectual elitism involved a large measure of contempt for artisans and their activities. But More's praise of work testifies to the existence of more profound changes in the collective attitudes of his era: work had become 'the principal right of man in his struggle for enrichment and mastery over his fate.'

It was in this atmosphere, when debates among municipal authorities over social reform and discussions among intellectuals about attitudes towards work and beggars, poverty and wealth were at their most heated, that Juan Luis Vivés wrote his treatise *De Subventione Pauperum*, the leading work of the humanist programme of reform. In dedicating it to the municipal councillors of Bruges he was paying homage to that city's efforts in the sphere of social reform; for his decision to write the treatise was influenced, he said, as much by his experience of Flanders as by that of Valencia, his native city. In the first book of the treatise he sets out the general principles of charity and defines the need to do good as a necessary condition for society's existence. He then goes on to analyse the reasons for the reticence sometimes evinced in this domain, citing false beggars, with their swindles and abuses of the law, as the principal cause; finally he lays down the rules of behaviour befitting the poor. The second book in its entirety deals with the details of a programme of urban social reform.

It is the duty of political rulers to care for the poor. This is Vivés' principal thesis, and he supports it with arguments of a general nature, invoking, for example, the need to maintain social harmony within the state; would a doctor, he asks, refuse to tend a patient's arms and legs on the grounds that they are too far away from the heart? The poor need looking after not only because it is harmful to the public interest if a large section of the population is idle, but also because they are spreaders of disease, and because theft, delinquency and prostitution flourish in their midst. In addition to criticizing beggars for their dishonesty and denouncing them as thieves and impostors, Vivés alludes to their neglect of Christian duties: they do not go to confession, nor even to mass, and they lead dissolute and disordered lives. It is apparent from his choice of arguments that Vivés is careful to stress his conformity with Christian doctrine; nevertheless the main point of his remarks about the duties of rulers is that secular authorities, rather than the Church, should be responsible for aid to the poor.

He develops this point with a number of detailed recommendations concerning the management and control of hospitals and other charitable institutions by the municipality. The authorities, he says, should begin by appointing special commissioners to take a census of all the poor, listing them according to their categories: residents of hospitals and shelters, the sick and the infirm, public beggars and vagrants, and those who simply live their lives of poverty at home, without begging. The next step should be to find work for all the able-bodied, mindful of God's commandment that our daily bread should be earned by the sweat of our brow: this should be impressed upon the recalcitrant. All the poor capable of working for a living should be trained in some useful trade. Many cities in Flanders complain of the lack of labour for their workshops; the authorities should therefore see to it that the poor find work with artisans and that artisans do not suffer from a lack of hands. The dissolute, the crooked, the thieving and the idle should be given the hardest work, and the most badly paid, in order that their example might serve as a deterrent to others. Those who are looking for work but have not yet had time to find it may be given temporary support to tide them over, but here, too, care should be taken that they do not remain entirely without occupation, lest they fall into the habit of idleness and sloth.

Hospitals and shelters should expel all those who have no good reason for being there; the rest may be given whatever forms of light work their sickness or disability permits. Once cured, they should immediately be put to work, lest they, too, acquire a taste for the idle life. Beggars from other cities whom the commissioners declare sound of body should in principle be sent back to their place of origin, with provisions for the trip but no more.

Vivés considers that, if the hospitals pooled all their revenues, the resulting fund would be able to finance all the municipal institutions of social aid, especially since it would be augmented by the proceeds from the work of the poor. To this end the municipal authorities should forthwith assume control over all the hospitals. In exceptional cases these funds might be supplemented by the contents of church collection boxes, but this should be limited to the city's three or four main churches, and should be resorted to only in an emergency. On the role of the Church in this programme the treatise remains remarkably discreet. The subject is dealt with in a few remarks praising the Church's past zeal in collecting and distributing alms; the hope is expressed that it will continue to play an important role by encouraging charity and compassion.

Vivés devotes a separate chapter of his treatise to refuting possible critics of his programme. There will be some, he thinks, who will want to defend the poor from the alleged threat of banishment; others will cite the gospels: 'Pauperes semper habebitis vobiscum.' Finally, the poor themselves will be reluctant to accept the need to work and the changes in their lives. But these objections cannot be taken into account if the plague of beggars is to be eliminated; one must press on firmly regardless, for the programme of reform will bring many benefits. Sanitary conditions in the city will improve and delinquency will be reduced once the constant influx of criminals into areas of poverty is stopped. A city without beggars is an object worthy of admiration, and its glory can only increase.

Vivés was perfectly well aware of the possible pitfalls attending so thorny a subject. He wrote in a letter to Cranevelt: 'I have neglected no precautions.' He was judicious in choosing his arguments in favour of prohibiting begging, and careful to make no allusion whatsoever to the mendicant orders, lest his criticism of beggars be perceived as a veiled attack on them. Despite his precautions he did not escape criticism; the first attack came in 1527, from the Franciscan Nicolas de Bureau, accusing him of heresy and Lutheranism. But his caution did shield him from any further consequences.

Some doubt nevertheless remained in Catholic circles as to whether the municipal reform of social aid, and in particular the prohibition of begging, were in conformity with the teachings of the Church, and whether they might not be considered heretical. It was for this reason that the authorities of Ypres, whose programme of reform had many points of similarity with Vivés' proposals, turned to the Sorbonne theologians to defend them against accusations of Lutheranism made by the mendicant orders. In 1531 the Paris theologians reached their conclusion: while they conceded that the new statute did not on the whole offend Christian piety, they firmly condemned the prohibition of begging as heretical, and made it clear, moreoever, that Church property, as well as the traditional rights of the orders, must be protected. Similarly, when the Lyons humanist Jean de Vauzelles developed his programme of municipal social reform in 1531, the local inquisitor, the Dominican Nicolas Morin, launched into accusations of impiety against the proponents of reform.

Vivés' proposals evoked a variety of responses in European Catholic circles. Konrad Wimpina, theological advisor to Joachim I of Brandenburg, extolled their virtues in a speech – almost a panegyric – delivered to the Augsburg Diet in 1530; this speech was also his last will and testament. Cellarius, a professor at the University of Louvain, criticized some of Vivés' ideas in a learned discourse consisting of twenty-one hexameters, but he, too, was generally in favour of municipal reform. The title of his discourse was a programme in itself: *Oratio contra Mendicitatem pro Nova Pauperum Subventione* ('Discourse against Begging and for a New Aid to the Poor'). In 1531 Pierre Papaus, also a professor at Louvain, spoke out in defence of Vivés' treatise; the fervour with which he spoke testifies to the violence of the criticism to which he was responding.

Vivés' doctrine had its roots in a complex variety of experiences: the Strasbourg and Nuremberg reforms had preceded its publication by a few years, and those of Ypres by only a few months. Vivés was certainly aware of the latter, and it is likely that the former were known to him as well. The remarks about Bruges in his preface show how closely he followed the municipal debates over the reform of social aid. In his presentation of the principles of his programme, his supporting ideological arguments and his advice to the municipal ruling elite he appears as a mere theoretician; but he was also, in the words of Marcel Bataillon, 'an extraordinary interpreter of the spirit of cities at that time'.[1] This spirit was evident in the excessive preoccupation with the problem of beggars on the part of the leading reformers, political figures and eminent literary men of the time: it was perceived as the chief evil of their age. It is also significant that the intellectual debates to which the problem of beggars gave rise coincided with a social crisis of great proportions: for it was precisely in the 1520s, years that were to be decisive for the evolution of social and economic structures in general and of charitable institutions in particular, that religious reformers, and above all Christian humanists, made their entrance on the political scene.

Nevertheless there is in Vivés' thought a certain lack of synchronism between the theory and the social reality. Although the Netherlands were his adoptive country of choice, he constantly refers to the experiences of Spanish cities, and particularly to those of Valencia, his native town. In so doing he remains faithful both to his feelings of national identity and to the humanist concept of cultural cosmopolitanism. The result, however, is that his diagnosis and his proposed remedies are the same for Castillian cities and those of the Netherlands, which exhibit widely different characteristics. Certainly there are some elements common to both: the erosion of traditional attitudes towards the poor, in part due to the bourgeois mentality and its hostility towards idleness, and the resulting municipal policy decisions, such as the expulsion of beggars and the prohibition of begging, based on considerations of hygiene and public safety. But at the core of Vivés' thinking was his programme of integrating the idle and the marginal into the city's economic life as a useful additional source of labour to increase economic productivity; and on this point Spain and the Netherlands differed widely. Putting the poor to work, whether that work is voluntary or forced, requires large and flexible demand. All the examples Vivés cites concern Flanders: the drapers of Armentières complain of the lack of labour; the silk weavers of Bruges would willingly hire children, even if only to turn the spinning-wheel, but there are none to be found, for they bring in more money for their parents by begging than by working. In the proto-industrial economy of Flanders the labour market had the necessary absorptive capacity, but there was no such demand on the Spanish market.

The popularity of Vivés' treatise in Europe, both in its Latin version and in translation, can be variously explained. It was useful to the municipal movement of reform in providing both ideological underpinnings and practical suggestions for dealing with beggars; it explained the technicalities of census-taking and proposed various methods of distinguishing between different categories of beggars. Its essential ideas were universal, and could be applied in all contexts, regardless of the level of economic development reached by any particular city or country. Among them was a hostility towards beggars that bordered on repugnance, and which he did not scruple to reveal in his descriptions of them; an insistence on the responsibilities incumbent upon secular authorities, both municipal and state, in the matter of social aid; a number of proposed repressive measures, forced labour being chief among them; and a proposed reorganization of hospitals so that their huge wealth might be used to finance aid to the poor. There is no mention, however, of secularizing the assets of the Church which formed the 'patrimony of the poor' — an example of Vivés' characteristic caution.

Despite the fact that some of his more specific recommendations were ill-adapted to socio-economic realities outside the Netherlands, Vivés' programme as a whole influenced at least two countries in important ways. In the second half of the sixteenth century it was widely adopted in Spain, where it provoked violent polemics; and it found fertile ground in Poland, where it met with the approval of Andrzej Frycz Modrzewski, the most illustrious Polish social thinker of the sixteenth century.

Frycz Modrzewski, in his treatise *De Republica Emendata* ('On the Reform of the Republic'), makes several attempts to tackle the problem of beggars. He devotes an entire chapter — 'On Custom' — to the praise of work and the condemnation of idleness, and it is here that the subject of beggars is broached. The essential principle of his social programme is expressed in the first paragraph: those capable of working should not be allowed to beg, and adequate support for the 'genuine poor' should be ensured. (It is worth remarking that this principle of the new social policy is drawn entirely from the medieval distinction between 'true' and 'false' beggars, and appears frequently both in legislation and in theoretical writings on the subject.) The first aim of social policy should be to weed out those who prefer a life of vice to honest labour and force them to work, on pain of expulsion from the city. Beggars unable to work should be placed in poorhouses.

As for wandering beggars, Frycz ventures, cautiously and almost timidly, to suggest that their presence should not be tolerated, for their begging is only a way of concealing the various crimes, murders and robberies that they commit.

Poorhouses cannot depend for their funds on individual donations alone; they must have another, permanent source of funding. Frycz suggests that part of the city's budget should be set aside for this purpose. In addition, individual donations should be encouraged by the placing of collection boxes outside churches and public places. This last suggestion is accompanied by a passage in praise of charity and an exhortation to remember the duties of the good Christian. Finally, Frycz touches on the most delicate and controversial issue, namely the use of Church revenues, in whole or in part, to finance aid for the poor. He is judicious in his arguments: recalling that ancient principle whereby a quarter of the bishop's revenues was set aside for the poor, he merely appeals to the good-will of men of the cloth and warns them of the threat of divine punishment; but he is careful to make no mention of obligatory contributions.

Like the municipal reforms, Frycz's proposed reform of charity involves the secularization of social aid. Aid to the poor should be organized by specially appointed 'guardians of the poor' (*pauperum curatores*), and it is they who are henceforth to be responsible for deciding which of the poor will receive support, and which must be sent to work. They will also have powers to apply repressive and coercive measures to the recalcitrant in the latter category, and will be responsible for the proper management of the poorhouses. Finally, it will be their task to collect the funds necessary for the efficient functioning of the social aid system; this will involve, among other things, reminding bishops of their duty to aid the poor, not an easy task in view of the fact that this aid must now take the form, not of alms distributions among beggars, but of substantial contributions to secular charitable institutions. Thus the guardians of the poor had a dual role to play in the lives of the poor: to protect as well as to police.

Behind Frycz's praise of charity a strong dislike and distrust of beggars is clearly visible. He recommends that the 'causes of each pauper's poverty' be examined in detail, in order to determine the correct treatment of every particular case: those who have sunk into poverty through their own fault should be 'fed more modestly and worked harder' than those that have become impoverished through sickness, for example; to them kinder treatment may be extended.

The aim of this policy is to instil into the social consciousness, and into the minds of the poor in particular, a conviction of the virtues of work and the evils of idleness. This is why Frycz, like Luther and Vivés before him, insists that the food given to the poor be just sufficient to satisfy their hunger: it is a way of deterring them from a life of idleness. When begging is profitable, work naturally suffers. The poor living in the protective custody of social aid institutions should therefore be treated in such a way as to discourage all thoughts of profiting from the work of others. They should also be made to work, each in accordance with his strength and abilities. Unlike Vivés, however, Frycz does not advise the creation of workshops in poorhouses – an understandable omission, given the different socio-economic conditions of the country for which his project was intended. But he does hint at the possibility of introducing gardening or crafts into the poorhouses when he speaks of providing an 'honest occupation' at which the poor might be employed, with pay, according to their strength. But the justification for this lay not in an excess of demand on the labour market, but rather in the hope that the harmful moral effects of idleness – 'debasement through sloth', as Frycz called it – might thereby be avoided.

Finally, Frycz approves of the idea of sending 'alien' beggars back whence they had come. This principle is an ancient one, dating back to the medieval doctrine whereby each Christian community was responsible for looking after its own poor. It was not until the late Middle Ages, however, that the practice of expelling 'alien' poor became current. Sixteenth-century reformers stressed that organized aid for the poor must include both institutionalized charity and a system of controls and repressive measures, and saw the expulsion of 'alien' poor as an integral part of municipal social policy.

The similarities between the arguments of Frycz and Vivés are sufficiently striking to permit the conclusion that Frycz simply adopted large parts of Vivés' programme as his own. But to what extent was such a programme applicable to the socio-economic realities of life in Poland at that time? In the sixteenth century Poland's main economic activities, and most of her social problems, were still concentrated in the countryside. The principal threat to the interests of the nobility, anxious to maintain their way of life and to preserve traditional agrarian structures, was the mobility of the poor. The struggle against 'vagrancy' arose from a perceived threat to public order; more precisely, it was inspired by the fear that the behaviour of 'vagrants' might infect the rest of the rural population, and ultimately lead to the collapse of the attempts then being made to revive and reinforce the feudal system of personal dependence, known as the 'second serfdom'.

But the towns, too, were coming up against the problem of beggars in much the same way as other cities in Europe. In Cracow, after a series of epidemics, the municipal authorities decided to implement severe measures against vagrants and to prohibit public begging entirely. The involvement of secular authorities in matters of social aid began to be visible in Polish towns in the late Middle Ages: officials were appointed to supervise the running and financial management of hospitals. After the Council of Trent the problem of how best to run hospitals and charitable institutions, and the issue of beggars in general, were taken up with renewed vigour. This was not in the spirit of Frycz's proposals, however, for social aid was declared to be the domain of the Church – indeed Frycz's programme was strongly criticized by Stanislaw Hozjusz, a leading figure in the Council of Trent and one of the main proponents of Tridentine policy. Nonetheless, from the second half of the sixteenth century the expulsion of 'alien' beggars from Polish towns was recognized as a practical necessity, and became routine. All beggars and pilgrims were required to carry appropriate documents (political considerations were partly responsible for this: beggars were often taken for spies, particularly Turkish ones), and repressive measures against vagrants became a generally accepted principle. All this is unlikely to have been the result of Frycz's influence, but it shows at least that many elements of the problem of beggars were the same and could be similarly dealt with in different societies, regardless of their economic structure.

Frycz's programme also has certain antecedents in Polish social thought. The struggle to extirpate public begging makes its first appearance as a theme in Polish literature in the fifteenth century; traces of repressive measures taken against beggars may also be found in legislative documents and court archives of the period. But the main source is Jan of Ludzisko, a leading figure in the intellectual circles of Cracow in the fifteenth century, whose work contains a remarkably clear and acute analysis of the problem. One of his subtle and elegant discourses foreshadows, in its praise of work and condemnation of idleness, the treatise Frycz was to write a hundred years later. He has nothing but scorn for beggars, whom he sees as vile, greedy, base creatures; his treatment of mendicant orders is equally contemptuous. With a pragmatism characteristic of Polish thought of the period, he sets out the principles by which he thinks social life should be guided: 'It would be most fitting, therefore, if the wretches who live in penury but have retained all their strength were forced to cultivate the land, so that they might have a source of income; and they should also be urged to learn a trade, so that they do not pass their time in idleness, wallowing in sloth.' Praise of work was hardly a new idea, being well rooted in the Christian tradition; but the writings of Jan of Ludzisko expose the link between this tradition and the modern work ethic, and show how bourgeois culture and ideology adopted this element of traditional Christian morality and brought it into relief. The condemnation of begging, on the other hand, was an entirely new idea; and here, too, Jan of Ludzisko foreshadowed Frycz to a remarkable degree:

> Since men have lost the habit of work, begging of the most contemptible sort, by able-bodied people, has proliferated all over the earth, as well as robberies, lootings and other misdemeanours; and in our own land, although there is food in plenty, and no lack of any of the other necessities of life, this base and ignoble distaste for honest toil brings detriment to the kingdom and does great harm in lands where the Christian faith has been recently adopted. This beggary is tolerated in spite of human and divine laws, in spite of the most worthy customs and ancient and present rituals of the holy Church, in all the most Christian nations and states. It is a source of great shame and untold harm, for the common people think it a noble and profitable thing. . . . the said habit of begging and avoiding work on the part of strong and vicious men should be firmly condemned and stamped out.[2]

The work of Jan of Ludzisko in the fifteenth century, and the writings of Frycz a century later, both seem detached from their social context, as if theoretical thinking were an autonomous domain, unconnected with direct observation of social realities. Frycz's work in particular is an example of this: in his treatise *De Republica Emendata* he assumes that the problem of beggars must be dealt with simply because it belongs to the canon of set themes which must be included in any systematic vision of how social life should be organized. Neither the fifteenth nor the sixteenth century in Poland witnessed pauperization on a scale comparable with that of other European countries, nor was there any reason to expect it in future; the interest that both Frycz and Jan of Ludzisko took in the problem of beggars cannot be traced back to any phenomenon of this kind. But it does not necessarily follow that their interest in the question was purely academic and theoretical; for, even when it did not assume the vast proportions characteristic no less of long-term structural change than of brief periods of acute crisis, poverty endured and made its presence felt in all European countries, regardless of their socio-economic structure. It influenced social morality and human relations; it was a problem with which all individuals and groups, families and social classes, institutions and states were constantly confronted, both in the realities of everyday life and in ideological debate.

Vivés' ideas had much more complex repercussions in Spain, where they provoked violent debate. This was partly owing to the paradoxical situation in which the Spanish empire found itself at the time: on the one hand, the flow of riches from the New World contributed in large measure to the maintenance of feudal structures and the resulting stagnation of the traditional economies of the Iberian provinces; on the other, Spanish rule extended over the Netherlands, the most urbanized country of Europe at that time, with a highly developed proto-industrial economy. In addition to this, the political influence wielded by the Church, and the Catholic orthodoxy which was the monarchy's constant political and ideological guide, reinforced a theocratic political system. In such a climate, doctrinal conflicts were inevitably sharp.

The first such conflict took place in the 1540s. Castillian cities were stepping up efforts to get rid of beggars and vagrants; Zamora, Salamanca and Valladolid promulgated laws on the reform of social aid. In 1540 Charles V issued his edict on the centralization of hospitals. A total prohibition of begging, in accordance with Vivés' programme, seemed to be the natural next step; in Flanders it was already municipal policy. The conflict finally broke out in 1545, the year of the opening of the Council of Trent. At the beginning of the year a treatise devoted entirely to the problem of beggars was published in Salamanca by the Segovian Dominican Domingo de Soto. It defended the traditional doctrine of charity and the Christian duty of helping the poor; it also argued, after an analysis of Spanish central and municipal legislation concerning beggars, that the measures taken by Spanish cities in this regard, particularly by Zamora and Valladolid, were far more radical than the imperial edict of 1540 had intended. While not denying the need to combat vagrancy as a threat to public order and an infringement of the law, de Soto insisted that a distinction be made between vagrants and poor people who wander about the country seeking alms simply in order to survive. He saw no reason to persecute poor people who had been forced to leave their native parts to seek support elsewhere. There is, he said, no moral or legal argument to justify repressive measures such as banishment; banishment is a punishment almost as severe as the death penalty, and yet poverty is no crime. Wandering beggars do not deserve such a fate. The kingdom being one body, it is quite natural for beggars to leave its poorer regions to seek support in wealthier areas and cities. Even if parishes were bound by law to support their own poor, some parishes would still contain greater numbers of poor than others, and would be unable to provide for everyone. Paupers should therefore be allowed to move about freely, and be received everywhere with kindness; for the gospels praise hospitality as a virtue. Toledo, Valladolid or Madrid should extend their aid to the poor who come to them from Asturia. De Soto also rejected the example of Ypres, often invoked by proponents of the reform of charity; indeed, he doubted that the Ypres reforms were really approved by the Sorbonne.

De Soto's discourse on the moral virtues of poverty as a condition follows traditional medieval doctrine. Charitable institutions should be guided in their treatment of the poor by love and compassion, not hatred and policies of repression. De Soto conceded that a distinction could be made between 'genuine' and 'false' poor, but he believed that the practice of charity could not rely on inquisitorial tactics and judicial procedure. The poor may sometimes resort to dishonest methods of evoking our sympathy and compassion, but they do this from necessity, in order to conquer indifference and soften hardened hearts. Sickness or physical infirmity are not sufficient criteria for distinguishing the 'genuine' poor from others; a pauper may have other, equally valid reasons for being unable to work, such as the loss of his tools, for instance, or his lack of professional training. And in any case, de Soto declared, it is far better to give alms to twenty vagrants than to repulse them and risk depriving the four genuine paupers among them of much-needed support. The policy of distinguishing between genuine and false paupers entailed too many moral risks to be acceptable to the Christian conscience. De Soto also insisted on maintaining the hallowed tradition whereby aid to the poor belonged to the domain of the Church and the clergy; he saw no reason to entrust the organization of this aid to secular authorities.

The controversies over poverty cannot be reduced to a simple conflict between modern and medieval attitudes. De Soto, one of the

most eminent theologians of the Council of Trent, was not a dogmat-
ist relying only on doctrine and the hallowed traditions of the past to
provide solutions to present problems; he was not blind to the social
realities of his day. His praise of poverty was not just a narrow and
abstract theological argument: it concerned crowds of flesh-and-blood
beggars who really existed and were becoming an increasingly frequent sight in European cities. His remarks about the possible causes
of unemployment, such as loss of tools or lack of training, testify to
his awareness of the problems of his age: the spread of poverty in cities
was indeed largely owing to the inability of new immigrants from the
countryside to adapt to urban life. Even as he defended traditional
Christian principles, the ideal of poverty and the interests of the
Church, he was acutely conscious, as conservative thinkers often are,
of the social injustices of the modern age.

In March 1545, a few months after the publication of de Soto's
treatise, a work by Juan de Medina de Robles, abbot of the Benedictine monastery of San Vincente in Salamanca, was issued by the same
printer. It was entitled *De la orden que algunos pueblos de España se ha
puesto en la limosna: para remedio de los verdaderos pobres* ('On the regulations concerning aid to the poor in some cities of Spain; and on
helping the true poor'). The title itself leaves no doubt as to the
abbot's allegiance: he was entirely in favour of municipal reform and
of the guidelines contained in the imperial edict of 1540. He had
some practical experience of the matter, for he had participated in
drawing up the poor law in Zamora. He insisted on the need to adapt
and find new solutions to the problems of the times; like Vivés, he
approved of municipal reform and sought to demonstrate its conformity with Christian piety. He was, however, strongly opposed to alms-
giving, and his treatise contains a violent diatribe against the
infamous conduct of beggars. The increase in the number of vagrants,
parasites and idlers was owing, in his opinion, to the lack of restraints
on begging and the failure to distinguish between mere idlers and
those in genuine need. Those who are genuinely unfit for work should
receive regular support, in exchange for which they must participate
in divine services; all others must be forced to work. The system of
social aid should be based on justice tempered with compassion; the
traditional principles of charity must be maintained, but applied
conscientiously, with due regard for justice and truth.

Juan de Medina also insisted on the need for a radical reform of
hospitals and charitable institutions, the administration of which

should pass into secular hands. Care for the poor being the domain of the secular authorities, he thought it fitting that the administration of hospital assets and the distribution of alms should also be entrusted to them, while the clergy saw to the proper running of these institutions. He listed the advantages of such a system: first, the proper care of the sick would prevent the spread of infectious diseases; second, 'false' beggars, who disregarded God's commandments and stayed away from mass and confession, would no longer be able to lead their dishonest and dissolute lives, and the more efficient use of alms would encourage benefactors to be more generous, for they would see that their money was being well spent; finally, as more people were forced to find work, the labour supply would increase.

In their interpretation of the doctrine of Christian charity, their conception of social policy and their attitudes towards poverty and the poor, de Soto and Medina represented opposite poles. They could not be reconciled, nor could one refute the arguments of the other, for the interpretation, social policy and attitudes of each were equally valid. Thus they continued to exist side by side, accepted by some, rejected by others. But social policy could not oscillate between two contradictory positions; solutions were needed, and a choice had to be made. The reform of social aid was emerging from its embryonic and experimental stages to become general practice. Thus in the second half of the sixteenth century, after the Council of Trent, the old polemics about aid for the poor were taken up with the same vehemence as before.

The first of these took place in Bruges, where the edict of Philip II had clearly and unambiguously restored to beggars the right to seek alms publicly. Twenty years after the death of Vivés, Bruges launched a second attempt at reform. It was grounded in Wyts's treatise *On Aid to the Poor at Home and on the Problem of Healthy Beggars*, published in 1562 in Antwerp. Among those who rose up in opposition to the projected reforms was one Lorenzo de Villavicencio, Spanish Augustinian, local preacher in Bruges and secret agent for Philip II in the Netherlands – in short, a typical product of his times. In a minor treatise on aid to the poor, published in 1564, he instigated an assault upon Wyts's treatise. He also condemned Vivés' treatise as heretical, because Vivés had dared to question the traditional prerogatives of the Church in the administration of hospitals and charitable institutions. He detected in the municipal reform of charity the taint of paganism and Lutheranism; he objected strongly to the plan of allowing the town council to organize aid to the poor and control the revenue of the Church on the pretext of ensuring its proper distribution among the poor, claiming that such a step would be an outrage against the Holy Scriptures and canonical law. He saw in the treatise of Vivés the source of all the errors committed by the councillors of Bruges. He urged the local populace to place their trust unreservedly in their bishops, who bore the whole burden of caring for the poor on their shoulders; and he invoked the situation of the poor in Spain as testimony to the continuing vitality and efficiency of the traditional system of charity, holding up the hospitals of Cordoba, Burgos, Granada and Valencia as examples to follow in Catholic countries. In an appendix to his treatise he attempted to refute, point by point, the main arguments supporting the programme of reform announced by the Bruges authorities in 1564. In attacking the reforms on theological grounds in this systematic way Villavicencio had a precise aim in view: to show that the proposed municipal reform of charity was contrary to the doctrine and teaching of the Church.

This was the last time that traditional attitudes and policies regarding the poor were to be so fiercely defended. In the last quarter of the sixteenth century all efforts in the domain of social thought were concentrated on finding a way to check the continuing and relentless deterioration of the living standards of Spain's poor. The great sixteenth-century debate over charity continued with the publication of a number of books and pamphlets advocating various programmes of reform. One such pamphlet, published in 1576, issued from the pen of Miguel de Giginta, canon of Elna. Addressed to the Cortes of Madrid, it contained detailed proposals for the reorganization of social aid; these were later expanded into a full treatise, which was published in Coimbra in 1579. Over the next few years Giginta was to produce a further three works dealing with charity and compassion. In all these works the traditional view of charity forms the basic assumption and starting-point of the argument. Giginta's praise of compassion and his defence of the right of the poor to seek alms may both be considered as part of his polemical stand against reform. He denounces as a violation of God's commandments the proposed expulsion of 'alien' poor – indeed, this was a measure about which even so enthusiastic a proponent of reform as Juan de Medina was moved to express some doubt – and rejects as illegitimate all measures intended to restrict the personal liberty of beggars, suggesting that efforts to deal with the problem of the poor would be better directed towards finding a means of providing regular support for those in genuine need. To this end he proposes the creation of 'Houses of Compassion' (*Casas de Misericordia*) in which they might be lodged. The funds for such houses would come from gifts and donations, from alms collected by the resident poor and from the profits on the sale of their work.

This project was something of a compromise between two different models of charity. While it did not rule out public begging, it assumed that the alms collected would be pooled in a common fund; and while it contained no definite moves towards the secularization of charity, it did contain some forceful criticism of the abuses committed by the Church in its administration of hospitals and of the misuse of funds destined for the poor. With its adoption of a centralized model of charity, the project as a whole was very much in the spirit of the reforms proposed by the municipal authorities. Indeed, in the matter of organizing work for the poor Giginta took up certain suggestions made by Vivés: the recommendation that all the poor in the Houses of Compassion should be usefully employed in some way, in accordance with their strength and abilities, and in particular that the children resident there should be taught and prepared for a trade, certainly had its origins in Vivés' treatise. In support of his project Giginta invoked the decisions of the Council of Trent and the creation, in 1563 in the papal State, of a house for beggars, in which the poor lived on alms and on the profits from their own work.

Giginta's proposals for a system of social aid were particularly important in that they provided, at a time of increasing pressure from the Counter-Reformation movement to preserve doctrinal purity, a way of reconciling the demands of orthodoxy with urban needs. They were also to influence the way in which the reform of charity was put into practice in Spanish cities. The idea of creating Houses of Compassion had its roots in the reform movement of the 1520s, while at the same time remaining very much in the spirit of the reforms of charity in post-Tridentine Europe, and indeed foreshadowing the programmes of social aid that were to be developed in the seventeenth century.

Giginta's proposals were also a source of inspiration for Cristobál Pérez de Herrera, whose *Discourse on Aiding the Poor* ('*Amparo de Pobres*') was published in Madrid in 1598. The 1590s were years of acute crisis, combining economic recession with a series of epidemics and bad harvests. Pérez de Herrera, a doctor from Salamanca and a high-ranking court dignitary, knew something of the social problems of those years. As chief doctor of the Spanish galleys, and thus a high-ranking state official, he learnt something of the functioning of state institutions. He also had the opportunity to observe the life of the poor, for in 1592 he was appointed royal physician to Philip II, who entrusted to him the task of drawing up a report on the problem of vagrants and beggars. Thus Pérez de Herrera, in addition to acquainting himself with all the literature on the subject, studied and assessed the functioning of charitable institutions, observed the life of beggars in Madrid, personally directed the work of the Brotherhood of Compassion in one of the Madrid parishes, and organized, together with some other dignitaries and officials, a shelter for the poor in the city, which was to become the model for similar institutions in other Spanish cities. In this way the programme of reform set forth in the *Amparo de Pobres*, built on these experiences and indeed incorporating the essays which Pérez de Herrera published in the course of his three years' work before the publication of the main treatise, began to be implemented under the benevolent eye of the old king, even before it appeared in print and became official doctrine.

The programme of reform was based on the principle of local organization: each parish was to be responsible for providing regular support, at home, for its sick and infirm, as well as for its 'shamefaced poor'. This aid was to be organized principally by Brotherhoods of Compassion of the type founded by Pérez de Herrera in St Martin's parish in Madrid. Each parish was to be divided up into quarters, and each quarter administered by specially appointed delegates (*diputados*), elected from the ranks of the rich, the famous and the particularly charitable. Aid for the poor organized on a local level would, in Pérez de Herrera's view, allow greater insight into the lives of the poor and the precise situation of each, ensure greater efficiency, and make it easier to collect the necessary funds.

This organization of aid on the parish level was not, however, the essential point in Pérez de Herrera's programme, nor the most controversial; nor, indeed, was it particularly instrumental in modernizing social aid. It allowed for the continuation of traditional methods of charity, and it was for precisely this reason that Pérez de Herrera made it part of his programme: it was a concession to the orthodox doctrine of charity in its strictest sense, that of alms-giving. The real focus of his programme, its most fundamental part, was the creation of shelters for the poor. First suggested twenty years earlier by Giginta and already established in several cities, they were now to become the main instrument of the new social policy. Moreover, Pérez de Herrera was now proposing to establish a network of such shelters on a nationwide scale. This was significant, for it meant going beyond local authorities to central government, at which point the whole question of social aid became a matter of national rather than municipal policy. Without such a shift no measures could be really effective: if the reforms remained on a municipal level, beggars and vagrants who wished to avoid the stricter control which such reform would impose on their lives could simply move, *en masse*, to another city. Pérez de Herrera therefore proposed that a census of public beggars – those who begged for alms in the streets and from door to door – be taken simultaneously in all the main urban centres in the kingdom. For this purpose the beggars were to present themselves at their local poor shelter, where the circumstances of each were to be examined in detail, so as to exclude vagrants and those who were fit to work. Those who, at the end of this census, were found deserving of aid were given special tags to wear, imprinted with a picture of the Virgin Mary and the city arms, and a certificate entitling them to beg for alms. Thus public begging was not to be entirely banned, but rather regulated and subjected to stricter controls. The poor shelters were to act as refuges for healthy beggars; henceforth the hospitals were to take in only the sick. The role of the hospital envisaged by this project is almost a modern one: it was no longer the traditional hospice and refuge for all the poor, but a place reserved for the sick.

Another principle essential to the project was that the poor shelters should also function as workhouses: work was to be the principal rule of their functioning. Vagrants were to be tracked down and imprisoned by special guards – *alguaziles* – appointed for the purpose by the city. Above all something had to be done about beggar children: they were to be educated and trained for some useful profession. Particularly severe were the measures aimed at female vagrants and women who led dissolute lives: the incorrigible were to be imprisoned in workhouses (*casas de trabajo y labor*) for a period of one to several years.

Pérez de Herrera was not a theologian. First and foremost he was a political writer who read widely and drew on his own experiences. It was, for him, a fundamental rule of social life that people be made useful members of society, according to their abilities and to the profit they could bring to the State. A number of Spanish economists, known collectively as the Salamanca School, saw productive work as the fundamental economic value. Pérez de Herrera wholeheartedly embraced this idea, and made it the leading principle and focal point of his new system of charity. At the same time he was perfectly well aware that, in venturing into an area strictly controlled by religion and by the Church, he was treading upon delicate ground. He therefore tried to deflect attention from the unequivocally secular nature of his reforms by praising parish charity and including representatives of the clergy among the administrators of his proposed institutions; and he stressed, in a further attempt to forestall attack, the spiritual benefits of reform: it would make the poor more pious, encourage compassion and have a salutary effect on morals in general. Indeed, the emblematic heading of his fourth discourse, devoted to women, contains the motto 'work improves morals'.

The discourses themselves provide ample evidence of the extent to which Pérez de Herrera was aware of the controversy his proposals had aroused: in one discourse, for example, he launched into an explicit and systematic defence of his programme in an attempt to parry possible attacks in advance. The great majority of his opponents saw themselves as guardians of the traditional doctrine of charity. They denounced the proposed reforms as dangerous innovations that violated ancient customs and laws. Pérez de Herrera replied to this charge by pointing to all the ancient laws, past Spanish legislation and council decisions intended to combat vagrants and control beggars. Among the eleven objections to which he responded, one is of particular interest. It concerns the special tags that beggars would be forced to wear for purposes of identification: they were, it was claimed, nothing less than marks of infamy. To this Pérez de Herrera replied — with, it must be said, a good deal of casuistry in his arguments — that they were merely signs of poverty, and that poverty, according to the gospels, is a blessed state; such tags were therefore signs of honour, symbols of the dignity of the poor man and of the respect which is his due. The elevated rhetorical style of these arguments, however, presents a great contrast with the stern, indeed pitiless argumentation of the first discourses, which speak only of the great harm done by beggars and vagrants to the public interest.

By the end of the sixteenth century the great controversy over charity had burnt itself out and the conflicts abated. This is not to say that they came to a definitive end, for the following century saw a continuation of the debate both on the practical and on the theoretical plane, and the subject was still a prominent one in religious and ethical literature. The reform of charity ceased, however, to be perceived as the 'municipal heresy', a threat to the interests of the Church. It became incorporated into the ideology of the modern State, and accepted as the State's prerogative; it was through the attempts to combat vagrancy and ward off the social dangers of poverty that the state apparatus of repression was shaped. The social and political changes of that time are reflected in the work of many other thinkers, polemicists and writers, in England, in France, in Germany. It was precisely the public nature of the reform of social aid, its institutionalization on the state level, that explains the widespread debates about poverty: in the century which formulated the concept and doctrine of *raison d'état*, the reform of charity became a political tool of the modern State and an integral part of its ideology.

6

Prisons of Enlightenment

In the evolution of the penal system the idea of prisons has a singular history. Ethnological studies show that the isolation of individuals, families and even groups which infringe the rules of the community is a widespread practice, adopted in a variety of cultures. All rulers aspire to a prison of their own, even if it is only a cellar, a dungeon or an underground chamber. Prison was not always seen as a punishment: it could be a temporary place of detention, or a way of isolating undesirable members of the elite. As late as the middle of the eighteenth century its role was still perceived in this way: a French lawyer of that period asserted that prison was not in itself a punishment, merely a place where wrongdoers could be temporarily held. This was indeed the case: the 1670 French ordinance which continued to define the rules of criminal procedure until the end of the *Ancien Régime* listed, in order of decreasing severity, all the possible types of punishment as follows: the death penalty, torture, life sentence to the galleys, life sentence of banishment, limited sentence to the galleys, the lash, the pillory and temporary banishment. Prison was not among them. It was widely used as a punishment by the Church, but the civil authorities resorted to it only when no other punishment – such as the galleys, for example – was possible or appropriate: for women and old men, for debtors or for blasphemers who could not afford to pay the fine. Prisoners had to be fed; those who did not have the money to pay for food went without. Thus the real punishment was not loss of liberty but hunger. While one does begin to come across the occasional prison sentence from as early as the late Middle Ages, it was not until the end of the nineteenth century that such sentences became common and were finally established, under the influence of the

English and American models, as the basis of the penal system. In his book about the origins of prisons,[1] Michel Foucault shows how profound an influence this change exerted on techniques of government and on the collective understanding of the ideas of 'punishment' and 'correction'.

Before prison became widespread as a method of punishing and re-educating offenders, it was used in modern Europe as an instrument in implementing social policy with regard to beggars. The forced isolation of lepers, and later the plague-stricken, in the Middle Ages, was extended to beggars and madmen. The 'great imprisonment' of beggars in the sixteenth and seventeenth centuries was the crowning point of the new social policy: the changing attitudes towards poverty were mirrored in the affirmation of the structures of the modern state.

6.1 The Roman Procession

On the Italian Peninsula the first attempts to centralize aid for the poor were undertaken at the end of the Middle Ages. In Milan, for example, in the final years of the fourteenth century, Gian Galeazzo Visconti introduced measures which brought hospitals under secular control and declared that they would henceforth house the city's beggars. In order to carry out this plan a special commission was appointed to study the situation in the city, draw up lists of beggars and 'ailing poor' and ensure that there was room for them in the hospitals. The *Officium Pietatis Pauperum*, created in Milan in 1406 to control the organization of aid to the poor, included both clergy and laymen, and was accountable to the vicar general of the Milan diocese.

In the middle of the fifteenth century bishops and Bernardine preachers initiated the reform and centralization of social aid. Centrally administered 'general hospitals' were created in Brescia in 1447, in Milan in 1448 and in Bergamo in 1449. Their creation was accompanied by a variety of other initiatives in the domain of charity: 'pious banks' were set up to protect the poor from unscrupulous money lenders; religious brotherhoods, like the Company of Divine Love, for example, combined aid to the poor with their religious activities; parish and diocese authorities exerted themselves to help the poor more efficiently; religious orders, both old and new, embarked with a new vigour upon their charitable work. In Italy, therefore, the Church played an extremely active and important role in this domain, carrying on its traditional charitable work, helping to implement reform and generally cooperating with the secular authorities. This new surge of charitable activity, combined with swelling numbers of pilgrims, was not without its negative aspects, as critics were quick to point out: at the time of the Reformation, opponents of traditional medieval doctrine and policy with regard to charity claimed that the profusion of alms, and the ease with which they could be obtained, had a demoralizing influence, and could be seen as an incitement to idleness.

The case of Venice, discussed earlier in this book, provides some examples of the wide variety of measures employed by the authorities in Italy at times of crisis, in an attempt to ward off famine, social unrest or the spread of an epidemic. The policies embarked upon at such times were not determined by the nature of the crisis alone; they were also influenced by a combination of ideology and religion, by the Christian work ethic and by a general conviction that the system of social aid was in need of reform. It was by such concerns that Girolamo Miani, a Venetian nobleman, was guided in his philanthropic and charitable ventures – ventures which were to spawn a large number of imitators throughout Italy. The orphanage he founded in Venice, and the institutions modelled on it which sprang up around 1530 in Verona, Brescia, Bergamo and Milan, were guided by a strict set of rules: begging was categorically forbidden, and the children, in addition to being taught the rules of proper conduct and instructed in the principles of the Catholic faith, were prepared for a trade. To this latter end master artisans were brought in to train them in production techniques; the skills they acquired in this way were to enable them, later on, to earn their living by honest work.

During this period the charitable institutions of Italy greatly enlarged the scope of their activities, and as they evolved they became aware of the need to modernize and reorganize the system of charity. They therefore appointed parish inspectors to take censuses of the poor and study their living conditions in detail. The consequence of this blossoming of interest in charitable activity was, paradoxically, a widespread tendency to ban begging and extirpate beggars.

Two factors influenced the hostile attitudes and repressive policies towards beggars and vagrants which were becoming increasingly visible on the Italian Peninsula: they were the Counter-Reformation and the development of the modern state. The Council of Trent, in defining more clearly the role of the diocese in the provision of aid for the poor, did much to integrate the reform of charitable institutions into Catholic doctrine. In accordance with its decisions, hospitals were to be brought entirely under the control of the bishops, and secular hospital administrators made accountable to them alone. In addition, the bishops were to be responsible for the proper use of all legacies in favour of the poor. The decisions which issued from the Council's debates were intended to restore the hospitals' charitable role and prevent corrupt members of the clergy from treating them as lucrative livings, to be used for appropriating the 'assets of the poor'. In some countries, however, attempts to put the Tridentine decisions into practice brought the Church into open confrontation with the lay authorities, who progressed from sporadic interference in the administration of hospitals to a systematic policy intended to bring them entirely under secular control. The Council's decrees had two important consequences: on the one hand, they forced the Church to assume a more active role in the organization of charity; on the other, they provided doctrinal support for the movement to reform the system of social aid.

No less significant to the process of reform were the new state structures now beginning to emerge. Vagrancy and begging disturbed the harmonious division of social roles; they created zones impervious to 'police' interference, gave rise to uncertainty and anxiety and threatened the public order. Beggars upset the divine order of things and infringed the rules and work ethic of Christian life: *in sudore vultus tui vesceris panem*. They were a source of impiety, a threat to the public interest and a menace to peaceful social coexistence. In this domain the arguments of the Counter-Reformation were in harmony with reasons of State; religion and politics met. They met in a particularly striking fashion in Rome, in papal policies towards beggars; the Pontiff's rule over the Eternal City combined both religious and state functions. Reasons of State and the Counter-Reformation model of Christian society were tightly connected here, and both pointed to the same conclusion: that radical means were needed to deal once and for all with the plague of beggars infesting the city.

Rome's special role had an influence on the social life of the city. In order to forge lasting bonds between the Christian world and its spiritual capital, popes gave absolution to all the faithful who came to Rome; as a result, pilgrimages to Rome were a constant target of satire in late medieval literature. The theme was taken up, with great vehemence, by writers and preachers of the Reformation, but their criticism only reinforced the Roman practice of indulgences and jubilees, and they became an important element in the confrontation between Catholicism and Protestantism. The number of pilgrims flowing into Rome was huge: in 1575 it was estimated at 400,000, in 1600 at 536,000 and by 1650 at 700,000. This was many times greater than the number of Rome's inhabitants, which at the beginning of the sixteenth century was not more than about 50,000, and by the beginning of the seventeenth had grown to 100,000. The initiators of charitable activities in Rome pointed out that the great majority of pilgrims were poor people: in 1575 the Santissima Trinità de' Convalescenti, a brotherhood founded by Philip Neri, provided shelter for about 165,000 pilgrims; in 1600 it took in 210,000 and in 1650 300,000. These were presumably either paupers or people who had accepted the condition of poverty along with the pilgrim's staff. Catholic critics of mass pilgrimages stressed that such journeys often served as a simple pretext for fleeing one's family and adopting the life of a vagrant. The estimated figures above are from jubilee years, when the number of pilgrims was particularly great; but even in normal years their numbers continued to grow steadily, and it is estimated that at least 30,000 came to Rome each year.

Of this mass of pilgrims flooding the city, some were poor people who blended in with the crowds of local beggars; there were others, however, who were comfortably off, rich even (some of these made their pilgrimage in a carriage), and, in accordance with the pious nature of their journey, distributed alms to the poor. Both groups of pilgrims, rich and poor, had their effect on the life of the city, increasing the instability of its social structures as well as the number of beggars.

Montaigne, in his journal of travels in Italy, remarked that all of Rome was like a great court at which everyone, in one way or another, participated in 'ecclesiastical idleness'. 'This city', he wrote, 'has no labourers or men who live by the work of their hands.'[2] Jean Delumeau, the historian of Renaissance Rome, has shown that this was not entirely true, for Rome's building works, as well as the need for goods and services, created considerable demand for labour and provided employment for many. It nevertheless remained true that those who worked with their hands constituted only a very small part of the city's social landscape; and of the plebeians in this landscape it was the beggars who occupied centre stage.

At the end of the seventeenth century one of the great reformers of charity, father A. Guevarre, wrote as follows: 'For many years now beggars have enjoyed full freedom in the city, and begging has assumed huge proportions, causing much disorder. As Rome is a capital, and in a sense the centre of the Christian world, the poor of all nations flock here to seek comfort in their misery. Many also come to do business, but when they run out of funds they take to begging, at first from necessity and later because they develop a taste for the profession.'[3] The profusion of alms and institutions of charity in Rome obviously favoured the spread of begging and attracted crowds of hopeful paupers. They swarmed over the city's streets and squares, loitering in front of churches and even inside them, disturbing the services and as good as forcing the faithful to give them alms. A. Guevarre wrote: 'It is astonishing to see the endless throngs of vagrants and idlers trailing from dawn to dusk over the whole city, from house to house and from church to church, pestering one person after another in order to wheedle, nay forcibly extort, alms which they then go on to use in a base and scandalous fashion.'[4]

Sixteenth-and seventeenth-century literature presents a similar image of Rome, and further embellishes the stereotype with the often expressed conviction that Rome's swarms of beggars were part of an organized clandestine structure with criminal aims. It was claimed that this organization controlled the alms market, appointed the places at which beggars were posted and formalized, almost to the point of institutionalization, the techniques of begging. In this picturesque and mostly hostile view of beggars the huge dimensions of the phenomenon are a constantly recurring theme.

In the second half of the sixteenth century the papacy renewed its efforts to purge the city of this infestation. Previous attempts to expel beggars from Rome had not been successful: they had involved only provisional measures, most of which in any case remained at the planning stage. In view of this a policy of imprisonment seemed the only possible solution.

Radical steps were taken under Pius IV (1559–65). The papal edict of 1561, 'on providing for poor beggars', introduced a total ban on begging in the streets of Rome and threatened offenders with imprisonment, banishment and the galleys. It was aimed precisely against 'beggars', not against 'vagrants'. The change in terminology may seem insignificant, for the rather fluid and imprecise category of vagrants was understood to include beggars, but it was symptomatic of an important change in attitudes towards poverty: scruples had been abandoned, and the edict of 1561 clearly and explicitly classed public begging as a misdemeanour. This policy of repression was nonetheless accompanied by an attempt to reorganize aid to the poor. An official was appointed to supervise the enforcement of both the repressive and the charitable aspects of the policy: the expulsion of beggars on the one hand, and the care of the sick and infirm on the other. All beggars, vagrants and persons without occupation or resources were summoned together in one place, where they were sorted into different categories: the sick were sent to hospitals, and those who were fit to work were given suitable employment. The effects of these measures cannot have been entirely satisfactory, however, for Pius IV's successors continued, each in his turn, to be faced with the same problem, as serious and troublesome as ever.

Pius V (1566–72) concentrated his efforts on providing aid to the sick and to the poor families of Rome. The project of concentrating beggars and paupers in four well-defined areas of the city is attributed to him. Officially this project had the purely practical aim of facilitating aid and alms distribution. The unspoken intention, however, characteristic of the changing attitudes of the age, was to remove beggars from the city's streets and isolate them from society by creating zones of poverty in which they would be confined. But implicit in this project was also the principle of separation which lay at the root of the phenomenon of the ghetto as a place for the community's outcasts.

Pope Gregory XIII (1572–85) continued the policy of isolating beggars. Rather than creating the zones of poverty planned by his precedessor, however, he sought inspiration in the proposals of Pius IV, and ordered the creation of a general hospital in which beggars might be lodged and fed. The organization of this plan he entrusted to the Brotherhood of the Holy Trinity, which was to draw up a list of Rome's beggars and install them in one of the buildings which had housed the old convent of San Sisto, having furnished it suitably for the purpose. The hospital was to be both a refuge and a workshop, and the able-bodied among the beggars were to be given work there. Thus in 1581, on 27 February, the beggars gathered together by the Brotherhood of the Holy Trinity were led to their hospital in solemn procession, witnessed and later described in colourful detail by Camillo Fanucci, chronicler of the philanthropic works of Gregory XIII and Sixtus V. At the head of the procession marched prelates and members of the brotherhood, attired in red robes and bearing candles. Behind them filed the cortège of beggars, two by two: first the able-bodied, who could walk unaided, then the blind; behind them came the invalids in their carts, wheeled along by other beggars, and finally, closing the procession, were fourteen carriages containing the seriously ill. All in all, according to this account, eight hundred and fifty beggars filed through the streets of Rome on their way to their new place of refuge.

Processions were an important element in the organization of public life: they endowed human dealings with a sacred dimension and they were a way of obtaining divine grace, part of a long and deeply entrenched tradition of magic ritual. At the same time they were a public affirmation of certain ruling or important values. Fanucci wrote that the beggars, as they filed past, seemed to walk in triumphal procession. The occasion was indeed a triumph – the extraordinary, baroque triumph of Christian compassion. Behind it lay a complex social reality and an equally intricate and carefully balanced policy towards the poor, a policy involving, on the one hand, the elimination of individual charity, achieved through the systematic and institutionalized work of the Arciconfraternità della Santissima Trinità de'Pellegrini, which was dedicated to this end, and, on the other, support for the poor on condition that they renounce public begging and allow themselves to be confined within the hospital.

The San Sisto hospital was a success, so much so that the convent building originally prepared for the purpose soon ran out of room, overwhelmed by the mass of beggars crowding at its doors, and additional space had to be found in some of the adjacent buildings. The Brotherhood of the Holy Trinity, however, was unable to cope with the cost and administrative work involved in an undertaking on such a scale, and soon appealed to the Pope to be released from its duties in running the institution. As a result the hospital closed and the beggars returned to the streets.

Nevertheless, the tendency to gather beggars in a separate place and forbid public begging remained dominant in social policy in Rome. In his bull *Quamvis infirma* of 1587, Sixtus V (1585–90) launched into a violent tirade against the dishonesty and base practices of the beggars and vagrants infesting the city's streets and squares: their cries and wailings disturbed the faithful at prayer in the churches; they roamed about like animals, always in search of food, thinking only of how to assuage their hunger and fill their bellies. Many of them simulated illness or infirmity in order to wheedle alms from passers-by, and would do anything to avoid honest work. These words were intended to justify the decision to forbid begging in the streets of Rome, on pain of the galleys. The Pope ordered a new refuge for the poor to be built near the Ponte Sisto, and over a thousand beggars were confined there. But this attempt, too, was doomed to failure: after Sixtus V's death everything went back to the way it had been before, and no more than a hundred and fifty beggars were left in the hospice. Its numbers rose briefly in 1590, when over a thousand beggars took refuge there; but that was an exceptional year, a time of particularly poor harvests, and the streets of Rome were filled with notices ordering the expulsion of vagrants, gypsies and the like.

At the end of the seventeenth century the papal administration renewed its efforts to rid Rome's streets of beggars. Innocent XII (1691–1700) founded the Ospizio Generale de'Poveri, housed in the Lateran palace. Both public begging and giving alms to beggars were strictly forbidden. A special congregation was entrusted with the task of implementing the reform and supervising the activities of the hospice. A census was taken, a list of the poor drawn up, and once again the beggars gathered to file through the streets of Rome in triumphal procession, on their way to the new hospice. Here they were given such work as their health allowed: weaving, making shoes and stockings, and working wood. The successors of Innocent XII developed this idea, founding similar hospices for orphans and old people. But the implementation of this policy was hampered by constant financial and administrative difficulties, by the reluctance of beggars to be confined and the refusal of individual benefactors to be bound by the new regulations; a papal decree of 1774 reveals that, in spite of the efforts of the authorities, beggars and vagrants were still to be seen in the city streets. Nevertheless, the idea of 'concentrating' beggars in one area had become a permanent element of social policy in Rome.

From the first, the implementation of this policy had required the use of force; beggars saw their confinement within the hospice as a form of imprisonment. In 1581 it was rumoured in the city that beggars had offered the pope the huge sum of 2,500 thalers in exchange for their freedom and the right to beg. Even if this was no more than a piece of sensational gossip spread by the *avvisi*, the news pamphlets of the period, it still revealed that the policy was generally felt to be one of repression. It was certainly true that constant police surveillance was needed to ensure that it was carried out; the municipal guards spent all their time chasing after beggars and vagrants in the streets. They knew that beggars tended to gather around the Piazza Navona, often for the night, and it was here that they organized periodic raids to hunt them down. During these raids it was sometimes difficult to distinguish vagrants from seasonal labourers, who tended to blend in with the crowds of paupers, but the guards found a simple and ingenious solution to this: they released all those whose hands were rough and calloused from work; those who remained were taken away to prison. Giambattista Scanaroti, bishop and lawyer, describes this method in his 1655 treatise on prisons, and considers it a sign that working hands had once again become an object of respect, as they had been in antiquity.

The fate of successive papal policies of this type bears witness to the extreme difficulties involved in running a centralized system of social aid and effectively enforcing a ban on public begging. It is significant, however, that in spite of these difficulties the idea of imprisoning beggars came to be seen as the obvious solution and an essential part of social policy in Rome. The arguments in the papal bull *Quamvis infirma* and the methods deployed by the police to control beggars in Rome exemplify the open hostility which characterized the papal administration's efforts to deal with the problem. This hostile attitude had wide repercussions in other countries of Catholic Europe, where the example of Rome was invoked to justify the introduction of similar policies. Thus the Roman processions symbolizing the triumph of compassion were above all symbols of a different triumph – a triumph over beggars.

6.2 'Labore nutrior, labore plector'

The gates of a workhouse in Hamburg bore the message: *Labore nutrior, labore plector* ('By work I am nourished, by work I am punished'). A similar notice, at the entrance to a workhouse in Dessau, read: *Miseris et Malis* ('For the Poor and the Wicked'). In 1667 the following words were posted at the door of a workhouse for women in Amsterdam: 'Be not afraid! I do not avenge wickedness; I compel goodness. My hand is heavy but my heart is full of love.' The juxtaposition of such slogans with the sombre reality of workhouses and 'houses of correction' is shocking. Their didacticism apart, however, they are excellent indicators of public attitudes and new trends in social policy. The 'concentration' and imprisonment of the poor were connected both with a visible and emphatic affirmation of the work ethic in countries embarking on the road to capitalism and with the development of modern penal doctrine: loss of freedom and forced work came together in re-educational policies aimed at criminals and the unemployed poor.

In the systematic application of policies of this kind Bridewell, in London, played a pioneering role. Its creation was the result of lengthy experiences with English social policy, all of which pointed to the conclusion that the most effective way of punishing 'able-bodied beggars' and vagrants was to force them to work. In 1552 a special commission called by Edward VI and Nicolas Ridley, Bishop of London, drafted proposals for a new policy on aid for London's poor: vagrants, idlers and parasites were to be confined to poorhouses in which a strict work regimen was imposed; it was hoped that this experience of forced work would cure them of their idleness and wicked tendencies. Before 1557 such a poor-house was established at Bridewell, a former residence of Henry VIII; the very name 'Bridewell' came to be so closely associated with the idea of a workhouse that it became synonymous with it, and within a short space of time about two hundred workhouses, all called 'Bridewell', sprang up all over England.

The London Bridewell was run like a well-guarded and strictly controlled workshop. Since the labour itself consisted of forced rather than voluntary recruits, the institution could function only with constant supervision and prison discipline. As a result of the reform of 1552–3, the task of dealing with vagrants and providing aid to London's poor was divided up among the city's specialized hospitals. Of the vagrants confined in Bridewell, the genuinely sick were transferred to St Thomas's or St Bartholomew's hospital. The hospitals formed part of a network of repressive institutions: at St Thomas's, for instance, vagrants were flogged as soon as they had recovered from their illness, and all hospitals saw to it that the ban on public begging was enforced. Bridewell, however, because it was a place of work, had a special status within this new system. A number of specialized workshops were created within its walls, run by master craftsmen under the general supervision of the appropriate guild. For example, the draper in charge of the textile workshops was responsible for supplying the raw materials, keeping the work tools in good condition and arranging for the distribution of the final product; in all this he was supervised by one of the Bridewell administrators. The guilds had priority in buying the finished merchandise, in order to protect local craftsmen from disloyal competition. Each workshop had its own cook, responsible for feeding all those employed in it. The worst vagrants, the incorrigibles and the recidivists, were sent to work at the mill and the bakery, where the work was hard and demanded no qualifications other than physical strength.

Bridewell was originally created to provide work for 'able-bodied beggars'. However, unemployment was so great that it was unable entirely to absorb the excess of supply. According to the available statistics, most of Bridewell's residents came from the London area and were young: a register from 1602 reveals, among the thirty-seven people whose age was supplied, only one above the age of twenty-one. The majority – over 70 per cent – were men, mostly journeymen and domestic servants of various kinds. The problem of forcing beggars to work was closely connected with the state of the labour market; it was a part of the general problem of unemployment, and Bridewell, constantly under a weight of financial difficulties, could not remedy the situation by creating new posts. At the beginning of the seventeenth century it found itself with almost a thousand vagrants on its hands; not being able to employ them all, the administration had no choice in many cases but to try them, fine them and send them away, a procedure which reinforced Bridewell's punitive and correctional role.

An administrator of one of London's hospitals wrote in 1587 that 'all London is but an hospital' because of the huge number of people receiving aid. He reserved some particularly harsh criticism for Bridewell, where servants, domestics, veteran soldiers and 'other worthy and upright younsters' without work were placed together with vagrants, beggars, thieves and all manner of idlers and scoundrels, so that 'there is no more distinction between good and evil, and the very name of Bridewell is so hateful to the people that all confidence [in it] has been lost and buried forever.'[5] The author of these words makes it clear that he is in no way opposed to punishing beggars and idlers, and wishes only to draw attention to the fact that Bridewell, once the inculcator of morality and good conduct, has degenerated into a place of depravity.

All the evidence indicates that this criticism was justified. Bridewell was indeed manifestly failing in its primary role, which was to put beggars and prostitutes to work and teach them an honest trade. Bridewell's registers from the beginning of the seventeenth century show that the percentage of recidivists was high: in 1602 they made up 22 per cent and in 1631 29 per cent of the vagrants sent there to be tried. One vagrant arrested in 1602 confessed to having been forty times arrested and confined at Bridewell; another, barely twelve years old, was there for the ninth or tenth time. Organizing forced labour turned out to be a costly rather than a profit-making exercise; certainly it could not finance itself. Nor was the programme of re-education simple to implement: like all prisons, Bridewell was a place where a social habits became ingrained. Bridewell's other role was to isolate those who had refused to live by the normal rules of society, but the administrators soon found that this, too, could be achieved by other means – for instance by deportation to the colonies. Accordingly, in 1618–19 they sent ninety-nine children, from nine to sixteen years old, to Virginia. Other transports followed, to Virginia, Bermuda and Barbados.

It was not until the end of the seventeenth century that England witnessed the creation of a network of workhouses which, because they were run on rational economic principles, managed to achieve a measure of success in their punitive and educational aims. The main branch of production developed in these workhouses was textile manufacture, and in particular the spinning of wool. Catherine Lis and Hugo Soly have pointed out how the economic usefulness of these workhouses was linked to certain disproportions in the structure of the textile industry at the time: until the technological innovations of the 1760s, the spinning of yarn was the bottle-neck of the textile trade, and manufacturers were understandably eager to increase yarn production, especially since the workhouses could supply it at a low price. In the first half of the eighteenth century there were close to two hundred such workhouses in England, and in 1723 a law was passed which gave parishes the right to refuse aid to those of their poor who refused to work in them.

This trend in social policy – punishment and education through work – had its origins in the modern reform of charity; its essential principles can be found in the work of Vivés, Sir Thomas More, Frycz Modrzewski and others. But the way in which these theoretical principles of humanism were gradually translated into reality, the varied experiences through which they emerged, show how great is the gap between reality and utopia. Between the founding of Bridewell as the first institution combining the functions of prison, hospice and place of forced work, and the creation of a network of workhouses throughout England, there were many attempts on the continent to establish workhouses and houses of correction of various kinds.

Among all such ventures attempted in Europe, Dutch experiments at creating houses of correction gained particular renown. In 1587 the Dutch humanist Dirck Vockertsz Coornhert published a treatise in which he argued that social and penal policy ought to combine forced labour and loss of freedom. The nobles of Amsterdam were quick to take up this idea, creating in rapid succession a workhouse for men, the Rasphuis, where the primary occupation consisted in working Brazilian wood, and another, the Spinhuis, for women, where the women and children were put to work spinning and sewing. Other cities soon followed Amsterdam's example, and similar workhouses were created in other parts of Holland, especially in cities which were industrial centres. As their usefulness as a source of cheap labour became apparent, the social and educational goals of their founders gradually fell by the wayside. The work was done in groups, and the workers were paid. The daily work schedule was strictly adhered to, and arranged so as to leave time for prayers and the reading (aloud) of religious texts. The Rasphuis in Amsterdam was from the first, more than anything else, a penal institution: in addition to the poor, young criminals and delinquents were imprisoned there, and their sentences could be reduced, for example from twelve to eight years, for good conduct.

The war against 'idleness' remained one of the primary tasks of these institutions, and it was waged with a vengeance. In the Amsterdam work-house, recalcitrant workers were locked up in a cellar which was gradually filled with water. In the cellar there was a pump, and the prisoner, in order to keep from drowning, had to work constantly at pumping out the water. This was considered an effective way of countering idleness and inculcating the habit of work.

In the wake of the Dutch houses came attempts at creating similar institutions in Germany. In the first decade of the seventeenth century workhouses were founded in Bremen and Lübeck, and then, in the following decade, in Hamburg. In the last thirty years of the seventeenth century workhouses mushroomed in dozens of cities of the Empire, among them one in Breslau, founded in 1670. As in England, they were run and financed by the municipality, or else leased directly to manufacturers, who then organized the production.

In either case they had, in addition to their penal and educational role, to satisfy the needs of the local economy, and their continued functioning, and sometimes even their creation, depended on their economic usefulness and on the state of the labour market.

Some historians have thought it significant that the idea of the workhouse should have been adopted as an integral part of social policy by countries and regions which were predominantly Protestant; they have argued that it was precisely the Protestant work ethic which lay behind the development of an institution combining production with punishment, education and social aid. Thus the German scholar A. Müller-Armack has pointed out that Catholic workhouses, in Cologne, Münster, Paderborn, Würzburg, Bamberg and Passau, were not created until the eighteenth century. Indeed, the disparity is striking: there were sixty-three Protestant workhouses to set against this small handful of Catholic ones.

The idea of incorporating forced labour into social policies and using it to combat public begging was not, in fact, a Protestant invention, nor was it limited to Protestant countries. We have seen it in papal efforts to clean up the streets of Rome in the sixteenth century; it played an important role in the evolution of Catholic social doctrine and in the local projects implemented by Catholic municipalities. The different forms which policies of imprisonment, isolation and 'education through work' could take were determined by the social and cultural context in which they were applied. Programmes of forced labour and re-education through work seem to have been implemented mostly in economically well-developed regions; hence their attribution to Protestantism, for the models of behaviour instilled by the Protestant work ethic were well adapted to the needs of emerging industrialized societies.

6.3 The General Hospital and the 'Great Imprisonment' in France

Centralized institutions of social aid in the modern era considered work as an essential instrument for adapting the poor to social life and its requirements. The social and psychological roots of seventeenth-century policies of imprisonment lay in what Michel Foucault has described as the 'myth of social happiness', a curious vision of an ideal social order in which police constraints and Christian principles reigned together. The history of the 'great imprisonment' of the poor in Catholic France in the seventeenth century provides ample evidence of this.

In France, the idea of combining imprisonment with forced labour arose from a mixture of practical experience and theoretical social policy programmes in the sixteenth century. A vigorous policy intended to extirpate vagrancy and public begging was launched at the beginning of the seventeenth century by Barthélemy de Laffémas, when he became the royal economist; it involved the creation of two 'public villages', one for men and the other for women, where the poor would be confined and made to work, if necessary by force. But the isolation of the poor on a large scale did not take place until the creation of 'general hospitals', later in the seventeenth century.

The first attempt to isolate and confine the poor of Paris took place under Marie de Medici when three hospices were created for this purpose, known collectively as the 'Hospital for the Imprisoned Poor' (*Hôpital des Pauvres Enfermez*). In the autumn of 1611 a decree was announced forbidding begging in Paris and ordering all non-resident beggars to leave the city; local beggars were required to find work immediately, or failing this to present themselves, on the day appointed by the decree, at the Place St Germain, to be taken to one of the hospices. This day, as well as subsequent attempts to enforce the decree, was described in a booklet published six years later, according to which the announcement of the decree 'so frightened the beggars that of the eight to ten thousand living in the city only ninety-one presented themselves at the appointed place.'[6] But the streets of Paris were under close surveillance, and in the end hunger forced the beggars to take refuge in the hospices. By the end of six weeks, eight hundred of them had been thus confined, and by 1616 they were two thousand, two hundred. Women who were caught begging were publicly flogged and had their heads shaved, while men were taken off to prison; the giving of alms was punishable by a fine.

The rules governing the running of the three hospices – one for men, one for women and children up to the age of eight and one for the seriously ill – were defined in a special statute. For both men and women they stipulated work from dawn to dusk, beginning at five o'clock in the morning in summer and at six o'clock in winter. The men were put to work in mills, breweries, lumber yards and 'other places of heavy labour', while the women and children sewed and spun, and made stockings and buttons and the like. A supervisor assigned a daily work quota, and those who failed to fulfil it were punished: their food rations were halved, and if they repeated their offence they were expelled from the hospital and imprisoned. Order and discipline were maintained by the supervisors and administrators, but also by a few specially designated beggars, each responsible for a group of twenty people. Builders could use the hospital as a source of hired labour, but the beggars who worked on the sites were given only a quarter of their pay, the rest going to the hospital. A special unit of guards was appointed to enforce the law against public begging, and there was a reward for the capture and imprisonment of vagrants.

In the eyes of the authorities and the general public, however, this microcosm of concentration was, for all its constraints and restrictions, an institution of charity. Admission to it was seen as a sort of privilege, one from which non-resident beggars were excluded, and which could be withdrawn for bad behaviour. Its withdrawal – expulsion – was perceived as a punishment. It could be considered simply as one on a scale of punishments, ranked according to severity: expulsion from the hospital meant a transfer from one prison to another that was even worse, for vagrants arrested in Paris were locked up in the dungeons of Châtelet. But the first article of the statute dealing with 'imprisoned poor' is quite clear in defining the difference between those poor who, armed with the required documents to show that they were born in Paris, were admitted to the hospital and all others who, lacking such documents, 'will be considered strangers to the city and punished'. The 1617 booklet, mentioned above, which describes this first large-scale imprisonment of beggars in Paris, stresses that the aim of the exercise was to provide the poor with work, religious instruction and training for a trade. The religious and charitable aspects of the policy of imprisonment were indeed significant. We have seen how charitable ventures of a religious nature were in fact motivated by social and political considerations; here we have a case of the inverse: the police surveillance and repressive measures which accompanied the imprisonment of the poor were motivated by feelings of Christian charity and inspired by the hope that the poor might, through being forced to work, learn to live a life of dignity. History abounds in examples of schemes to thrust happiness upon men by force; there have been many such ideologies. Accordingly, if we are to understand the reactions to this repressive policy towards the poor, we must take account of the intentions which lay behind it.

For it must be said that, although its more repressive aspects met with some hostility, on the whole it rejoiced in the warm approval and even active support of the general public.

After the Religious Wars, the Counter-Reformation, seeking to rekindle the religious spirit in France and strengthen the position of Catholicism, laid particular stress on the role of the Church in the dispensing of charity and the care of the poor in general. The Society of the Holy Sacrament, created in the 1620s as a strong, efficient and secret political and religious organization with a nationwide presence, launched a crusade against the 'dangers of the age', among which dangers vagrancy and beggary, the 'disorder of the poor', occupied a prominent position. In 1631 this society adopted the policy of imprisoning the poor in general hospitals as part of its social programme. The intended effect of the policy was to render charity more efficient by providing genuine assistance to the poor at a lower cost, and at the same time to avert the threat of social revolt emanating from vagrancy at the time of the Fronde. 'The poor man who, by the circumstances of his birth, is fated to serve the rich' will soon, if he fritters away his youth in begging, vagrancy and general idleness, sink irrevocably into a life of vice – proclaims a booklet describing the plans for a general hospital in Toulouse. Here the 'social training' scheme which lay behind the creation of general hospitals is made quite explicit. The concrete measures which it involved, and which began to be implemented in Toulouse in 1647, served their aim well: almost all the poor, including small children, were to be imprisoned and made to work, and begging, as well as individual alms-giving, was forbidden.

The society's most important achievement was the creation of a general hospital in the capital. Previous attempts at founding an institution of this type had left their mark, and the experience could be drawn upon. In addition, social tensions in the city were running high, and the problem of the poor had once again been brought into sharp relief; new measures were urgently needed. According to Henri Sauval, a Parisian chronicler of the seventeenth century, the number of poor in the city had grown to forty thousand. The Society of the Holy Sacrament organized alms distributions and religious instruction, founded the *Magasin Général Charitable*, and ensured that local brotherhoods and charitable organizations provided permanent and regular support for the poor in their parish. When a General Hospital was created in Paris by a royal ordinance of 4 May 1656, members of the society accounted for almost half of the twenty-six seats on its governing board. One of the first measures taken by this board was to create a special police unit to arrest beggars and vagrants. Begging was forbidden on pain of flogging; recidivists would be sent to the galleys.

By 1657 about six thousand paupers were living in this hospital, and most of them had come there of their own free will; beggars who had had to be brought in by force, as prisoners, were a minority. The suppression of individual alms-giving and the threat of punishment proved to be successful means of persuasion. Emanuel Chill, in his work on the imprisonment of beggars, rightly remarks that, while traditional forms of charity and care for the poor endured in the selfless and devoted efforts of the most pious members of the Society of the Holy Sacrament, and indeed in the religious writings of the time, individual compassion had no place within the stark, gloomy and menacing walls of the General Hospital. Although the hospital had room to house only a small percentage of the beggars in the capital, its prison regimen and threatening aspect must have succeeded in cowing and terrifying them all. Its residents, if they infringed the rules of discipline, or if any fault was found with their work or their obedience to religious duties, could be flogged, pilloried or locked up in the cellars. Their clothes consisted of grey habit-like robes with hoods; on each were sewn the emblem of the hospital and the prisoner's number.

The hospital outlived its founders, and continued to thrive and even to expand long after the Society of the Holy Sacrament, known to its enemies as the 'cabal of pietists', had been dissolved by Mazarin. The various hospitals and poorhouses attached to it gradually developed their own particular fields of specialization. Thus the Pitié Hospital, which housed the administration of the General Hospital as a whole, took in mainly children and young girls; in 1663 it had about one thousand residents, of whom two hundred and thirty-six were seriously ill and bedridden, six hundred and eighty-seven were employed in workshops, and the remainder, three hundred and fifty-one girls and one hundred and twenty boys, were sent every day to school. The Salpêtrière Hospital, so called because it was housed in the buildings of the old Arsenal, built under Louis XIII, had room for six hundred and twenty-eight beggars in a total of four hundred and sixty-three beds, and was for women only. Over the years a number of additions to it were built, including a correctional institution for prostitutes; in

1666 it had more than two thousand, three hundred residents, and by 1679 almost four thousand. The Bicêtre Hospital, originally built as a refuge for disabled war veterans, became a hospice for men; the number of residents at any one time was between one thousand and fourteen hundred. Finally, the Savonnerie was turned into a hospice for school-age boys, and the so-called House of Scipio into a refuge for infants and mothers about to give birth. By the end of the seventeenth century the total number of poor housed in the various institutions which made up the General Hospital was close to ten thousand.

By 1666 each of these institutions had its own workshops. A booklet published in that year states that, 'despite considerable resistance, there is now no pauper in any of the buildings of the Hospital who sits idle, apart from the bedridden or the totally infirm. Even old men, cripples and paralytics are forced to work; and since this principle of work for all was instituted there has been greater discipline, order and piety among the poor.' Work was obligatory even in the children's hospices, and in the House of Scipio the women knitted and spun.

Work in these hospitals was organized in one of three ways: some of the workshops were run by the hospital itself; others were run as cooperatives: others still were leased out to traders and manufacturers, who signed a contract with the hospital. By the terms of these contracts the merchants were bound to pay over a certain sum of money to the hospital. Similarly, when residents were 'leased out' for work of various kinds, for example on building sites, two-thirds of their pay was to go to the hospital.

An important point to remember about the work done in these hospitals is that it brought no profit. 'It should not be imagined', we read in a pamphlet published in 1666, 'that such manufacture could, now or at any time in the future, ensure the upkeep of the hospital or bring it any real profit.' Indeed, such work, far from bringing in any profit, was an additional strain on the hospital's budget. Nevertheless, the aim of the exercise being not to derive economic profit from the labour of the residents, but rather to instruct them in religion and morals and instil in them a proper respect for honest work, this additional financial burden was readily assumed by the hospital authorities. The same pamphlet of 1666 describes the effects of the work regimen as follows: 'Many of the poor grew to enjoy their work, and one may safely say that they were all fitted to it; but their long-ingrained tendency to idleness and base behaviour frequently gained the upper hand not only over their own promises and assurances of reform but also over the efforts of the hospital's governors and administrators.[7] Thus the idea of imprisonment and forced labour in the General Hospital was conceived as a way of reaffirming the work ethic, and its universal enforcement was assured through the use of force, threats and fear. The spectacular acts of repression which characterized social aid in the modern era had a well-defined ideological role to play.

Nevertheless, the hospital's creation and the methods of its functioning gradually began to evoke a certain unease among the general public, which disapproved of its manifestly repressive, prison-like regime. Indeed, this unease was shared even by some of the hospital's original founders. Vincent de Paul, who was connected with the Society of the Holy Sacrament, expressed great reservations about the policy of expelling 'alien' beggars from cities, and indeed about the idea of the General Hospital itself: initially in favour of the plan, so much so that he made available for the hospital's use the buildings which had formerly housed the Salpêtrière and the Bicêtre refuges of the poor, and which were subject to his authority, he came to have doubts about the enterprise as it proceeded. He refused to assume the directorship of the hospital, unsure whether the imprisonment of the poor was in accordance with God's will. In this he was not alone, for the policy of imprisonment continued, in the course of the seventeenth and eighteenth centuries, to be questioned by various religious groups in France. It also met with considerable hostility from the populace, by some sections of which the imprisonment of beggars was on occasion physically opposed. The decrees which ordered the creation of general hospitals stated clearly and repeatedly that acts of violence against hospital staff would not be tolerated, and sometimes authorized such staff to bear arms. Jean-Pierre Gutton, a historian of social aid in France, has found that among those who provoked riots and disturbances to defend the poor from imprisonment were craftsmen, servants and labourers, and that their motives for engaging in these protests were varied, ranging from feelings of social solidarity, through anger at the unfair competition created by the hospital workshops, to simple defiance and hostility towards the authorities. At the same time they were expressing traditional attitudes of compassion and respect for poverty as a holy condition. This feeling of solidarity was also the result of high unemployment and the precarious state of the labour market: the uncertainty of life from one day to another, and the very real possibility that they, too, might at any

moment find themselves amongst the ranks of the unemployed, reduced to begging for a living, naturally bound the working population to these paupers. The threat of prison hung over them all. The
files of the Paris police in the eighteenth century, of which a study has
been made by Arlette Farge, contain records of riots in which the
populace resorted to violence in order to prevent police action against
beggars. In 1758 a group of two hundred and fifty pavers, on their
way to collect their pay, wrested a captured beggar from the hands of
the police. On another occasion, a captured beggar shouted, 'Masons,
help!' or, 'Boys, help me!' A labourer on a building site, seeing a
group of hospital guards leading a sixty-year-old cripple whom they
had arrested for begging, cried out, 'The swine, they arrest a man who
had the misfortune to fall from the roof while he was working, but
they don't touch the other beggars.' For people of that time the
imprisonment of beggars was associated with police repression of the
poor in general. Indeed, beggars would sometimes be sent to the
galleys, like ordinary criminals. In 1704, for instance, the provost of
Orléans sentenced a peasant from Jussy-en-Bourbonnais to the galleys
because 'the man', he said, 'although healthy and sound of body, is a
beggar and a vagrant, and has threatened a number of people who
refused to give him alms or shelter for the night, saying that he would
burn their house down.' The man was sentenced to three years in the
galleys, and died in 1707 in the galley-slaves' hospital. The ambivalence which characterized the policy of imprisonment, considered
by the authorities not as a punishment but as an expression of charity
and compassion, naturally led to spontaneous outbursts of protest.

During the French Revolution, in the first days of September 1789,
the Paris mob stormed the prisons, freeing some prisoners and lynch-
ing others. It also forced its way into the buildings of the General
Hospital, as menacing and prison-like in their aspect as they had been
a hundred years previously. Restif de la Bretonne, the 'nocturnal
observer' of Paris life, has left us an account of bloody battles with the
hospital staff and of the liberation of the women's hospital in the
Salpêtrière, where almost eight thousand people were being held.
This is his description of the young girls' wing in this hospital:

> It is a sad life that these unfortunate creatures lead here. Always at
> school, in constant fear of the matron's rod, condemned to eternal
> celibacy and to foul and revolting food, their only hope is that some-
> one might take them on as servants or as apprentices in some hard and

strenuous profession. And even then, what a life! At the smallest complaint from an unjust master they are sent back to the hospital to be punished. . . . [They are] degraded, humiliated creatures, and if by some happy chance they are ever thrown back into society, they will always occupy the meanest position.[8]

In the eighteenth century these institutions continued to function, but social policy underwent a significant change. The combination of repression and charity practised by the general hospitals in the seventeenth century, without any distinction between the two, became the object of widespread criticism in the eighteenth. There were calls for a humanitarian reform of social aid that would allow a distinction to be made between professional vagrants, who should be imprisoned as criminals, and the merely poor, who should be given support or employment. The poor, it was said, ought to be allowed their freedom to learn an honest trade, while forced labour in hospital workshops should be reserved as a punishment. The General Hospital in Paris was accused of being nothing more than a 'detention centre for beggars', a *dépôt de mendicité*, a new institution recently created in other parts of the country.

For much of the eighteenth century, the fundamental role which general hospitals played in social policy continued to be reflected in royal legislation. A decree of 1724 ordered all unemployed to present themselves at the hospitals, where work of some sort, probably on public works, would be found for them. Begging was considered a criminal offence, punishable by at least two months in the General Hospital in the case of a first arrest, three months – along with a reminder, in the form of the letter 'M' (for *mendiant*), with which the beggar was marked – for a second offence, and five years in the galleys (or, for women, in the General Hospital) if the offender was caught for a third time. This last could be extended to a life sentence at the discretion of the court. In 1764 and 1767 two further laws against beggars were issued, defining as a vagrant and a criminal anyone who had been out of work for six months and did not possesses a certificate of morality. 'Beggars' detention centres' began to supplant general hospitals as places of internment for vagrants and able-bodied beggars, while the general hospitals took in the simply poor. In 1784 Necker estimated that the thirty-three detention centres then in existence had seven or eight thousand beds between them. During the period up to 1773, 18,523 beggars were arrested in the Paris area (the

Généralité de Paris), of whom 11,895 were set free, eighty-eight were drafted into the army, 3,158 died and 1,963 escaped. The detention centres in which arrested beggars were held were intended as temporary quarters for those who had families or employers to seek them out. Only vagrants and professional beggars were held there for longer periods: a law of 1785 authorized their use as places of detention for periods as long as several years. All the prisoners were forced to work from dawn to dusk, and each centre was equipped with workshops for this purpose. Riots and disturbances of all kinds were of course frequent in these paupers' prisons, and sometimes, as in Rennes in 1782, erupted into bloody revolts. At the same time, funds for the maintenance of the centres were inadequate, a state of affairs which was a subject of constant complaints from all the provinces. The complaints registers (*cahiers de doléances*) also mentioned the incompetence of these institutions in enforcing the laws against public begging. With the Revolution the brief existence of the detention centres was brought to an end.

The policy of imprisonment had a profound effect on the evolution of modern society in Europe. The singular amalgam of charitable intentions and repressive measures which it involved marked a fundamental step in the reaffirmation of the work ethic. Work, both in Protestant and in Catholic countries, both in economically advanced societies and in those which, still agrarian, were only embarking on the road to industrial revolution, became a form of social education, a way of adapting people to the structures of economic life. The combination of prison and manufacture was in some sense the basis for the functioning of the modern factory, with its discipline, strict rules and organization of work. Even in its external aspect, which left such a deep imprint on the urban landscape that traces of it persisted well into the twentieth century, it resembled a prison.

7

Poverty and the Contemporary World

The closer we approach to the present day, the more the march of history seems to speed up: events, processes and attitudes seem clearer and better defined. It is true that the industrial revolution changed the rhythm to which societies evolved, and in this sense the pace of history has indeed quickened; but it is equally true that our view of the past is deformed by a natural tendency to see recent events as more significant and more transparent than those in the distant past.

The processes discussed in this book – the confrontation of the medieval doctrine of charity with social realities, and the birth of modern social policy – took place in the far distant past and spanned a period of almost a thousand years. It was within this time period that pre-industrial Europe witnessed the birth of all the social attitudes towards poverty, and some of the main social policy programmes, that exist in modern industrial society. The social history of the last two hundred years, however, has seen considerable changes in the quantitative relations between wealth and poverty. Bonds of solidarity have come to encompass broader or different groups, and the problem of poverty has become firmly and explicitly set in the context of industrial development.

7.1 Pauperization and the 'Discoveries' of Poverty

Gianmaria Ortes, considered by Marx as one of the greatest economic thinkers of the eighteenth century, wrote in 1774: 'The wealth of a nation corresponds to its population, and its poverty to its wealth.

The work of some is the cause of idleness in others. The poor and the idle are the inevitable product of the rich and the industrious.'[1] He meant that poverty is a natural phenomenon, and part of the social order. But this view is quite distinct from the medieval theory according to which the poor had a necessary place in the system of distribution of tasks and functions in Christian society. Nor does it have anything in common with the way in which early modern socio-economic literature dealt with the problem of the poor. By the second half of the eighteenth century the emphasis had shifted: the question was no longer how to do away with the masses of beggars and vagrants which had become a scourge for society, but how to define their place in the modern economic system by analysing and coming to understand the causes of poverty as a mass phenomenon. This shift of attitude towards the problem of poverty belongs to the domain of the history of social thought, and can be approached only within the context of the intellectual trends of the period. But this is not to say that the social realities of the day had no influence on the new direction taken by theoretical thought on the subject. Both the nature and the scale of poverty were so changed, and its proportions so vast, that a certain amount of the anxiety and uncertainty it evoked also crept into theoretical reflections and cast doubt on the nature of historical progress.

The pace of processes of social change in the eighteenth and nineteenth centuries was much more varied than it had been before. Although industrialization did much to quicken the evolutionary rhythm, local factors intervened, and the pace and scale of evolution were ultimately determined by the conditions prevailing in particular cities, regions and countries. With time, however, as commerce and transport developed, the labour market expanded and, later, professional brotherhoods, which sought to protect the rights both of workers and of employers, intervened with regulatory mechanisms of their own, a certain equilibrium was restored, and the more glaring discrepancies between wage and price levels were eliminated. Nevertheless, there were some extreme situations not revealed by the statistics: sudden moments of prosperity and equally sudden periods of sharp decline which affected centres of production, cities and regions and particular branches of industry. Economic crises could also have some unexpected effects: even in earlier periods, and outside the context of the first accumulation of capital, we have seen how poverty, the social price paid for economic growth, could favour urbanization and industrial development. The fundamental question, however, and one that has generated considerable controversy, concerns the general direction in which the living standards of modern societies evolved. It is a twofold question, for it involves not only the historical issue, discussed in the preceding chapters, of the relation between pauperization and the birth of capitalism, but the more general socio-economic issue of whether the impoverishment of the masses in an absolute sense is the direct and unavoidable result of capitalist development.

Karl Marx, in considering the different forms of relative over-population in capitalist societies, attempted to analyse the phenomenon of poverty and pauperization. Leaving aside the lumpenproletariat, he distinguished three categories of poor: those capable of work, children, and paupers incapable of work. The poor as a group he defined as a 'house of infirm veterans of the active army of workers and the dead weight of an industrial army of reservists.'[2] He saw constant pauperization as a necessary condition of capitalist production, and treated the problem of poverty as part of a more general analysis of the accumulation of capital. The example of England, the most highly industrialized society of his time, provided him with ample proof that 'the accumulation of riches at one pole means an equal accumulation of poverty, suffering, slavery, ignorance, savagery and moral degradation at the opposite pole.'[3]

This conception of poverty as a necessary evil may be found in the writings of many European thinkers of the eighteenth and early nineteenth centuries. 'The poor of a State are like the shadows in a painting: they provide the necessary contrast', wrote the French doctor and moralist Philippe Hecquet in 1740.[4] Joseph Townsend, an English priest, remarked in his *Dissertation on the Poor Laws* (published in 1786) that poverty is the best guarantee of a constant supply of manual labour for the heaviest work, since hunger, 'while exerting a gentle, silent but relentless pressure, also inclines people to great effort, for it is the most natural motive for work.' A similar opinion was expressed as early as the beginning of the eighteenth century by Bernard of Mandeville, who thinks it quite natural that poverty should in itself constitute a guarantee of labour supply: 'No man', he wrote in his *Fable of the Bees*, 'would suffer to be poor or work hard for his living if it were open to him to do otherwise. It is his need for food and drink, and, in a cold climate, for clothing and a roof over his head, that resigns man to suffer all that he can bear. Without these needs no one would work.' From this argument for the necessity of poverty

Mandeville concludes that, 'in a free nation, where slavery is forbidden, the surest treasure is the existence of large numbers of working poor.'[5]

The vast dimensions of poverty at this time were remarked on not only in the context of arguments which presented it as a necessary evil ('there is a curse upon the earth', wrote Mandeville, 'and we have no other bread than that which we are obliged to eat in the sweat of our brows')[6] or simply as the natural and inevitable consequence of the division of social functions. They were also invoked to bolster another type of argument, namely that poverty is a threat to public order and a hindrance to the proper functioning of the social system. Malthus is perhaps the best example of this line of reasoning: according to him, pauperization is caused by a surplus in the working population. Its growth is steady and relentless, for it follows patterns of demographic growth which are almost impossible to control. For this reason it represents a threat to social equilibrium.

Industrialization absorbed most of the rural immigrants who had been the main cause of pauperization in the previous era. At the same time, however, it changed the face of poverty. The working masses, composed of the urban and rural proletariat, henceforth delineated the social zone of indigence. Workers were assimilated to the poor; their housing and living conditions, their state of health, their large families, their appearance and behaviour, in short, all the characteristics of poverty, identified them as belonging to that social category. The process of proletarization was swift: in France, by 1790, the proletariat made up at least 40 per cent, if not more, of the rural population, and of the urban population between 45 and 60 per cent were hired labourers. The assimilation of workers to 'the poor' as a class hugely increased the social dimensions of poverty, and pauperization became truly a mass phenomenon.

Of the factors responsible for the progressive deterioration of the lives of the working masses, unemployment was probably the most important. In 1784 the clergy of Lyons expressed their anxiety at the tense social situation which had developed in the silk industry, which was the city's main branch of production and depended for its smooth running not only on the supply of raw materials, fluctuations in demand and competition with other centres, but also on royal decisions concerning foreign trade. As a result the level of employment was never stable: 'Today', it was said, 'sixty thousand workers barely suffice, while tomorrow twenty thousand might be too many.' Each fluctuation brought with it extremely serious social consequences, and the spectre of unemployment permanently haunted the lives of the working classes. Hence the frequency with which workers, and especially their wives and children, were to be found among those listed as recipients of aid.

A disparity in the movement of prices was also a factor in the decline of living standards among the masses. The Polish historian Witold Kula has shown that 'products of the poor', in other words food staples, rose in price much more quickly than less basic necessities; similarly, when price fluctuations occurred, periods of high prices tended to last longer than those during which prices fell. The price of non-essential items, in other words luxury goods, which took up a considerable part of the budgets of the rich, tended, on the contrary, to fall, sometimes not only in relative but also in absolute terms; and this of course widened still further the rift between rich and poor. It was only in the later stages of economic development, as the consumption of goods other than basic necessities became gradually more generalized, that this factor ceased to contribute to the impoverishment of the masses.

Looking at the social reality of nineteenth-century Europe one is left with the impression that the living standards of the working classes were in permanent decline. Without delving into the deeper reaches of the old and lengthy debate on pauperization and its processes, we should nevertheless stop to mention three conclusions arrived at in the course of this debate, simplistic though they may sound. They are, firstly, that throughout the nineteenth and twentieth centuries the living standards of the working population gradually improved, and 'workers' ceased to be identified with 'the poor'; secondly, that socio-economic life was characterized by periods of profound and more or less general crisis, as a result of which the living standards of the working population, or of a particular section of that population, suffered a decline; and thirdly, that economic progress erases neither social inequalities nor disparities in the division of global revenue.

Nevertheless, the habit of referring to workers as 'the poor' persisted well into the second half of the nineteenth century. The problem of poverty and pauperization remained closely linked to the 'workers' question' throughout the nineteenth century, and even in the twentieth the two issues were connected: questions of social aid were determined by the state of the labour market, and considered alongside the respective merits of welfare and job creation and the duties of the community towards those for whom it has been unable to provide a means of subsistence. Uncertainty about tomorrow hung constantly over the lives of working people. Factories in the mid-nineteenth century were health hazards, and working in them often meant risking life and limb; but they offered opportunities for more stable employment, and factory workers were on the whole, all things considered, better off than those who were not members of the 'industrial proletariat'. In France, around 1840, only thirty-one thousand workers were employed at yarn factories equipped with spinning machines, while the weaving industry, where traditional methods of cloth production persisted and where the risk of unemployment was constant, employed half a million people. The worst-off in this respect were manual and unskilled labourers of all categories. In London, before the First World War, only 2 per cent of factory workers were unemployed, but among dockers, on any given day, 36 per cent would be out of work and forced to rely on state support in order to feed their families.

The fundamental question in the industrial era was the degree to which different social groups should share in the benefits brought by economic growth. As Wilhelm Abel has shown, a German worker's wages generally rose twelvefold between 1801 and 1951, while during the same period the price of iron doubled and that of wheat tripled. The comparison may seem somewhat arbitrary and simplistic, but it defines the general tendency quite well: workers' wages rose in real terms, the working day became shorter, and overall work and living conditions improved. At the same time, however, disparities between different groups became so glaring that more and more people perceived them as being against nature. The way in which poverty was perceived, and in particular the way in which the poor themselves perceived and felt their own poverty, played an enormously important role, quite independently of objective definitions of poverty and empirical methods of establishing the 'poverty line'. The great twentieth-century surveys and studies of poverty in industrial societies made use of both objective and subjective criteria.

In 1904 the American Robert Hunter, an activist in social and philanthropic organizations, published a book on poverty in the United States. Its subtitle, 'Social Conscience in the Progressive Era', is revealing, although Hunter himself saw his book above all as a sociological study. He defined poverty as a syndrome the constituent elements of which were material need, physical helplessness and a way of life which was socially and psychologically marginalized (this latter being characteristic particularly of vagrants and immigrants). The annual family income he adopted as his poverty line was four hundred and sixty dollars in the industrialized North and three hundred in the South: in this he differed from the president of the miners' union at the time, who considered an annual income of less than six hundred dollars as being below the poverty line. Hunter calculated, while taking account of periodic unemployment, that, of the eighty-two million inhabitants of the continental United States, ten million lived below the poverty line. Among these he distinguished two categories: the merely 'poor', whose incomes enabled them to subsist on a basic level, and 'paupers', who had to rely on state and private aid. Regardless of statistical markers, he considered as poor all those who were 'underpaid, underfed, underclothed, badly housed and overworked'.

Almost sixty years later, in 1962, Michael Harrington again sounded the alarm with his book *The Other America*, in which he attempted to alert public opinion to the huge proportions poverty was assuming. The social context of poverty in the United States in the 1960s was no longer the same as it had been at the beginning of the century. Social policy and attitudes had also changed: it was the mentality of a 'society of abundance' that was under attack in this book. Hunter's main aim, in 1904, had been to free society of its conviction that poverty was the price to be paid for lack of talent, a life of sin and moral decadence; by 1962 the social and economic causes of poverty were clear, and the main aim was to show that poverty could be fought, and that it was the duty of society to fight it. Hunter's study spoke of the possibility of famine, for in the United States at the turn of the century, as in pre- and proto-industrial Europe, the fear of hunger was still present at and below the poverty line. The poor of the 1960s, on the other hand, no longer feared hunger, nor even chronic malnourishment; what marked them out as poor was rather their way of life, which diverged sharply from the norm in the 'society of abundance'.

On the day after the great crisis of 1930, Franklin D. Roosevelt declared that a third of the population of the United States was malnourished and underclothed. Thirty years later, Michael Harrington estimated that between 20 and 25 per cent of the population lived in poverty. A number of American studies, undertaken in the wake of Harrington's book and other efforts to fight poverty in the United

States, attempted to use annual income as a statistical criterion of poverty. Thus in 1965 a study by M. Orshansky adopted an annual income of three thousand dollars for a family of four, or fifteen hundred dollars for a single person, as the poverty line. Ten years later, when these figures had been appropriately adapted, the proportion of poor families in the United States was found to have decreased somewhat. A similar attempt to establish the poverty line on the basis of annual income was also made in England, where about 10 per cent of the population were found to be living below the poverty line. But income proved insufficient as a criterion; more accurate results were obtained by relying on a combination of two factors – income and structure of expenditure. This method was based on the theory, put forward in 1857 by Engels, that the amount of space allocated in a family budget to expenses on food is inversely proportional to the level of wealth.

All these techniques for measuring poverty, however, proved at one stage or another to be less than reliable, and none was flexible enough to allow for a comparison between different periods. B. Seebohm Rowntree's study of poverty in York in three different years – 1900, 1936 and 1950 – showed that accurate comparison between them was impossible because so many factors, such as the degree of public awareness, the amount of information available to the participants in the surveys and the conception of what constituted basic needs, were constantly changing. Critics of income-based techniques have pointed out that the problem of poverty in the United States is to a large degree a sociological and psychological one: the fact that the poor perceive themselves as poor, and feel cut off from the rest of the population, is more important than the actual, measurable extent of their poverty. Nor does the 'discovery' of poverty in modern industrial societies imply a general trend towards pauperization in the evolution of those societies. Such 'discoveries' were the result of a heightened awareness of social inequalities and disparities of income: they were signs that people had become more sensitive to the existence of social problems and felt that it was possible to succeed in the fight against poverty. One should not assume that countries which have not 'discovered' poverty are really untouched by it.

It is characteristic of these 'discoveries' that their object has not been the material situation or living conditions of families or individuals in need of support, but the situation of social groups and classes seen as underprivileged, deprived of their fair share in the division of goods and living below what is generally accepted to be the minimum level necessary to ensure the satisfaction of basic needs.

7.2   The Idea of Philanthropy

As attitudes towards poverty evolved in the modern era, the weight given to ethical and religious considerations gradually declined, and the problem of poverty came to be analysed almost exclusively in terms of social policy, collective interest or reasons of State. This shift of emphasis was owing among other things to the development of economic thought, which saw it as one of its tasks to evaluate the dimensions of poverty and investigate its causes. The various views of poverty, some of which we have discussed above, are all united by a common thread: the conviction that the proper role and duty of the poor, the condition for which they are naturally fitted, is work. Creating opportunities for work was one of the ways of providing social aid; it was also a way of combating moral decadence. Utopian visions of a new social order, so abundant in modern European literature, present work as a kind of panacea, a remedy for poverty and crime alike. For modern man, the moral degradation born of poverty goes hand in hand with the depravity born of a life of idleness. Obligatory work is therefore a frequent recourse in the modern search for effective social policies, and the most common form of state intervention in matters of social aid. The French *dépôts de mendicité*, a system which combined education with repressive measures in dealing with beggars and paupers, is a good example of such intervention; it was reintroduced after the Revolution, and the Napoleonic administration extended it to Italy. In England, the Workhouse Act of 1723, in allowing the creation of joint workhouses by several parishes, abandoned the principle whereby each parish was to be responsible for 'its' own poor; it also expressed the hostile attitude of the rich towards idleness among the poor. The rules of discipline in the first factories were similarly inspired. Work was seen as a form of re-education, a universal remedy for social ills.

Arguments for state intervention in matters of social aid first become clearly formulated in the eighteenth century. Montesquieu argued that the State had a duty to provide all its citizens with adequate living conditions and a means of subsistence, and that the guarantee of work for all should be the principal means of accomplishing this. 'A man who has nothing, and who is forbidden to beg', wrote the French encyclopedists, 'has the right to demand that he be allowed to work for his living.' This recognition of society's responsibilities towards the poor led to the emergence of a centralized social policy, formulated by the State and directed in practice towards the creation of a state system of social aid or state control of charitable institutions. The extent of state intervention depended on a number of different factors. In the nineteenth century liberal doctrine decreed that it must be limited; in the twentieth the tendency was rather to broaden it. It also varied from country to country: in France, for example, state intervention in matters of social aid in the eighteenth and nineteenth centuries was certainly far greater than in England, where it was limited mainly to combating vagrancy; the organization of aid for the poor was left to local authorities and, in Scotland, to the Presbyterian Church.

The so-called New Poor Law, passed by the English Parliament in 1834, may be said to represent the decisive victory of the principle that social aid must be subordinated to the needs of the labour market; from that moment on the two were inextricably bound. Severe repressive measures were intended to dissuade the idle from their ways, and aid to the poor was pronounced to be harmful if it presented a more attractive alternative to working for a living. In workhouses, prison discipline became a frequent means of intimidation; it was certainly effective, as Dickens's vivid evocations indicate. At the same time, the labour force had become more mobile, and fear of the workhouse drove surplus rural labour to seek work in the city. It was thought that the role of the State in matters of social policy and aid to the poor might, by such measures, be limited to a basic minimum. But the socio-economic situation in England, and in other countries where similar legislation had been passed, nevertheless required the creation of a system of social aid. The poor laws fell gradually into disuse, and in England were repealed completely in 1929. At the same time, governments began to develop systematic policies with regard to the poor, and to organize efficient health care, child care, pensions and unemployment benefits.

The various welfare doctrines of the industrial era, as well as public opinion about aid to the poor, were characterized by two principal beliefs. The first of these was the conviction that poverty was something dangerous and threatening, and must therefore be strictly controlled and limited. This attitude was by no means incompatible with the by now familiar view that poverty had a necessary and proper place in society because it forced people to work. The French doctor Philippe Hecquet, who thought that poverty and differences of fortune were necessary to the proper balance of society, and ought therefore to be allowed to persist, also wrote: 'It is therefore necessary that the poor should exist; nevertheless, paupers [*misérables*] should not be allowed to exist; for while the former constitute an integral part of the political economy, the latter bring nothing but shame to humanity.'[7] The view according to which the only poor acceptable to society were the working poor – or those who, if not working, were only temporarily unemployed – became a literary stereotype in the late eighteenth and early nineteenth centuries.

The second widely accepted belief about poverty was that it went hand in hand with crime. Fielding wrote in 1753: 'The suffering of the poor is less visible than their crimes, and this diminishes our compassion for them. They die from hunger and cold among others like themselves, but the wealthy notice them only when they beg, rob or steal.'[8] It is a common prejudice to accuse the poor of all manner of crimes; it is nonetheless true that there have always been links between the poor and criminal elements, and that poverty contributes to the spread of crime. The image of the poor quarters of nineteenth-century Paris in the novels of Balzac, Eugène Sue and Victor Hugo is confirmed to an astonishing degree by the crime statistics and trial testimonies of the period. The French historian and demographer Louis Chevalier has pointed out that in the first half of the nineteenth century in Paris the so-called dangerous classes and the 'working' part of the population were closely intertwined. In addition, European societies in the industrial era harboured the conviction that welfare benefits encouraged idleness and crime in enormous numbers of people who were perfectly capable of working for a living. Historical research has shown this view to be ill-founded: we know, for example, that in a region of England in the early nineteenth century over half of those receiving welfare benefits were children below the age of fifteen, and that only 20 per cent of them were healthy and capable of working. But stereotypes, in order to take root, have never required a particularly firm grounding in reality.

These two ways of seeing the poor – as beasts and as criminals – lay at the root of the repressive measures and discriminatory social programmes which were aimed at them. Near the end of the eighteenth century a professor at the faculty of medicine in Halle proposed, in a Malthusian spirit, that beggars be sterilized. Although hostility towards the poor rarely assumed such drastic forms, the tendency, born in the early modern era, to base social policy on repression and coercion lasted until the twentieth century.

In the last few centuries, however, and especially with the humanitarian ideals of the eighteenth century, such attitudes coexisted with equally strong attitudes of compassion towards the poor. The philosophers of the Enlightenment believed that social progress was linked to human solidarity and to education; accordingly, they saw poverty as the result of ignorance on the part of the poor and lack of solidarity on the part of the rich. Condorcet, Godwin and Wolff argued that aid to the poor was a fundamental way of expressing human feelings, and that repressive measures against the poor were a denial of the principle of brotherly love. According to Thomas Paine,

> There is something wrong in a system of government when old men are sent to the workhouse and young men to the gallows. External appearances in such countries would seem to testify to total happiness; but, hidden from the eye of the average observer, there is a mass of poor who can expect little more than to die of hunger, and in infamy. Paupers enter life already bearing the marks of their destiny; we cannot punish them until we find a cure for poverty.[9]

Compassion towards the poor was expressed above all through the creation of schools for poor children. This was an idea initially suggested by Renaissance thinkers, and put into practice both in Catholic Venice and in Calvin's Geneva; indeed, in this domain the Protestants were much more systematic and efficient than the Catholics. The Philanthropium of Dessau, founded by J. B. Basedow and run by him from 1774 to 1785, was an example of how the principle of brotherly love, in other words Philanthropy, can be put into practice. The philanthropic movement stressed the importance of private charity, relying on it to fund schools and other forms of aid for the poor. It was a principle of the philanthropic movement that funds for the poor come from private sources, for it was thought that in this way higher goals could be realized than those set by public institutions of aid to the poor, and a solid foundation for social peace might be laid. Given that poverty was considered the result of a disorderly life, schools were seen as the best way of educating the poor to obedience and inculcating industriousness and respect for the law.

Humanitarianism and the philanthropic movement tried to find a base for charity in secular principles; just as the municipal reform movement of the sixteenth century wanted to secularize charitable institutions, the philanthropists and humanitarians now tried to secularize the commandment to love one's neighbour. The result, in both cases, was a sort of mingling and readaptation of the old and the new. Similarly, a new form of coexistence emerged between private charity and public aid, the two complementing each other, each searching, in its own way, for happiness and social harmony. The development of secular philanthropy also injected a new vigour into traditional Christian charity, both individual and institutional. There can be no doubt as to the benefits of this philanthropic activity: it brought real aid to the needy, softened blows of fate and the effects of deteriorating living conditions, fought against demoralization and tried to prevent social disorder. Nevertheless, given the huge proportions of poverty it was, and could only be, a palliative, not a remedy.

One of the negative characteristics of philanthropy, one which did perhaps the most damage to its reputation, was its paternalism. In addition, the philanthropists' frequent sermons on the duty of the rich to come to the aid of the poor turned out in many cases to be no more than empty rhetoric. This, too, did much to discredit the movement. The connection made in the modern era between poverty and the lot of the working classes – the identification of 'poor man' with 'working man' – placed the problem of poverty in a well-defined social context; and with the development of class consciousness among the workers, and the creation of trade unions, rich men's charity came to be looked upon with growing distaste and hostility.

David W. Griffith's 1916 film *Intolerance*, a classic of the silent screen, is a powerful condemnation of how charity is doled out to a city's poor. With withering irony, Griffith depicts the hypocrisy of philanthropists and charitable institutions, the enormous gap between the expectations of the poor and the charitable programmes devised for them, so ill-adapted to their needs, and the accompanying repressive measures, which included strict control – almost police surveillance – over the lives, morals, religious practices, personal hygiene and everyday behaviour of the poor. All this served only to confirm and reinforce the general perception of the poor as base, despicable, degraded creatures. The philanthropists condemned all forms of entertainment and recreation for the poor as leading to depravity and idleness. As a result, philanthropic activity was increasingly regarded by the poor, and even by the socialist movement, with hostility and suspicion.

In the course of the twentieth century, poverty – material poverty – was considerably reduced as living standards improved for workers in industrialized countries and official forms of welfare were organized. The just distribution of goods no longer belonged to the domain of charity; it was henceforth a socio-political issue.

7.3 The Poverty of Nations

Charitable programmes have always depended to a great extent on local institutions and community ties. The earliest economic treatments of poverty already recognized how closely linked was the feeling of community to that of collective responsibility for the community's members. As government intervention in matters of social aid became more frequent and broader in scope, so too the concept of local responsibility was broadened, until it encompassed the entire nation or State. In the mid-eighteenth century an English author, writing about charitable programmes for sailors, remarked: 'British benevolence, together with British enthusiasm, will spread the true spirit of patriotism throughout our kingdom.'[10]

Politicians throughout the ages have used a variety of arguments involving an appeal to some sort of community: they have appealed, for instance, to reasons of State, the power of the State, military needs and foreign competition. Philanthropists and humanitarians appealed to human solidarity and the unity of the human race, but even they did not venture beyond their own national horizon. It was religion which provided the broadest kind of solidarity: the faithful were bound by ties which not only went beyond local communities but crossed the frontiers of nations. Such bonds of solidarity were particularly strong among minority groups; the institutions of charity developed within Jewish communities are a good example. Occasionally, during the twentieth century, attempts were made by philanthropists, both secular and religious, to extend their activities beyond Europe. Such attempts, although of little significance by themselves, nonetheless testified to a certain awareness on the part of industrial societies of the existence of a world beyond their own borders. In the modern world, the poverty of nations on all four continents is the direct concern of industrialized countries; the social ills of such nations have become above all a political issue, for poverty is one of the main features which define and set apart the so-called Third World.

The techniques for measuring poverty currently in use in industrialized societies have proved ill-adapted to conditions in Asia, Africa and South America: the difference in economic evolution between countries in these regions and the industrialized world is just too great to allow for comparisons on the same scale. The gap becomes all to evident when one calculates in terms of per capita income: for example, when the poverty line in the United States, based on per capita income, was established at 1,500 US dollars, the average per capita income in Third World countries was 520 US dollars – in 1950 it was half that. Nor is the structure of consumption, another basis for establishing criteria of poverty in the Western world, of much use in Third World countries, where the poverty line is simply a question of survival. Hunger and chronic malnutrition are present here on a huge scale, and few of these countries have succeeded in eradicating them permanently from the daily lives of their citizens. The populations of India, Cambodia, Somalia and Uganda continue to suffer from regular famines; an estimated 25 to 30 per cent of the population of South Asia and Africa suffer from chronic malnutrition. Despite a degree of industrialization and economic progress, hunger and malnutrition in the Third World are not declining; on the contrary, as population growth exceeds economic growth, they are increasing.

The figures cited by international organizations, and constantly repeated in the press, are horrifying: of the world's population of four billion, almost half live in poor countries with a low national revenue. Half a billion suffer from hunger. Half a billion can neither read nor write. Over a billion have no access to drinkable water or medical care. According to demographic estimates, the world's population will increase by another two billion by the year 2000 – in 1925 two billion was the entire world population. This massive increase will take place mainly in the poorest countries of the Third World, those with the lowest national revenue. In the 1970s the GNP of developing countries, inhabited by 66 per cent of the world's population, represented no more than 12.5 per cent of the gross world product. Modernization has done little to soften the contrast with the industrialized world, but it has widened and accentuated differences between particular groups or regions within these countries. Since the 1960s Brazil, whose national revenue currently places it, according to international statistics, in the middling category, has managed to quadruple its GNP to become the leader among developing countries; but in its north-eastern regions, which are inhabited by a third of the country's total population of a hundred and thirty million, the poverty is comparable with that in Bangladesh. At the same time the country's highest and lowest salaries stand in a ratio of 1 to 500. Added to this is the stunning indifference so often displayed by the elites of Third World countries in the face of the contrast between their own wealth and the poverty of the population as a whole.

The problem of poverty in the Third World should be analysed in terms of international relations and strategies for their development. Its causes vary from country to country and continent to continent, and the possible remedies will vary accordingly. But in international politics, and to a certain degree in the collective consciousness as well, it is perceived as a global phenomenon which concerns the world as a whole. The historian, if he follows the debates about what policies should be adopted by industrial countries with regard to poor ones, will be surprised at the similarity between such debates and the socio-economic arguments advanced at the beginning of the modern era for various ways of combating poverty in Europe. Some of these arguments appear again and again, confirming the similarity in a particularly striking way.

It is often asked, for example, whether international aid to poor countries might not be counter-productive, in that it discourages such countries from taking active steps to lift themselves out of their own misery and reinforces attitudes of passivity and dependence. Instead of seeking to increase their own production, countries of the Third World are encouraged to rely entirely on foreign aid. An American journalist wrote in 1978: 'Aid is simply charity – it does nothing to stimulate local productivity. Aid encourages poor nations in their indifference to human suffering and growing poverty.'[11] A policy of aid, according to its critics, serves only to reinforce the social and psychological attitudes which generate poverty.

Proponents of aid to Third World countries, on the other hand, maintain that poor countries have the right to demand support. Both medieval and modern arguments in favour of the 'rights of the poor' were based on the teachings of the Scriptures, and even defended the poor man's right to steal if he did so from dire need. In the case of the

Third World, arguments based on an interpretation of such 'rights' combine medieval and humanitarian traditions. A former president of the World Bank, Robert McNamara, has said that poor countries have a 'fundamental right to a minimum of food, medical care and education'. Critics of this line of reasoning argue that it neglects the interests of rich countries and absolves poor countries of all responsibility for their present, as well as their future, state. One can only talk of rights and collective responsibility, say these critics, within a well-defined context, a system of values and institutions which have the power to establish, strengthen or weaken such rights and responsibilities. The idea of a global community belongs to the realm of wishful thinking, intentions rather than reality; poor countries must fight their own battle with poverty. This argument, too, echoes the great moral debates about the ethos of wealth. Just as Calvinists and Puritans maintained that wealth is a reward for good deeds, and poverty a punishment for a misspent life or the result of idleness, so others today resort to similar arguments in order to justify, with reference to economic policy or social ethics, the current state of imbalance between the wealth of some and the poverty of others.

Policy with regard to the Third World is also characterized by an element of fear, for poverty poses a threat to world peace and stability. Fear of the beggar and the vagrant in modern Europe was sometimes used as an argument to increase charitable activity; more often, however, it led to policies of repression and isolation of the poor. In the modern world poverty remains a threat, and a threat which increases daily with demographic expansion. Fear of this threat provides the main motivation for rich countries to come to the aid of poor ones and seek solutions to their poverty; in this case a policy of isolation and repression, apart from being impossible to realize, would quite simply be unthinkable.

The poverty of nations has become the subject of international policy, of the policy of States and blocs, international organizations and institutions. Little by little, the feeling that the modern world is a united whole has also been seeping through to the collective consciousness. Some of the arguments advanced by opponents of aid to the Third World have received massive popular support in industrialized countries, and have been influential in forming collective attitudes: the so-called Cartierist movement in France in the 1960s, named after a *Paris Match* journalist known for his opposition to Third World aid, is one such example. At the same time, however, greater awareness of poverty in other countries has induced a corresponding change in Western public opinion, and encouraged social and political movements, groups and organizations to take an active part in fighting poverty on a global scale. Indeed, the very expression 'the global poor', which has now entered common usage, shows the extent to which attitudes have changed. When we speak of the 'global poor', we leave the terminology of politics and socio-economic strategy and enter the realm of ethics: the expression symbolizes a feeling of brotherhood and solidarity with all members of the human race.

The idea of the 'global poor' also implies that the world of poverty is a world apart, and that the lives of the poor are very different from our own. When the poor themselves become aware of their otherness, their own sense of identity is reinforced; a common feeling of injustice and inequality strengthens the bonds which unite them. The ideologies and social movements of the Third World, like all great historical movements, arise from a conviction that poverty is born of exploitation, and that the 'damned of the earth', by revolting against the rest of the world, will finally succeed in liberating themselves from the shackles of poverty.

Conclusion

Can feelings have a history? The French historian Lucien Febvre, defying the positivists, claimed that they can, and considered them a proper and worthy subject of historical research. Historians of literature, culture and ideas gradually began to take an interest in this new field, delving into the history of the idea of love and the idea of happiness, the history of laughter, and, most exhaustively of all, the history of fear. Despite the undoubted importance of such studies for our knowledge of past cultures and societies, the field is one in which a degree of arbitrariness is difficult to avoid; a real history of feelings would have to investigate processes of biological evolution, processes far too slow for the historian to observe and impossible to analyse with the aid of research techniques proper to the historian's craft. Nevertheless, in studying the motivations of human behaviour and the external expressions of human feelings (rather than the feelings themselves), the historian is able to distinguish certain patterns: some attitudes and types of behaviour are more socially acceptable at certain periods than others, and the intensity with which they are expressed will also vary from one period to another.

The historian feels safest when dealing with the theoretical and ideological underpinnings, and the corresponding behavioural patterns, of a particular era; once one begins to delve into their social ramifications one is in less familiar territory. The task here is doubly difficult, for patterns of social behaviour tend to be very long-lasting: they become entrenched, often outliving the ethical and cultural codes and attitudes in which they had their origin. As a result, one is liable to assume that patterns of behaviour reflect genuine attitudes when in fact they have long ceased to do so. A good example of the durability of behavioural models is the persistence, even in times of 'great fear', of the idea of courage as a virtue. Similarly, the commercialization of the marriage contract proceeds even in times when great importance is attached to bonds of affection; we conceal our selfish motives, for we know that altruism is the generally accepted virtue. In every civilization, feelings, or at least certain kinds of feelings, are classified according to a hierarchy of values, and this hierarchy is a very durable one. Thus compassion towards the weak and the needy seems to have been firmly established as a virtue in European civilization, persisting even as, at the beginning of the modern era, the shadow of the gallows came to darken the reality in which they had been nourished.

Few European writers have gone further than Bernard de Mandeville in exposing human hypocrisy; it was not without reason that his contemporaries rejected him as a cynic. His treatment of compassion was deliberately iconoclastic. He considered charity to be one of the principal virtues, but only if the people towards whom we practise it, by transferring to them 'some of that pure and sincere love which we feel for ourselves', are not bound to us by ties of friendship or kinship of any kind.[1] Pity, on the other hand, he considered a false virtue, only superficially related to charity. Like anger and fear, pity is a sudden and spontaneous outburst of feeling, uncontrollable and independent of our will; it is therefore a sort of passion, albeit a perfectly benign one. At least, it is benign as long as it does not lead us to neglect our natural duties; for it is precisely pity which, along with pride and vanity, is responsible for senseless and unreasonable foundations, donations and legacies. Such practices ought to be opposed: 'No harm would come to the Public if men were prevented from the vanity of putting an excess of treasures into the Dead Fund of the Kingdom.'[2] Even charity can be harmful, for if it becomes too widespread and excessive it can foster idleness and a disinclination to work. It is therefore in the public interest for us to control our own feelings and passions and our desire for virtue. We must recognize that the happiness of a nation requires the presence of large numbers of beggars, and that pity towards the poor may sometimes entail cruelty towards the rich. The wise law-giver, therefore, will 'cultivate them [the poor] with the greatest care, and guard against their lack, just as he guards against the lack of food.'[3] Acording to Mandeville, then, feelings of charity, too, can be pernicious, no less than its practice; and the moral value placed on feelings and behaviour depends both on individual motives and on the true interest of the community.

Attitudes towards poverty are shaped essentially by the idea of mutual aid and solidarity, both in the context of the family and the local community and in professional relationships; in both cases, a group comes to the aid of those of its members who are unable to provide adequately for themselves. Even at times of widespread poverty, this principle of local responsibility has retained its hold, influencing present attitudes towards the problems of the Third World as well as the reform of charity in the sixteenth century. In addition to being rooted in feelings of group solidarity, aid to the poor also contains an eschatological aspect: alms-giving can be perceived as a sort of sacrifice, a form of communication between man and God. The act of true charity, charity in the fundamental sense of *caritas*, or love, must be completely disinterested; nevertheless, in social attitudes to charity, motives of self-interest are often intertwined with genuine love of one's fellow man: true charity and contemptuous pity exist side by side. The alms given to a beggar who makes an ostentatious display of his poverty and his infirmity may be inspired by a mixture of pity, which is a spontaneous and temporary reaction, genuine compassion in the face of need, and the hope of obtaining one's just reward on the eschatological plane. Similarly, philanthropy, as well as expressing a genuine desire to help one's fellow man, can also be a way of displaying one's wealth and affirming one's social prestige. Thus charity is a complex feeling, and its practice involves a number of different motivations.

In considering the evolution of attitudes to charity over a thousand years of European history, we have attempted to trace the history of institutions and social policies, of their ideological underpinnings and the theoretical discourse within which they evolved, and, to some extent, of behaviour in the face of poverty; we have also tried to contrast and confront this history with the history of poverty as a social phenomenon. It was from the confrontation of these two parallel histories that a picture of evolution emerged – an evolution in which shifts in social and moral codes could be seen as a response to corresponding changes in the social reality. At the same time, however, social and ethical models of behaviour retained a certain degree of autonomy: the proponents of the new social policy, for example, clearly did not abandon their firm attachment to traditional forms of charity; nor did individual acts of charity disappear when repressive measures against beggars and vagrants were intensified. If feelings of charity can endure even in such difficult times, they must be very firmly rooted; for this reason the history of feelings has a bearing on our understanding of the history of attitudes towards poverty.

It is also partly for this reason that interpretations of the problem of poverty, the debates and ideological polemics surrounding it, and even the types of behaviour displayed in response to it, have been so similar at different periods. The medieval ethos of poverty was gradually weakened until, on the threshold of the modern era, it disintegrated completely; but it left so strong a mark on Christian civilization that it persists in European culture as an undercurrent, as one possible solution among many, waiting to be resuscitated. In the 1960s and 1970s the model of the life of poverty and renunciation of worldly goods reappeared as one of the responses to the ideological crisis of the 'civilization of plenty'; but this stand has never received the kind of official, ideological and institutional backing it enjoyed in the Middle Ages, and remains no more than an expression of individual choice. The world seems always, in every age, to have been peopled by proponents of voluntary poverty as well as by those who exalt the virtues of work, thrift and material wealth; by those for whom charity and compassion are the supreme virtues, and those for whom poverty is a matter of indifference, a problem to be solved by a policy of repression. It is only the relative proportions of these attitudes that change.

The birth of modern society was accompanied by a sharp deterioration in human relations – the social price, according to some social and economic historians, of the expansion of capitalism. Whether or not this price was too high, it was paid, and it would be vain, in the twentieth century, to speculate about the extent to which it was morally justified. What is certain, on the other hand, is that the social policy implemented at the beginning of the modern era, a policy based on 'measures of the rich', enjoyed widespread support at the time; few reacted with outrage when prison and the gallows supplanted charity and compassion. The virtues we consider supreme, the feelings and values we prize above all others, surface in us and influence our behaviour only when reality permits. But at such moments we also reject and condemn all past actions which violated or failed to respect these most precious feelings and values, for even historical necessity cannot justify depriving individuals and groups of their natural rights.

Notes

Introduction: What is Poverty?

[1] B. Seebohm Rowntree, *Poverty and Progress: A Second Social Survey of York*, London, 1941, p. 102.

[2] Alfred Marshall, *Principles of Economics*, 8th edn, London, 1903, p. 2.

[3] J. K. Galbraith, *The Affluent Society*, Boston, 1958, p. 259.

[4] D. Matza, 'Poverty and disrepute', in *Contemporary Social Problems*, ed. R. K. Merton and R. A. Nisbet. 2nd edn, New York, 1966, p. 657.

[5] C. L. Waxman, The stigma of poverty: a critique of poverty, *Theories and Policies*, New York, 1976, p. 71.

[6] D. Matza, op. cit., p. 668.

Chapter 1 The Middle Ages: is Poverty Necessary?

[1] Monumenta Germaniae Historica, Legum sec. II, vol. I. p. 106, a. 802.

[2] Patrologia Latina, vol. LXXXVII, col. 533.

[3] Cf. F. Graus, 'The poor of the city and the poor of the country in the late Middle Ages', *Annales E.S.C.*, 16, p. 1055, n. 2.

[4] Patrologia Latina, vol. CXVIII, col. 1625.

[5] Cf. B. Tierney, 'The decretists and the "deserving poor"', *Comparative Studies in Society and History*, I. 4, 1959, p. 365.

[6] Cf. A. Murray, 'Religion among the poor in the thirteenth century; France: the testimony of Humbert de Romans', *Traditio*, XXX, 1974, p. 307.

[7] Cf. J. Batany, 'Les pauvres et la pauvreté dans les revues des "estats du monde"', in *Études sur l'histoire de la pauvreté*, ed. M. Mollat, Paris, 1974, p. 478.

[8] Ibid., p. 483.

[9] Fazio Degli Uberti, *Liriche edite ed inedite*, ed. R. Renier, Florence, 1883, p. 178.

[10] 'Death can indeed take away a man's life, but not fame or high virtue which, happy and real, remains alive in the world for ever. But he who descends to your depths, [O Poverty], however magnanimous and noble, will always be considered a vile thing; and therefore, let him who sinks into your abyss abandon all hope of ever spreading the wings of esteem.'

[11] *Cosmae Pragensis Cronica Boemorum*, ed. B. Bretholz, Berlin, 1923, I, ch. III.

[12] *Erzählungen des Mittelalters*, ed. J. Klapper, Breslau, 1914, p. 178.

[13] Jean, sire de Joinville, *Histoire de Saint Louis*, ed. N. de Wailly, Paris, 1868, p. 248.

[14] Cf. G. Uhlhorn, 'Vorstudien zu einer Geschichte der Liebestätigkeit im Mittelalter', *Zeitschrift für Kirchengeschichte*, IV, 1881, p. 71.

[15] Cf. G. Cohen, 'Le thème de l'aveugle et du paralytique dans la littérature française', *Mélanges Émile Picot*, vol. II, Paris, 1913, p. 393.

[16] G. Duby, 'Les pauvres des campagnes dans l'Occident médiéval jusqu'au XIIIe siècle', *Revue d'histoire de l'Église de France*. LII, 1966, p. 25.

[17] Monumentz Germaniae Historica, Formulae, I, p. 258. Cf. M. Mollat, *Les pauvres au Moyen Age: etude sociale*, Paris, 1978, p. 44.

[18] Chrestien de Troyes, *Yvain ou le Chevalier au Lion*, ed. Foerster, Halle, 1891, v. 5300.

Chapter 2   The Disintegration of Medieval Society

[1] H. Hauser, *Les origines historiques des problèmes historiques actuels*, Paris, 1930; *La modernité du XVIe siècle*, Paris, 1930.

[2] Giovanni, Matteo and Filippo Villani, *Croniche*, vol. II, Trieste, 1858, pp. 9–10.

[3] *The Society of Renaissance Florence: A Documentary Study*, ed. G. Brucker, New York, 1971, p. 102.

[4] Cf. F. Braudel, *La Méditerranée et le monde méditerranéen à l'époque de Philippe II*, Paris, 1966, vol. I, p. 471.

[5] E. Le Roy Ladurie, *Les paysans de Languedoc*, Paris, 1966, p. 278.

[6] J. Delumeau, *Rome au XVIe siècle*, Paris, 1975, p. 107.

[7] G. King, *Natural and Political Observations* (1696), London, 1801; cf. P. Laslett, *The World We Have Lost*, London, p. 36.

[8] Vauban, *Projet d'une Dixme royale* (1707) ed. É. Coornaert. Paris, 1933, pp. 77–81.

Chapter 3   Reformation and Repression

[1] *Registres des déliberations du Bureau de la Ville de Paris*, ed. F. Bonnardot, Paris, 1883, vol. I, p. 227.

[2] 'Livre de rason de Me Nicolas Versoris, avocat au Parlement de Paris (1519–1530)', ed. G. Fagniez, *Mémoires de la Société de l'histoire de Paris*, vol. XII (1885), Paris, 1886, p. 118.

[3] *I Diarii di Marino Sanudo*, Venice, 1879–1903, vol. XLVI, cols. 308, 550, 612.

[4] Ibid., vol. XLVII, col. 148.

[5] *Documents parlementaires et discussions concernant le projet de loi sur les établissements de bienfaisance*, Brussels, 1857, vol. I, p. 332.

Chapter 4   The Reform of Charity

[1] *Recueil des ordonnances des Pays-Bas*, 2nd series, Brussels, 1893, vol. III, pp. 157–61.

[2] Ibid.

[3] C. de Robillard de Beaurepaire, *Cahiers des États de Normandie sous le règne de Henri III*, Rouen, 1887–8, vol. II, pp. 161–2.

4   *Documents concernant les pauvres de Rouen*, ed. G. Panel, Rouen Paris, 1917, vol. I, p. 16.
5   Ibid., p. 41.
6   Ibid., p. 121.
7   G. Paradin, *Mémoires de l'histoire de Lyon*, Lyons, 1573, p. 292.
8   Cf. P. Slack, *Poverty and Politics in Salisbury, 1597–1666: Crisis and Order in English Towns, 1500–1700*, ed. P. Clarck and P. Slack, London, 1972, p. 182.
9   Ibid., p. 194.

Chapter 5   Charitable Polemics: Local Politics and Reasons of State

1   M. Bataillon, J. L. Vivés: réformateur de la bien-faisance*, Bibliothèque d'Humanisme et de Renaissance, XIX, 1952, p. 142.
2   Joannes of Ludzisko, *Orationes*, ed. H. S. Bojarski, Wroclaw, 1971, p. 103.

Chapter 6   Prisons of Enlightenment

1   M. Foucault, *Surveiller et punir: naissance de la prison*, Paris, 1973.
2   M. de Montaigne, *Journal de voyage en Italie (1580–1581)*, Paris, 1946, p. 229.
3   A. Guevarre, *La mendicità provveduta nella città di Roma*, Rome, 1693, p. 19.
4   Ibid., p. 109.
5   *Tudor Economic Documents*, ed. R. H. Tawney and E. Power, London, 1924, vol. III, pp. 431, 439.
6   Cf. C. Paultre, *De la répression de la mendicité et du vagabondage en France sous l'Ancien Régime*, Paris, 1906, p. 138.
7   Ibid., p. 189.
8   N. Restif de la Bretonne, *Les Nuits de Paris*, ed. P. Boussel, Paris, 1963, p. 287.

Chapter 7   Poverty and the Contemporary World

1   G. Ortes, *Della economia nazionale, libri sei*, Venice, 1774.
2   K. Marx, *Capital*, 1. I, part VII, ch. XV, 4.
3   Ibid.
4   Cf. J. Kaplow, *The Names of Kings: the Parisian Labouring Poor in the Eighteenth Century*, New York, 1971, p. 27.
5   B. de Mandeville, *The Fable of the bees or Private vices, public benefits, with an essay on charity and charity-schools, and a search into the nature of the society, 1705–1723*, London, 1740.
6   Ibid.
7   Cf. J. Kaplow, op. cit., pp. 59–60.
8   H. Fielding, *A Proposal for Making an Effectual Provision for the Poor* (1753), in *Works*, New York, 1902, vol. XIII, p. 141.
9   Cf. B. Inglis, *Poverty and the Industrial Revolution*, London, 1971, p. 36.
10 Cf. A. W. Coats, 'The relief of poverty: attitudes to labour and economic change in England, 1660–1782', *International Review of Social History*, 21, 1976, p. 111, n. 2.
11 *The Washington Post*, 27 July 1978.

Conclusion: a Return to Compassion?

[1]   B. de Mandeville, op. cit., vol. II.
[2]   Ibid.
[3]   Ibid.

Bibliography

Introduction

ABEL, W., *Massernarmut und Hungerkrisen im vorindustrieellen Europa: Versuch einer Synopsis*, Hamburg, 1974.

BENDIX, R., *Work and Authority in Industry*, Berkeley, 1974.

CLARK, K. B. and HOPKINS, J., *A Relevant War against Poverty*, New York, 1970.

GEREMEK, B., 'La réforme de l'assistance publique au XVIe siècle et ses controverses idéologiques', in *Domanda e consumi: atti della sesta settimana di studi*, Florence, 1978, pp. 187–204.

GEREMEK, B., 'Povertà', in *Enciclopedia Einaudi*, X. Turin, 1980, pp. 1054–82.

HARRINGTON, M., *The Other America: Poverty in the United States*, New York, 1962.

KINCAIRD, J. C., *Poverty and Equality in Britain*, London, 1973.

LEWIS, O., *La cultura della povertà et altri saggi di antropologia*, Bologna, 1973.

LIS, C. and SOLY, H., *Poverty and Capitalism in Pre-Industrial Europe*, Hassocks, 1979.

MENCHER, S., 'The problem of measuring poverty', *British Journal of Sociology*, XVIII, 1967, pp. 1–12.

MERTON, R. K. and NISBET, R. A., ed., *Contemporary Social Problems*, New York, 1966.

MOYNIHAN, D. P., ed., *On Understanding Poverty*, New York, 1968.

POLANYI, K., *The Great Transformation*, Boston, 1971.

ROWNTREE, B. S., *Poverty: A Study of Town Life*, London, 1901.

ROWNTREE, B. S., *Poverty and Progress: A Second Social Survey of York*, London, 1942.

ROWNTREE, B. S. LAVERS, G. R., *Poverty and the Welfare State: A Third Social Survey of York*, London, 1951.

TITMUSS, R. M., *Income Distribution and Social Change*, London, 1962.

TOWNSEND, P. ed., *The Concept of Poverty*, London, 1970.

VALENTINE, C. A., *Culture and Poverty*, Chicago, 1968.

WAXMAN, C. L., *The Stigma of Poverty: A Critique of Poverty. Theories and Policies*, New York, 1976.

WEAVER, T. and MAGID, A., *Poverty: New Interdisciplinary Perspectives*, San Francisco, 1969.

WEBER, M., 'Die protestantische Ethik und der Geist des Kapitalismus', in *Gesammelte Aufsätze zur Religionssoziologie*, I, Tübingen, 1922.

Chapter 1

BATANY, J., 'Les pauvres et la pauvreté dans les revues des "estats du monde" ', in *Études sur l'histoire de la pauvreté*, ed. M. Mollat, Paris, 1974, pp. 469–86.

BIENVENU, J.-M., 'Pauvreté, misères et charité en Anjou aux XIe et XIIe siècles', *Moyen Âge*, LXXII, 1966, pp. 389–424; LXXIII, 1967, pp. 5–34, 189–216.

BOSL, K., '*Potens* und *Pauper*: Begriffsgeschichtliche Studien zur gesellschaftlichen Differenzierung im frühen Mittelalter und zum "Pauperismus" des Hochmittelalters', in *Alteuropa und die moderne Gesellschaft: Festschrift für Otto Brunner*, Göttingen, 1963, pp. 60–87.

BRANDT, A. VON, 'Die gesellschaftliche Struktur der mitellalterliche Lübeck', in *Untersuchungen zur gesellschaftlichen Struktur der mittelalterlichen Städte in Europa*, Konstanz and Stuttgart, 1966.

CARABELLESE, F., 'Le condizioni dei poveri a Firenze nel secolo XIV', *Rivista Storica Italiana*, XII, 1895, pp. 401–18.

CHAREWICZOWA, L., *Klęski zaraz w dawnyn Lwowie*, Lvov, 1930.

CIPOLLA, C. M., *Clocks and Culture*, London, 1967.

COHEN, G., 'Le thème de l'aveugle et du paralytique dans la littérature française', in *Mélanges Émile Picot*, Paris, 1913, II, pp. 393–404.

CONGAR, Y., 'Les laïcs et l'ecclésiologie des ordres', in *I laici nella societas christiana dei secoli XI e XII*, Milan, 1968.

COURTENAY, W. J., 'The king and the leaden coin', *Traditio*, XXVII, 1972, pp. 188–203.

COURTENAY, W. J., 'Token coinage and the administration of poor relief during the late Middle Ages', *Journal of Interdisciplinary History*, III, 1972–3, pp. 275–95.

COUVREUR, G., *Les pauvres ont-ils des droits? Recherches sur le vol en cas d'extrême nécessité depuis la* Concordia *de Gratien (1140) jusqu'à Guillaume d'Auxerre († 1231)*, Rome, 1961.

CURSCHMANN, F., *Hungersnöte im Mittelalter*, Leipzig, 1900.

DE LA RONCIÈRE, C., 'Pauvres et pauvreté à Florence au XIVe siècle', in *Études sur l'histoire de la pauvreté*, ed. M. Mollat, Paris, 1974, pp. 661–745.

DEVISSE, J., ' "Pauperes" et "paupertas" dans le monde carolingien: ce qu'en dit Hincmar de Reims', *Revue du Nord*, XLVIII, 1966, pp. 273–89.

DUBY, G., 'Les campagnes françaises à la fin du XIIIe siècle', *Bolletino dell'Instituto Storico Italiano per il Medio Evo*, 74, pp. 161–73.

DUBY, G., 'Les pauvres des campagnes dans l'Occident médiéval jusqu'au XIIIe siècle', *Revue d'Histoire de l'Église de France*, LII, 1966, pp. 25–32.

FLOOD, D., ed., *Poverty in the Middle Ages*, Werl, 1975.

FOSSIER, R., *La terre et les hommes en Picardie jusqu'à la fin du XIIIe siècle*, Paris, 1968.

GAIER-IHOEST, J., *L'évolution topographique de la ville de Dinant au Moyen Âge*, Brussels, 1964.

GÉNICOT, L., 'Sur le nombre des pauvres dans les campagnes médiévales: l'exemple de Namur', *Revue historique*, CCLVII, 1977, pp. 273–88.

GEREMEK, B., 'I salari e il salariato nelle città del Basso Medio Evo', *Rivista Storica Italiana*, LXXVIII, 1966, pp. 368–86.

GEREMEK, B., *Le salariat dans l'artisanat parisien aux XIIIe-XVe siècles*, Paris, 1968.

GEREMEK, B., *Les marginaux parisiens aux XIVe et XVe siècles*, Paris 1976.

GIEYSZTOR, A., 'La légende de saint Alexis en Occident: un idéal de pauvreté', in *Études sur l'histoire de la pauvreté*, ed. M. Mollat, Paris, 1974, pp. 125–39.

GONAGLE, S. H., *The Poor in Gregory of Tours: A Study of the Attitude of Merovingian Society towards the Poor*, New York, 1936.

GRAUS, F., 'Au bas Moyen Âge, pauvres des villes et pauvres des campagnes', *Annales E.S.C.*, 16, 1961, pp. 1053–65.

HARTUNG, F., 'Die Augsburger Zuschlagsteuer von 1475', *Jahrbuch für Gesetzgebung, Verwaltung und Volkswirtschaft im Deutschen Reich*, 19, 1985, pp. 95–136.

HOBSBAWM, E., 'Poverty', in *International Encyclopedia of Social Sciences*, XII, New York, 1968.

HOLZAPFEL, H., *Die sittliche Wertung der körperlichen Arbeit im christlichen Altertum*, Würzburg, 1941.

KUSKE, B., *Die städtische Handels-und Verkehrsarbeiter*, Cologne, 1914.

LALLEMAND, L., *Histoire de la charité*, III: *Le Moyen Âge*, Paris, 1906.

LAMBERT, M. D., *Franciscan Poverty (1210–1223): The Doctrine of the Absolute Poverty of Christ and the Apostles in the Franciscan Poverty*, London, 1961.

LASLETT, P., 'Mean household size in England since the sixteenth century', in *Household and Family in Past Time*, ed., P. Laslett, Cambridge, 1972, pp. 125–58.

LAZZARINO DEL GROSSO, A. M., *Società e potere nella Germania del XIII secolo: Gerhoch di Reichersberg*, Florence, 1974.

LECLERCQ, J., 'Pour l'histoire du vocabulaire de la pauvreté', in *Mélange Dieb*, Bayreuth, 1967, pp. 293–308.

LECLERCQ, J., 'Aux origines bibliques du vocabulaire de la pauvreté', in *Études sur l'histoire de la pauvreté*, ed. M. Mollat, Paris, 1974, pp. 35–43.

LE GOFF, J., 'Les paysans et le monde rural dans la littérature du haut Moyen Âge (v^e–vi^e siècle)', in *Settimane di Studio del Centro Italiano di Studi sull'Alto Medioevo*, XIII, Spoleto, 1966, pp. 723–41.

LITTLE, L. K., *Religious Poverty and the Profit Economy in Medieval Europe*, Ithaca, 1978.

MANSELLI, R., 'Evangelismo e povertà', in *Povertà e ricchezza nella spiritualità dei secoli XI et XII* (Convegni del Centro di Studi sulla Spiritualità Medievale, XIII), Todi, 1969, pp. 11–41.

MARTIN, H., 'Les religieux mendiants de Bretagne et l'assistance aux pauvres au Moyen Âge, *Actes du 97e Congrès national des sociétés savantes*, Nantes, 1972, Philologie et Histoire, pp. 347–57.

MASCHKE, E., 'Die Unterschichten der mittelalterlichen Städte Deutschlands', in *Gesellschaftliche Unterschichten in den süd-westdeutschen Städten*, Stuttgart, 1967.

MAY, A. N., 'An index of 13th century peasant impoverishment', *Economic History Review*, 2nd ser., XXVI, 1973, pp. 389–402.

MICCOLI, G., 'Ecclesiae primitivae forma', *Studi Medievali*, 3rd ser., I, 1960, pp. 470–98.

MOLLAT, M., *Les Pauvres au Moyen Âge: etude sociale*, Paris, 1977.

PAGE, F. M., 'The customary poor law of three Cambridgeshire manors', *Cambridge Historical Journal*, III, 1929–31, pp. 125–33.

PATLAGEAN, E., 'La pauvreté à Byzance au temps de Justinien: les origines d'un modèle politique', in *Études sur l'histoire de la pauvreté*, ed. de M. Mollat, Paris, 1974, pp. 59–81.

PHELPS BROWN, E. H. HOPKINS, S. V., 'Seven centuries of the prices of consumables compared with builders wage-rates', *Economica*, XXIII, 1956, pp. 296–314.

PIRENNE, H., 'Un prétendu drapier milanais en 926', *Studi Medievali*, new ser., I, 1928, pp. 131–3.

RAPP, F., 'L'Église et les pauvres à la fin du Moyen Âge: l'exemple de Geiler de Kaysersberg', *Revue d'histoire de l'Église en France*, LII, 1966, pp. 39–46.

ROUCHE, M., 'La faim à l'époque carolingienne', *Revue historique*, CCLIII, 1973, pp. 295–320.

RUGER, W., *Mittelalterliche Almosenwesen: die Almosenordnungen der Reichsstadt Nürnberg*, Nuremberg, 1932.

SAPORI, A., 'La beneficenza delle compagnie mercantili del Trecento', in *Studi di storia economica*, 3rd edn, Florence, 1955, pp. 839–58.

SCHMITT, J.-C., *Mort d'une hérésie: l'Église et les clercs face aux béguines et aux béghards du Rhin supérieur du* XIVe *au* XVe *siècle*, Paris, 1978.

SCHÖNBERG, G., *Finanzverhältnisse der Stadt Basel im XIV und XV Jh.*, Tübingen, 1879.

SUDECK, E., *Bettlerdarstellungen vom Ende des XV Jahrhunderts bis zu Rembrandt*, Strasbourg, 1931.

TIERNEY, B., *Medieval Poor Law: A Sketch of Canonical Theory and its Application in England*, Berkeley, 1959.

TIERNEY, B., 'The decretists and the "deserving poor",' *Comparative Studies in Society and History*, I, 4, 1959, pp. 360–73.

TOUBERT, P., *Les structures du Latium médiéval*, Rome and Paris, 1973.

TREXLER, R. C., 'Charity and defence of urban elites in the Italian communes', in *The Rich, the Well-Born and Powerful*, ed., F. C. Jaher, Urbana, 1974, pp. 64–109.

UHLHORN, G., *Die christliche Liebestätigkeit*, I–III, Staugart, 1882–90.

Chapter 2

ABEL, W., *Crises agraires en Europe* (XIIIe–XXe siècle), Paris, 1973.

ANDERSON, P., *Lineages of the Absolutist State*, London, 1974.

BAIROCH, P., 'Écarts internationaux des niveaux de vie avant la révolution industrielle', *Annales E.S.C.*, 34, 1979, pp. 145–71.

BEIER, A. L., 'Vagrants and the social order in Elizabethan England', *Past and Present*, 64, 1974, pp. 3–29.

BLOCKMANS, W. P. and PREVENIER, W., 'Armoede in de Nederlanden van de 14e tot het midden van de 16e eeuw', *Tijdschrift voor Geschiedenis*, LXXXVIII, 1975, pp. 501–38.

BOIS, G., *Crise du féodalisme*, Paris, 1976.

BRAUDEL, F., *Civilisation matérielle, économie et capitalisme,* XVe–XVIIIe siècle, Paris, 1979.

BRENNER, R., 'Agrarian class structure and economic development in pre-industrial Europe', *Past and Present*, 70, 1976, pp. 30–75.

CHAMBERS, J. D., 'Enclosures and labour supply in the industrial revolution', *Economic History Review*, V. 3, 1953, p. 119 ff.

CIPOLLA, C., *Money, Prices and Civilization in the Mediterranean World*, Princeton, 1956.

COORNAERT, É., *La Draperie-sayetterie d'Handschoote (XIVe–XVIIIe siècle)*, Paris, 1931.

DE MADDALENA, A., 'Rural Europe, 1500–1750', in *Fontana Economic History of Europe*, II, Glasgow, 1974.

FOURASTIÉ, J., 'Osservazioni sui prezzi salariali dei cereali e la produttività del lavoro agricolo in Europa dal XV al XX secolo', *Rivista Storica Italiana*, LXXVIII, 1966, pp. 422–30.

FOURQUIN, G., *Les campagnes de la région parisienne à la fin du Moyen Âge*, Paris, 1964.

GASCON, R., 'Économie et pauvreté aux XVIe et XVIIe siècles: Lyon, ville exemplaire et prophétique', in *Études sur l'histoire de la pauvreté*, ed. M. Mollat, Paris, 1974, pp. 747–60.

GEREMEK, B., 'La popolazione marginale tra il Medioevo e l'èra moderna', *Studi storici*, IX, 1968, pp. 623–40.

GEREMEK, B., 'La lutte contre le vagabondage à Paris aux XIVe et XVe siècles', in *Richerche storiche ed economiche in memoria di Corrado Barbagallo*, Naples, 1970, II, pp. 211–36.

HAMILTON, E. J., *American Treasure and the Price Revolution in Spain*, Cambridge, MA, 1934.

HELLEINER, K. F., 'The population of Europe from the black death to the eve of the vital revolution', in *Cambridge Economic History of Europe*, IV, ed. E. E. Rich and C. H. Wilson, Cambridge, 1967, pp. 1–95.

KULA, W., *Théorie économique du système féodal*, Paris, 1970.

LASLETT, P., *The World We Have Lost*, London, 1971; 3rd edn, London, 1986.

LEADAM, I. S., *The Domesday of Inclosures, 1517–1518*, London, 1897.

LE ROY LADURIE, E., *Les Paysans de Languedoc*, Paris, 1966.

MALOWIST, M., *Studia z dziejów rzemiosla w okresie feudalizmu w zachodniej Europie w XIV i XV wieku*, Varsovie, 1954.

NEVEUX, H., *Les grains de Cambrésis (fin du XIVe–début du XVIIe siècle)*, Lille, 1974.

POSTAN, M. M., *The Medieval Economy and Society*, London, 1972.

POUNDS, N. J. G., 'Overpopulation in France and the Low Countries in the later Middle Ages', *Journal of Social History*, 3, 1970, pp. 225–47.

PROCACCI, G., *Classi sociali e monarchia assoluta nella Francia della prima meta del secolo XVI*, Turin, 1955.

PUTNAM, B. H., *The Enforcement of the Statutes of Laborers*, New York, 1908.

RAU, V., *Sesmarias portuguesas*, Lisbon, 1946.

RAVEAU, P., *L'agriculture et les classes paysannes dans le Haut-Poitou au XVIe siècle*, Paris, 1926.

RAVEAU, P., *Essai sur la situation économique en Poitou au XVIe siècle*, Paris, 1931.

RIBTON-TURNER, C. J., *A History of Vagrancy and Beggars and Begging*, London, 1887.

ROGERS T., *A History of Agriculture and Prices in England*, Oxford, 1866–1902.

ROMANO, R., *Tra due crisi: l'Italia del Rinascimento*, Turin, 1971.

SAUVY, A., *Théorie générale de la population, I: Économie et population*, Paris, 1956.

SCHMOLLER, G., 'Die Einkommensverteilung in alter und neuer Zeit', *Jahrbuch für Gesetzgebung, Verwaltung und Volkswirtschaft im Deutschen Reich*, 19, 1895, pp. 1067–94.

SIMIAND F., *Le salaire, l'évolution sociale et la monnaie*, Paris, 1932.

SLICHER VAN BATH, B. H., *De agrarische geschiedenis van West-Europa (500–1850)*, Utrecht, 1962.

SOSSON, J.-P., *Les travaux publics de la ville de Bruges, XIVe–XVe siècle*, Brussels, 1977.

TAWNEY, R. H., *The Agrarian Problem in the Sixteenth Century*, London, 1912.

THIRSK, J., *Tudor Enclosures*, London, 1959.

THIRSK, J., ed., *The Agrarian History of England and Wales*, London, 1967.

TOPOLSKI, J., *Narodziny kapitalizmu w Europie XIV–XVII wieku*, Varsovie, 1965.

VAN DER WEE, H., *The Growth of the Antwerp Market and the European Economy*, La Haye, 1963.

Chapters 3–5

BATAILLON, M., 'J. L. Vivés, réformateur de la bienfaisance', *Bibliothèque d'Humanisme et de Renaissance*, XIX, 1952, pp. 140–59.

BENNASSAR, B., *Valladolid au siècle d'or*, Paris, 1967.

BONENFANT, P., *Le Problème du paupérisme en Belgique à la fin de l'Ancien Régime*, Brussels, 1934.

CAVILLAC, M., 'Introducción', in C. PÉrez de Herrera, *Amparo de pobres*, Madrid, 1975, pp. vii–cciv.

COYECQUE, É., 'L'assistance publique à Paris au milieu du XVIe siècle', *Bulletin de la Société de l'histoire de Paris et de l'Île-de- France*, XV, 1888.

DARIVAS, B., 'Étude sur la crise économique de 1593–1597 en Angleterre et la loi des pauvres', *Revue d'histoire économique et sociale*, XXX, 1952, pp. 382–98.

DAVIS, N., *Les cultures du peuple: rituels, savoirs et résistances au XVIe siècle*, Paris, 1979.

DELUMEAU, J., *Vie économique et sociale de Rome dans la seconde moitié du XVIe siècle*, Paris, 1957–9.

EHRLE, F., *Beiträge zur Geschichte und Reform der Armenpflege*, Freiburg am Breisgau, 1881.

FOSSEYEUX, M., 'Les premiers budgets municipaux d'assistance: la taxe des pauvres au XVIe siècle', *Revue d'histoire de l'Église de France*, XX, 1934, pp. 407–32.

GRIMM, H. J., 'Luther's contribution to sixteenth-century organisation of poor-relief', *Archiv für Reformationsgeschichte*, LXI, 1970, pp. 222–34.

GUTTON, J.-P., *La Société et les pauvres en Europe, XVIe–XVIIIe siècle*, Paris, 1974.

GUTTON, J.-P., *La Société et les pauvres: l'exemple de la généralité de Lyon, 1534–1789*, Paris, 1971.

HAMILTON, E. J., 'The history of prices before 1750', in *XIe Congrès international des sciences historiques, Rapports*, I, Stockholm, 1960.

HILL, J. E. C., *Society and Puritanism in Pre-Revolutionary England*, London, 1964.

JIMÉNEZ SALAS, M., *Historia de la asistencia social en España en la edad moderna*, Madrid, 1958.

JORDAN, W. K., *Philanthropy in England*, London, 1959.

JORDAN, W. K., *The Rural Charities of England*, London, 1961.

KAMEN, H., *The Iron Century: Social Change in Europe, 1550–1650*, London, 1971.

LEONARD, E. M., *The Early History of English Poor Relief*, London, 1900; repr. 1965.

MEUVRET, J., 'Les crises de subsistance et la démographie de l'Ancien Régime', *Population*, I, 1946, pp. 643–50.

MULLER, A., *La querelle des fondations charitables en Belgique*, Brussels, 1909.

NOLF, J., *La réforme de la bienfaisance à Ypres au XVIe siècle*, Gand, 1915.

PIKE, R., *Aristocrats and Traders: Sevillan Society in the Sixteenth Century*, Ithaca, 1972.

PIRENNE, H., *Histoire économique de l'Occident médiéval*, Brussels, 1951.

POUND, H. F., 'An Elizabethan census of the poor', *Historical Journal*, VIII, 1962, pp. 135–61.

POUND, J., *Poverty and Vagrancy in Tudor England*, London, 1971.

PULLAN, B., 'The famine in Venice and the poor law, 1527–1529', *Bolletino dell'Istituto di Storia della Società e dello Stato Veneziano*, V–VI, 1963–4, pp. 141–202.

PULLAN, B., *Rich and Poor in Renaissance Venice: The Social Institutions of a Catholic State to 1620*, Oxford, 1971.

PULLAN, B., 'Catholics and the poor in early modern Europe', *Transactions of the Royal Historical Society*, ser. V, XXVI, 1976, pp. 15–34.

RUMEAU DE ARMAS, A., *Historia de la previsión social en España*, Madrid, 1944.

SALTER, F. R., *Some Early Tracts on Poor Relief*, London, 1926.

SCHOLIERS, E., *De Levensstandaard in de XVe en XVIe eeuw te Antwerpen*, Antwerp, 1960.

SLACK, P., 'Poverty and politics in Salisbury, 1597–1666', in *Crisis and Order in English Towns, 1500–1700*, ed. P. Clarn and P. Slack, London, 1972, pp. 164–203.

SOLY, H., 'Economische ontwikkeling en sociale politiek in Europa tijdens de overgang van middeleewen naar nieuwe tijden', *Tijdschrift voor Geschiedenis*, LXXXVIII, 1975, pp. 584–97.

STEINBICKER, C. R., *Poor Relief in the Sixteenth Century*, Washington, 1937.

TAWNEY, R. H., *Religion and the Rise of Capitalism*, London, 1936.

VENARD, M., 'Les œuvres de charité en Avignon à l'aube du XVIIe siècle', *XVIIe siècle*, 90–1, 1971, pp. 127–46.

VILAR, P., 'Les primitifs espagnols de la pensée économique', in *Mélanges Marcel Bataillon*, Paris, 1962, pp. 261–94.

WEBB, S. and WEBB, B., *English Poor Law History*, I *The Old Poor Law*, London, 1927.

WINCKELMANN, O., 'Über die ältesten Armenordnungen der Reformationszeit', *Historische Vierteljahrschrift*, 1914, pp. 187–228, 361–400.

Chapter 6

AYDELOTTE, F., *Elizabethan Rogues and Vagabonds*, Oxford, 1913.

BLOCH, C., *L'Assistance et l'État en France à la veille de la Révolution*, Paris, 1908.

CHILL, E., 'Religion and mendicity in seventeenth-century France', *International Review of Social History*, VII, 1962, pp. 400–25.

COATS, A. W., 'The relief of poverty, attitudes to labour and economic change in England, 1660–1782', *International Review of Social History*, XXI, 1976, pp. 98–115.

DEYON, P., *Amiens, capitale provinciale: étude sur la société urbaine au XVIIe siècle*, Paris, 1967.

DEYON, P., *Le temps des prisons*, Lille, 1975.

FAIRCHILDS, C. C., *Poverty and Charity in Aix-en-Provence, 1640–1789*, Baltimore, 1976.

FARGE, A., 'Le mendiant, un marginal? Les résistances aux archers de l'Hôpital dans le Paris du XVIIIe siècle', in *Les marginaux et les exclus dans l'histoire*, Paris, 1979, pp. 312–29.

FOUCAULT, M., *Folie et déraison: histoire de la folie à l'âge classique*, Paris, 1961.

FOUCAULT, M., *Surveiller et punir: naissance de la prison*, Paris, 1973.

GRENDI, E., 'Pauperismo e albergo dei poveri nella Genova del seicento', *Rivista Storica Italiana*, LXXXVI, 1975, pp. 621–65.

GUTTON, J.-P., 'À l'aube du XVIIe siècle: idées nouvelles sur les pauvres', *Cahiers d'histoire*, X, 1965, pp. 87–97.

HUFTON, O. H., *The Poor of Eighteenth-Century France, 1750–1789*, Oxford, 1974.

KAPLOW, J., *The Names of Kings: The Parisian Laboring Poor in the Eighteenth Century*, New York, 1972.

O'DONOGHUE, E. G., *The Story of Bethlehem Hospital from its Foundation in 1247*, London, 1914.

PASCHINI, P., *La beneficenza in Italia e la 'Compagnia del Divino Amore' nei primi decenni del cinquecento*, Rome, 1925.

PAULTRE, C., *De la répression de la mendicité et du vagabondage en France sous l'Ancien Régime*, Paris, 1906.

ROMANI, M., *Pellegrini e viaggiatori nell'economia di Roma del XIV al XVII secolo*, Milan, 1948.

SELLIN, T., *Pioneering in Penology: The Amsterdam Houses of Correction in the 16th and 17th Centuries*, Philadelphie, 1944.

SOTHMANN, M., *Das Armen-Zucht-und Werkhaus in Nürnberg*, Nuremberg, 1970.

TACCHI-VENTURI, P., *Storia della Compagnia di Gesù in Italia*, Rome, 1910–51.

TAYLOR, G., *The Problem of Poverty, 1600–1834*, London, 1969.

ZYSBERG, A., 'La société des galériens au XVIIIe siècle', *Annales E.S.C.*, XXX, 1975, pp. 43–65.

ZYSBERG, A., 'Galères et galériens en France de l'âge classique aux Lumières', in *Les marginaux et les exclus dans l'histoire*, Paris, 1979, pp. 354–86.

Chapter 7

CONHERD, G., *Political Economists and the English Poor Laws*, Athens, 1977.

ELLIOTT, C., ed., *Pattern of Poverty in the Third World*, New York, 1975.

HUNTER, R., *Poverty: Social Conscience in the Progressive Era*, New York, 1904.

INGLIS, B., *Poverty and the Industrial Revolution*, London, 1971.

KOCH, L., *Wandlungen der Wohlfahrtspflege im Zeitalter der Aufklärung*, Erlangen, 1933.

KULA, W., 'O pewnym aspekcie postepu gospodarczego', *Roczniki Dziejów Spolecznych i Gospodarczych*, X, 1948, pp. 173–83.

MARSHALL, J. D., *The Old Poor Law*, London, 1968.

MOHL, R. A., *Poverty in New York, 1783–1825*, New York, 1971.

MURATORI, L., *Della carità cristiana in quanto essa è amore del prossimo*, Modena, 1723.

ORSHANSKY, M., 'How poverty is measured', *Monthly Labour Review*, 92, 1969, pp. 37–41.

OWEN, D., *English Philanthropy: 1660–1960*, London, 1965.

PLUM, W., *Diskussionen über Massenarmut in die Frühindustraliesierung*, Bonn, 1977.

PONI, C., 'All'origine del sistema di fabbrica: tecnologia e organizzazione produttiva dei mulini da seta nell'Italia settentrionale (sec. XVII–XVIII)', *Rivista Storica Italiana*, LXXXVIII, 1976, pp. 444–97.

ROACH, J. K., and ROACH J. L. ed., *Poverty: Selected Readings*, London, 1972.

STEAMS, P., *European Society in Upheaval*, New York, 1975.

THOMPSON, E. P., *The Making of the English Working Class*, London, 1970.

WEISBROD, B. A., ed., *The Economics of Poverty: An American Paradox*, New York, 1965.

WILKINSON, R., *Poverty and Progress: An Ecological Model of Economic Development*, London, 1973.

WOOLF, S. J., 'The treatment of the poor in Napoleonic Tuscany, 1808–1814', *Annuario dell'Istituto Storico Italiano per l'Età Moderna e Contemporanea*, XXIII–XXIV, 1971–2.

WOOLF, S. J., 'La formazione del proletariato (secoli XVIII–XIX)', in: *Storia d'Italia, Annali*, I, Turin, 1978, pp. 1049–78.

Index